BEYOND THE
NECESSARY GOD

AAR

American Academy of Religion
Reflection and Theory in the Study of Religion

Editor
Mary McClintock Fulkerson

Number 15
BEYOND THE
NECESSARY GOD
Trinitarian Faith and Philosophy
in the Thought of Eberhard Jüngel

by
Paul J. DeHart

BEYOND THE NECESSARY GOD

Trinitarian Faith and Philosophy in the Thought of Eberhard Jüngel

by
Paul J. DeHart

Scholars Press
Atlanta, Georgia

BEYOND THE NECESSARY GOD
Trinitarian Faith and Philosophy in the Thought of Eberhard Jüngel

by
Paul J. DeHart

Library of Congress Cataloging in Publication Data

DeHart, Paul J., 1964–
    Beyond the necessary God : Trinitarian faith and philosophy in the thought of Eberhard Jüngel / by Paul J. DeHart.
        p. cm. — (Reflection and theory in the study of religion ; no. 15)
    Includes bibliographical references and indexes.
    ISBN 0-7885-0624-2 (pbk.)
        1. Jüngel, Eberhard—Contributions in concept of God. 2. God—History of doctrines—20th century. I. Title. II. Series.

BT98.J86 D44   1999
231'.044'092—dc21   99-056823

08 07 06 05 04 03 02 01 00 99   5 4 3 2 1

Printed in the United States of America
on acid-free paper

To my mother

Virginia Jackson DeHart

and in loving memory

of my father

Earl Waymon DeHart

1933-1977

TABLE OF CONTENTS

ACKNOWLEDGMENTS

I wish to thank first of all my teachers, those who taught me what it means to think, and especially those among them who taught me what it means to think as a Christian theologian. I must remember in particular Louis Dupre, Robert Clyde Johnson, Richard Hays, Brevard Childs, Brian Gerrish, Bernard McGinn, Kathryn Tanner and David Tracy. The last three named read this work in its initial form as a doctoral dissertation presented to the Divinity School of the University of Chicago.

I would also like to thank the administration and the members of the faculty of Vanderbilt Divinity School, above all my colleagues in the areas of theology and historical studies. Without their kindness and wisdom in helping me to make the transition to full-time teaching, the task of seeing this work through revision and publication would have been close to impossible.

Gratitude for close reading and critical commentary is due to my series editor Mary McClintock Fulkerson and the two anonymous readers assigned by Scholars Press. Coming under this heading as well is the superb work of Scott Seay, my indefatigable editorial assistant.

Chapter Two appeared in an earlier form in the journal *Theological Studies*. It is reprinted here with the kind permission of the journal.

The dedication page records my most personal note of thanks. The encouragement and generosity of my mother have not failed to this day, and her support has made possible on so many levels the course of my education. My father's life exemplified a rare combination of professional excellence, quiet moral integrity and intelligent religious faith, characteristics which I have come to know more fully only through the medium of those who love to remember him. It is an honor to dedicate this work to my parents.

CHAPTER ONE

INTRODUCTION

The question of God's "death," after sporadic appearances in various religious and philosophical contexts, has been a topic of special concern to Christian theology since the Sixties. Of course, the question can mean very different things depending on one's theological premises and the problems one seeks to address. Consequently in recent times it has had several manifestations as a theological motif. One was the so-called "Death of God" theology which caused a furor in English-speaking circles, albeit for a relatively short time. Another originated in the German-speaking countries, in this case taking up Barthian and Lutheran motifs in the interest of a radical incarnational theology. Jürgen Moltmann's book *The Crucified God* became for many the definitive statement of this kind of "*Kreuzestheologie*", but there had already appeared in 1968 an article on this theme by Eberhard Jüngel entitled "On the Death of the Living God."[1] This article bore a curious subtitle: it claimed to be a "poster" or "placard" (*ein Plakat*), an announcement of bigger things to come. Something did indeed come, and it was indeed large: Jüngel's *magnum opus* appeared in 1977, entitled *God as the Mystery of the World*.[2]

---

[1] Jürgen Moltmann, *Der gekreuzigte Gott: Das Kreuz Christi als Grund und Kritik christlicher Theologie* (Munich: Christian Kaiser Verlag, 1972). English translation of the second edition by R. A. Wilson and John Bowden as *The Crucified God: The Cross of Christ as the Foundation and Criticism of Christian Theology* (New York: Harper & Row, 1974). Eberhard Jüngel, "Vom Tod des lebendigen Gottes. Ein Plakat," in *Unterwegs zur Sache: Theologische Bemerkungen* (Munich: Christian Kaiser Verlag, 1972), 105-125.

[2] Eberhard Jüngel, *Gott als Geheimnis der Welt: Zur Begründung der Theologie des Gekreuzigten im Streit zwischen Theismus und Atheismus*, 6th ed. (Tübingen: J. C. B. Mohr [Paul Siebeck], 1992). English translation of the third German edition by Darrell L. Guder: *God as the Mystery of the World: On the Foundation of the Theology of the Crucified One in the Dispute between Theism and Atheism* (Grand Rapids, MI: William B. Eerdmans, 1983). On the interpretation of "*Plakat*" see Hans Küng, *The Incarnation of God*, trans. J. R. Stephenson (New York: Crossroad, 1987), 550. Throughout this study, all translations of Jüngel are my own unless specifically stated otherwise. (Note: although I have striven in my own writing to avoid gender-specific language for the deity, I have made no attempt to

It is perhaps a tribute to the continuing influence of Karl Barth that much of the current discussion of God's death (or of what Paul Fiddes, in a fine recent study, calls the "creative suffering of God") remains intimately connected to the problem of trinitarian discourse.[3] Jüngel himself at the time of his article on God's death was already well-known in German-speaking circles for his brilliantly executed interpretation of Karl Barth's doctrine of the Trinity.[4] It is impossible to understand Jüngel's exercise in what I will be calling "theistic (re)-construction" without grasping that for him there is a fundamental connection between trinitarian doctrine and the notion of God's suffering and death. But the exposition of that connection in detail is properly the task of a dogmatic theology; it is as a prolegomenon to that task that Jüngel's important contribution to the doctrine of God will be explored here. The following study is an attempt to identify and delineate that contribution in terms of a particular reconstruction of the concept of divine being which is basic both to Jüngel's trinitarianism and to his doctrine of the God who can die.

There is a twofold problem here. On the one hand, the actualization and perpetuation of Christian faith demand the continual shaping and reshaping of a concept of God; faith must learn how to "think" God if it is to preserve itself as faith. On the other hand, thought is an historically situated endeavor; it cannot take place except in the form of a critical encounter with the various intellectual traditions informing it (GGW 270-1 [199-200]). More will be said on this problem of "thinking God" in a moment, but it is mentioned here to render more precise the limitations of this study.

---

impose this restriction when translating Jüngel's own language.) Because of the large number of references to *Gott als Geheimnis der Welt*, it will be cited wherever possible in abbreviated form (GGW) in the text and not in the footnotes. The German page numbers of this work will be followed by the corresponding pages of the English edition in brackets. Unfortunately, the English translation of this book is marred by numerous lapses of judgement and many outright errors; it should be used with great caution.

[3] Paul S. Fiddes, *The Creative Suffering of God* (Oxford: Oxford University Press, 1988). This important work unfortunately came to my attention too late for its insights to be incorporated into this study.

[4] Eberhard Jüngel, *Gottes Sein ist im Werden: Verantwortliche Rede vom Sein Gottes bei Karl Barth: Eine Paraphrase*, 4th ed. (Tübingen: J.C.B. Mohr [Paul Siebeck], 1986). English translation by Horton Harris as *The Doctrine of the Trinity: God's Being is in Becoming* (Grand Rapids, MI: William B. Eerdmans, 1976).

The doctrine of the Trinity is the church's attempt to formulate the being of the God revealed to it and presupposed in its faith and proclamation. As a theological doctrine it is already a product of reflection and interpretation. But in order to carry through theology's reflection on this doctrine, it is necessary to clarify its special conceptual structure and implications as much as possible. For thinking which is both historically-situated and responsible to the present this implies a critical dialog with the theological and philosophical traditions and the changing concepts embedded in them. This is in order to appropriate what is useful in that legacy and, perhaps more importantly, to prevent unexamined concepts from being taken up into theological reflection and occluding the particular nature of its object.

This study is concerned to discover and expound the basic conceptual structure which Jüngel has devised in his own dialog with the traditions of theological and philosophical theism: the notion of divine simplicity or ontological unity. In order to clarify and render coherent the implications for thought of the doctrine of the Trinity, Jüngel has sought to recover and reformulate the traditional doctrine of divine simplicity understood as the identity of essence and existence in the divine being. Although it is not immediately apparent, the notion of divine simplicity will be shown to be central both to his reading of the collapse of traditional metaphysical theism and to the theistic conception he offers in response to that collapse.

Accordingly, what follows is not a direct exposition of Jüngel's trinitarianism; it is a treatment of the way he tries to develop a conceptuality of the divine being within the context of modern intellectual and cultural atheism, a context shaped by the collapse of "metaphysical theism" in both its philosophical and theological forms. One more preliminary point is in order. When this theistic conceptuality is spoken of as basic or fundamental, it is being accorded a structural or formal priority within Jüngel's theological reflection, not a genetic or epistemological priority. In other words, philosophical terminology is used to elucidate God's being as witnessed to by faith and as formulated dogmatically in the doctrine of the Trinity. Far from being an attempt to "ground" faith within a given philosophical scheme, theistic construction within the context of an evangelical theology is itself "grounded" in the God proclaimed and believed in by the community. It is "basic" in its abstractness, its striving for a maximum of formality and clarity with respect to competing concepts of divine being.

Before moving to state more fully the direction and scope of this project it will be helpful to orient the reader briefly by offering some relevant facts about Jüngel, his development, important works and influences. Born in 1934 in Magdeburg, he was raised in a completely non-religious household.[5] His turn to Christian faith was closely connected with his resistance to the conformity and mendacity of state socialism in the German Democratic Republic (DDR). Early studies in Kant and logic gave way to a fascination with Heidegger, prompted by his New Testament teacher at the *Kirchliche Hochschule* in Berlin, Ernst Fuchs. His dogmatics professor there was Heinrich Vogel, a student of Karl Barth. It is significant that his doctoral dissertation under Fuchs, *Paul and Jesus*, was an exercise in theological interpretation of the New Testament; it sought to probe the common ground between Jesus' proclamation of the Kingdom, especially the parables, and Paul's proclamation of the "righteousness of God."

Jüngel's teaching career began under hectic and bizarre circumstances. Only a few weeks after he received his doctorate, the Berlin wall went up, bisecting the city and disrupting the seminary by separating students and professors. Jüngel (on the eastern side) was thrown into the breach, appointed a professor with scarcely any time to prepare himself. His habilitation thesis on the idea of analogy in Heraclitus and Parmenides was produced at great speed and appeared just six months later. Jüngel taught at Berlin from 1961 to 1966, when he was called to the chair of Systematic Theology and History of Dogma at the University of Zürich which had been vacated by Gerhard Ebeling (who had himself been called to Tübingen to replace Adolf Köberle). Jüngel's book on Barth's trinitarianism, which had appeared in 1965, generated great interest and no doubt lay behind the invitation. Somewhat surprisingly, the East German authorities allowed Jüngel to leave the country and take up the position. A short three years later Jüngel moved again, this time to the chair of Systematic Theology and

---

[5] For what follows see Eberhard Jüngel, "Toward the Heart of the Matter," trans. Paul Capetz, *The Christian Century* 108 (1991): 228-233. Also Volker Spangenberg, "Eberhard Jüngel," trans. D. Sutherland, in *A New Handbook of Christian Theologians*, ed. Donald Musser and Joseph Price (Nashville: Abingdon Press, 1996), 244-252.

Philosophy of Religion at Tübingen which he holds to this day. (In a rather odd *pas de deux*, Ebeling at that time returned to his earlier chair in Zürich.)

A number of significant features of Jüngel's thought are foreshadowed in this sketch. His experiences as a Christian convert under the conditions of East German communism gave him a strong sense of Christian proclamation as an uncoerced discourse, the utterance of the truth and freedom of God in opposition to human blindness and enforced conformity. It also perhaps informs the uneasiness he is rumored to feel at the *de rigueur* leftism of many of his Tübingen students and colleagues, including Moltmann. Though committed to social justice and not opposed to socialism in principle, Jüngel is deeply wary of collectively imposed ideologies and distressed at what he sees as the naive political enthusiasms which sometimes threaten careful critical thinking in theology. His training in New Testament exegesis continues to shape a vital interest in the role of scriptural interpretation in theology, and indeed in the phenomena of interpretation and language in general. (He is director of the Institute of Hermeneutics at Tübingen, which Ebeling founded.) Finally, his habilitation research (and his current title) bespeak a lifelong interest in philosophy, its history and its impact on theology.

There was one particular event during the period of Jüngel's theological training which throws considerable light on his dominant intellectual influences. Jüngel managed to spend the Winter Semester of 1957-8 outside of the DDR; he shuttled between three different universities in a theological "grand tour": Zürich, Basel and Freiburg. Zürich was home to Gerhard Ebeling, prominent as the guiding light (along with Fuchs) of the "New Hermeneutic". While Jüngel's mentor Fuchs represented the exegetical side of the movement, Ebeling's contributions were in historical and systematic theology. These two thinkers decisively shaped Jüngel's great interest in language and hermeneutics. His understanding of the historical and linguistic mediation of both human and divine existence can be traced in large part to their influence.

Basel was of course the lair of Karl Barth, a place of pilgrimage for many young theologians at that time. Jüngel participated actively in Barth's seminar. He was at first regarded with suspicion as a Bultmannian interloper. Indeed, when recalling his spirited defense of Bultmann in this hostile setting, Jüngel seems a bit

surprised at his own "audacity."[6] Nonetheless, his intelligence and
skill as an interpreter of Barth's own work won over the older man.
Barth's influence on Jüngel is enormous, and constantly acknowledged by
the latter. Even so, it is unwise to label him a "Barthian" given the
rather dismissive and derogatory implications which that term often
has; his "take" on Barthian themes is sufficiently adventurous to
arouse the suspicion of the master's more obedient pupils. In addition to
God's Being is in Becoming, Jüngel has also published an important
collection of articles on Barth. His first published essay after his
dissertation was on Barth's doctrine of analogy, and one of his most
important Christological contributions stems from the Festschrift for
Barth's 80th birthday.[7] The present study will treat one point on
which Barth's influence on Jüngel is decisive: the trinitarian
interpretation of God as free subject of God's own being, and the
consequent rejection of general metaphysics or ontology as a framework
for faith's understanding of God.

The third city Jüngel travelled to was Freiburg, home to
another "grand old man": Martin Heidegger. Heidegger must probably
be counted as Jüngel's most important philosophical influence.
Heidegger's works with their continual forays into the history of
philosophy were the school in which Jüngel learned the deconstruction
of the Western metaphysical tradition. Also influential was
Heidegger's insistence that theology and philosophy are strictly
distinct modes of thought, a theme taken up by Jüngel in his very first
published article.[8] This latter point highlights the danger of
exaggerating Heidegger's influence on Jüngel's explicitly theological
positions. Jüngel followed Barth's path in his use of being-language for

---

[6] Jüngel, "Toward the Heart," 231. Cf. Eberhard Busch, *Karl Barth: His Life from Letters and Autobiographical Texts*, trans. John Bowden (Philadelphia: Fortress Press, 1976), 429.

[7] Eberhard Jüngel, *Barth-Studien* (Gütersloh: Gütersloher Verlagshaus Gerd Mohn, 1982); idem., "Die Möglichkeit theologischer Anthropologie auf dem Grunde der Analogie: Eine Untersuchung zum Analogieverständnis Karl Barths," in *Barth-Studien*, 210-32; idem., "Jesu Wort und Jesus als Wort Gottes: Ein hermeneutischer Beitrag zum christologischen Problem," in *Parrhesia: Karl Barth zum 80. Geburtstag*, ed. E. Busch, J. Fangmeier, and M. Geiger (Zürich: EVZ-Verlag, 1966).

[8] Eberhard Jüngel, "Der Schritt zurück: Eine Auseinandersetzung mit der Heidegger-Deutung Heinrich Otts," *Zeitschrift für Theologie und Kirche* 58 (1961): 104-22.

God, rejecting Heidegger's strictures against any kind of theological ontology.[9] Even so, when Jüngel's philosophical presuppositions are in question, the Heideggerian influence is usually manifest. Nor should the mediation of Heidegger via Fuchs and Ebeling be forgotten.

With regard to twentieth-century influences on Jüngel there is one city missing from this list: Bultmann's Marburg. Perhaps Jüngel could not successfully negotiate a fourth sojourn in the brief time available to him, or perhaps the fact that Bultmann had retired from active teaching (in 1951) made such a trip undesirable. Nevertheless, Jüngel's deep admiration for Bultmann has continued throughout his career. One result of that admiration was the editing for publication of Bultmann's lectures on theological encyclopedia, from which sprang a long interpretive essay.[10] Jüngel was influenced by Bultmann's students in the "New Hermeneutic" and he sought to engage the master's thought directly as well. Bultmann's greatest achievement in Jüngel's eyes is his break with traditional notions of faith. Bultmann's existential model of faith as self-understanding was marked by an anthropological holism, interpreting it as a response of the total human person to the proclaimed word. The moment of will or praxis and the moment of knowledge are not played off against one another but integrated.[11] Clarity on the question of faith was the secret to the "integrity" or "honesty" of Bultmann's talk of God.[12]

We have now indicated the chief contemporary influences on Jüngel, but the "placement" of his thought would be incomplete without invoking two figures from earlier periods. Besides Heidegger, the

---

[9] In my opinion Zimany's interpretation of Jüngel's thought makes claims for the influence of Heidegger's ontology which need some qualification. See Roland Zimany, *Vehicle for God: The Metaphorical Theology of Eberhard Jüngel* (Macon, GA: Mercer University Press, 1994). Cf. my review of this book in the *Journal of Religion* 77 (1997): 480-1.

[10] Rudolf Bultmann, *Theologische Enzyklopädie*, ed. E. Jüngel and K. W. Müller (Tübingen: J.C.B. Mohr [Paul Siebeck], 1984); English translation: *What Is Theology?*, trans. Roy A. Harrisville (Minneapolis: Fortress Press, 1997). Eberhard Jüngel, "Glauben und Verstehen: Zum Theologiebegriff Rudolf Bultmanns," in *Wertlose Wahrheit: Zur Identität und Relevanz des christlichen Glaubens: Theologische Erörtungen III* (Munich: Christian Kaiser, 1990), 16-77.

[11] Jüngel, "Glauben und Verstehen," 61-8.

[12] See Eberhard Jüngel, "Redlich von Gott reden: Bemerkungen zur Klarheit der Theologie Rudolf Bultmanns," *Evangelische Kommentare* 7 (1974): 475-7.

philosopher who has proven most important to Jüngel is probably Hegel.[13] A long section of *God as the Mystery of the World* is devoted to tracing the various guises of the death of God throughout Hegel's development as a thinker. Three Hegelian motifs are of particular importance to Jüngel. First is the explicit identification of the death of God as a theological concept springing from Christology. The second is the theological significance of atheism as the negation of theism, an historical and epistemological "moment" to be incorporated into the idea of God itself.[14] The third, closely related to the two preceding, is his "grand theological accomplishment": a conceptual integration of Christology and trinitarian thought which the theological tradition proper had for the most part glaringly failed to achieve, a "philosophically thought-out theology of the Crucified *as* a doctrine of the Triune God" (GGW 124 [94]).

The last figure is one whose influence on Jüngel is hardest to pin down precisely because it is so many-sided and pervasive: Luther. Themes from Luther's theology appear everywhere in Jüngel's thought. These include justification as the determination of human nature, the freedom of the Christian in faith, and the fundamental distinction between gospel and law. However, if we limit attention to the question of theistic reconstruction, the concern of the present study, the key idea is without doubt the revelation-in-hiddenness of God's being in the cross of Christ. In this Luther and Hegel in spite of all their differences complement one another. Jüngel clearly wishes to place his own work in the context of that "recent theology instructed by Luther's Christology and Hegel's philosophy."[15]

That instruction has come to fruition most strikingly in the centerpiece of Jüngel's published work, *God as the Mystery of the*

---

[13] Any list of philosophical influences would also have to include two figures whose influence is more muted but nevertheless vital: Schelling and Nietzsche.

[14] For these first two points, see GGW 128 (97) and cf. GGW 511 (373) note 19 on Hegel's "decisive breakthrough" with respect to fully incorporating change and negativity into the divine being.

[15] GGW 511 (373). Ironically, theology had to be reacquainted with this Lutheran line by a Swiss Reformed thinker: "In this respect only the older Karl Barth dared to travel decisively the paths of thought opened up by Luther and Hegel -- something which has nevertheless remained largely unnoticed by the theological public" (GGW 51 [40]).

World. It is a long and difficult work, but one of tremendous insight and power. Because Jüngel's theistic reconstruction is a central concern of this book, and because this book in turn is central to Jüngel's thought as a whole, it is necessary to say a word or two about its overall structure and argument. The thrust of the entire work is an attempt to confront cultural and intellectual atheism, the modern "death of God," with its own origins in Christian faith, that is in the theological "death of God" represented by the Christ-event. This confrontation and the resulting rethinking of God's being are the necessary prolegomena to a dogmatic theology which transcends the theistic traditions called into question by modern atheism.

The book has five parts. In the introductory part Jüngel begins by sketching a hypothesis with a quite contemporary ring: that knowledge of God ultimately depends on God's "speakability," that is on the mode of God's presence in human language.[16] Having modestly set the tone for the whole work, he leaves this possibility hanging in the air in order to begin exploring how the God putatively absent from modern speech is actually present in the discourse of God's "death." After showing how the "absolute" and "necessary" God of theological and philosophical tradition was discovered to be quite unnecessary for modern human beings, he defends this as an authentic insight, fully in accord with the dignity both of humanity and of God. God serves no necessary worldly "function" but is completely self-grounded. Traditional theology has misunderstood this self-grounding in terms of divine "absoluteness"; it was this absolute God which did not survive its clash with modern self-consciousness.

The second part probes God's death more deeply.[17] The discourse of God's death has a dual provenance: Christian theology made such an idea possible, but it was the absolute God of metaphysical theism whose death was actually demanded. Lurking behind the talk of God's death is the question of God's essence or true nature; when this question arose in modern culture, it was already a sign that the absolute God was dying. But rather than dismiss the atheistic discourse of God's death, Jüngel undertakes a detailed analysis of how it originally "migrated" from theology into philosophy via the

---

[16] "Introduction," GGW 1-54 (3-42).

[17] "Talk of God's death as an expression of the aporia of the modern idea of God," GGW 55-137 (43-104).

thought of Hegel (eventually issuing in Feuerbach), and also how the deep insights of the imprisoned Bonhoeffer represent its "homecoming," its return into theology. Jüngel's conclusion from this analysis is that the "aporia" or perplexity of modern thought confronted with the traditional thought of God lay in its inability to conceive an absolute essence, insulated from mortality and temporality.

This ushers in the third part of the book, which is of particular importance to Jüngel's theistic reconstruction.[18] Jüngel wishes first to show how the growing perplexity at the idea of God issued in the disintegration of the traditional concept of the divine as a being in which existence and essence are identical. Descartes' influence was pivotal because he accepted this tradition but drastically reconceived thought in such a way that the positing of existence was secured and grounded in the human subject. A divine existence so secured could no longer be conceived in identity with an absolute essence, and Jüngel traces how the idea of God collapsed in various ways, represented by Fichte, Feuerbach and Nietzsche. But this disaster is actually an opportunity for reconstructing the thought of God theologically; Jüngel offers a theology of revelation as the way out of the contemporary difficulties, basing the thought of God on the addressing word of the gospel and the decentering trust or faith in that word which "desecures" the subject. The actual result for the concept of God is a refashioned unity of essence and existence which conceives God's redeeming presence in the transitoriness and negativity of history.

Having removed an obstacle to thinking God, Jüngel turns in the fourth part to removing another traditional obstacle, one which hinders that talk of God upon which thought feeds.[19] If the gospel is God's word in human words, then to silence human speech about God is to silence God's own word. Jüngel wants to show that certain classic theological traditions sought to preserve a particular understanding of the divine mystery by foreclosing any possibility of authentic speech about God's being. Paradoxically, even the doctrines of analogical language used to insure that the Church's talk did not lapse into silence succeeded only in reinforcing the negative mystery of divine ineffability. In response, Jüngel formulates an analogy based on God's

---

18 "On the thinkability of God," GGW 138-306 (105-225).

19 "On the speakability of God," GGW 307-408 (226-98).

already having come to speech and constantly coming again in the proclaimed word of God's unity with the crucified. He focusses on the parabolic structure of that proclamation and its role in shaping the concrete subject who is addressed; in so doing, he rejects the model of an inauthentic speech always lagging behind an ineffable thought in favor of an analogy in which God's being can give itself to human language because it is self-imparting word. God is identified in the word and being of Jesus; not the ineffability of divine being but its humanity is the first and last word which thought follows after.

At last the ground has been prepared for beginning to speak of God's being concretely on the basis of the Christ-event, the concern of the fifth part of the book.[20] In a "hermeneutical preface" Jüngel asserts the necessity of temporal language (narrative) in the discourse of God's being. He then turns to a definition of God's being as love, and to the need for faith in God's identity with love as a safegaurd against merging God and humanity. He next moves to bring out the trinitarian form of God's being-as-love through a concentration on the story of the crucified Jesus. It is only on the basis of this story that God's being can be properly narrated in its interplay of self-differentiating and self-corresponding relations, Father, Son and Spirit. Jüngel concludes the work with a meditation on faith, love and hope as those human acts corresponding to the revelation of God's being. The mystery of human love is thus a participation in the divine mystery. Indeed, that mystery does not point to a second "world" alongside ours; it is the mystery of this world.

This study will be largely though not exclusively concerned with this book, as it represents Jüngel's deepest and most sustained explorations into the concept of God. Obviously, then, the purpose of the present investigation is not a general overview of or introduction to Jüngel's thought and writing. It restricts its attention to a particular problem: the basic conceptual issue at stake in Jüngel's dispute with the tradition of metaphysical theism. The thesis to be set out and defended is that for Jüngel the task of thinking God's being requires a reconception of its unity of essence and existence, what I have already called God's "simplicity" or "ontological unity."

---

[20] "On the humanity of God," GGW 409-543 (299-396).

This task is related to but distinct from the dogmatic task of thinking God as triune; it is concerned with the peculiar ontological status or "placement" of divine being insofar as this can be formulated in critical dialog with general ontological thought. I will argue that for Jüngel the philosophical and theological conception of God's simplicity is centrally implicated in the collapse of traditional theistic models in post-Cartesian metaphysics. For that reason, Jüngel undertakes a reconstruction of the concept of divine simplicity; moreover, further investigation will show how this concept is an ordering and structuring principle in Jüngel's various theological elaborations on God's identity as constructed by faith.

Some preliminary points need to be made in order to clarify this thesis. With regard to terminology, I will be using the term "theism" to refer to the way in which God's being is defined and elaborated within a given system of thought and practice. In other words, the term in this work is value-neutral; it thus differs from Jüngel's own pejorative usage where the term refers to those classical, metaphysically-informed understandings of divine being which he wishes to deconstruct (GGW 55-6 [43]). As already noted, "ontological unity" or "divine simplicity" refers to the unity of essence and existence which characterizes God's being. "Simplicity" is being used in this narrowly defined sense for the sake of convenience; in reality, the monotheistic tradition has had quite varied reasons for asserting the simplicity of divine being.[21]

The terms "metaphysics" and "metaphysical" will occur often, as will the terms "tradition" and "traditional" (or "classical"). My usage here follows Jüngel's, but it must be admitted that these terms are often applied in a loose and vague manner. Sometimes, for example, Jüngel can speak neutrally of metaphysics as an ongoing or perennial concern with which theology must come to terms. At other times, probably influenced by Heideggerian usage, he is referring to the particular course of Western metaphysics from its origins in ancient Greece to its putative dissolution in the modern period. This latter usage is sometimes problematic in the same way that Jüngel's talk of

---

21 For reflections on the complex of ideas in patristic thought related to simplicity ("indivisibility," "self-identity," etc.) see G. L. Prestige, *God in Patristic Thought* (London: William Heinemann, Ltd., 1936), esp. 9-13. See also the various arguments for God's simplicity in Aquinas, *Summa Theologica* I q. 3.

"the tradition" is; both terms tend to treat past intellectual history monolithically, eliding many important distinctions. Hence arguments involving such terms should best be treated as historical hypotheses pending confirmation from a greater variety of sources. Jüngel, historically sensitive thinker that he is, cannot be unaware that he sometimes risks oversimplifying the past in his zeal for the new.

Another question concerns the phrase (rather awkward in English) "thinking God." For Jüngel this activity is decisively determined from the direction not of its subject but of its object. The best entry into this idea lies in the irreducible narrativity of divine being. God's being is a path, a "way" which God travels; indeed in an unsurpassed sense God's being is understood as a "coming." Human thought which attempts to "think God" must accordingly be "taken along" this path with God; such thinking is always a reflecting upon God's path, a "thinking after" (*Nachdenken*). But to think God in this way presupposes that even if one does not allow oneself to be "taken along" one at least understands its meaning, which is nothing other than existence in correspondence to God's revelation, i. e. faith. If faith is the immediate form of being taken along, then the thought which reflects on faith in order to reflect on God's path must be seen as a mediate form of being taken along with God (GGW 224 [167]).

Two points must be made on this "thinking after." First, it is thinking, genuinely human thinking. As such it is a free human act, which each person must accomplish for him- or herself. There is here no submission to heteronomous authority, nor any submersion of thought in a quasi-mystical fog. Nor should the fact that thinking God requires "thinking after" faith be construed to mean that the personal actualization of belief in an individual is a prerequisite for conceiving God at all. Rather, Jüngel means that thought must grasp faith as constitutive of any true thinking of God; it must understand that the idea of God cannot be "constructed" without thinking God as the subject of God's self, and therefore as the one known only in response to God's address (GGW 213 [159]). "Reason can, therefore, only think God in that it follows after faith. It does not itself believe. It thinks." But in its thinking it comes to realize that "with the thought of God the thought of the necessary interrelationship of faith and God has been thought" (GGW 219 [163]).

The second point follows closely on the first, for this thinking must follow, it is a thinking *after*.

> Thus, theological thinking cannot first of all abstract from God
> himself in order to achieve (via the path of a self-consideration of
> thought which occurs in detachment from theology's proper
> object of thought) something like a thought of God which would
> then have a limiting function for the determinations of God based
> on revelation.[22]

Jüngel's notion of theological thinking involves the complete rejection
of any "limiting-concept" (*Rahmenbegriff*) of divinity constructed on
"purely" rational or general empirical lines which would presume to
have some basic legislative function for theology.[23] Jüngel insists that
in order for theology to think God as God is, it must proceed on the basis
of God's revelation because "God gives himself to be thought" (GGW
214 [160]). Thought "thinks after" God's self-gift.

"In theology, then, to think means just this: to try to correspond
to God with the faculty of human reason" (GGW 214 [160]). These brief
comments cannot hope to clarify completely this difficult element of
Jüngel's thought. They are intended only as an indication of the role of
conceptual thought in theology. Theological thought is the attempt to
grasp by means of concepts the complex formed by the revealing word
and faith's response to it. On this basis it must conceive God as the
utterer of this word. And it must do so within its own historical
situation, critically utilizing the conceptual resources bequeathed to it.

> There is only progress in thinking when thought follows its
> object (*Sache*) in reflection (*Nachdenken*) *and* in so doing
> considers the historical context of thought and the spirit of its
> own age in such a way that the demands upon thought arising from
> the object lead at once to a conversation with the spirit of the age

---

22 GGW 213 (159): "Theologisches Denken kann also nicht zunächst
einmal von Gott selbst absehen, um über den Weg einer Selbstbesinnung des
Denkens, die sich losgelöst von dem in der Theologie eigentlich zu Denkenden
vollzieht, zu so etwas wie einem Gottesgedanken zu gelangen, der dann eine Art
Rahmenfunktion für die aufgrund von Offenbarung gewonnenen Bestimmungen
Gottes hätte."

23 He has Pannenberg particularly in mind on this point. See Eberhard
Jüngel, "Nihil divinitatis, ubi non fides. Ist christliche Dogmatik in rein
theoretischer Perspektive möglich? Bemerkungen zu einem theologischen Entwurf
von Rang," *Zeitschrift für Theologie und Kirche* 86 (1989): 204-35 at 225.

and the perplexities (*Aporien*) of thought arising from it (GGW
271 [200]).

This is precisely the context in which the question of God's ontological
unity arises. The divine simplicity (as traditionally conceived)
became a stumbling block for modern thought; Jüngel's attempt to think
God in the present involves a reconsideration of simplicity as a basis for
reconstructing the concept of God.

But why if it has proven so problematic should a doctrine of
ontological unity be retained at all? In a sense this entire study
represents the answer to this question in that it will show the
centrality of that unity to all Jüngel's concepts of the divine. For now it
will suffice to point to the presuppositions of a radically incarnational
theology such as Jüngel's. God's essence is God's identity, that which
makes God to be God. God's existence is the act of God's being, God's
self-actualization, which is also the sphere of potential interaction
with actualities other than (i. e. created by) God. For Jüngel, the basic
axiom of a "theology of the word" is that God has revealed God's self
within the sphere of human or worldly existence through a free
identification of God's being with what is not God, the person and
history of Jesus. The perfect freedom in which God acts, which implies
the indistinguishibility of God's act and God's being, makes this
"identification" with historical existence not the simple disclosure of
an already "given" divine identity but a self-identification in a much
deeper sense: an act of ontological self-determination, whereby God is
in fact choosing and bestowing an identity upon God's own being.

The traditional idea of God's simplicity was formally correct
in equating God's essence with God's act of existence. The problem lay
in attempting to determine the mode of God's existence on the basis of a
prior determination of God's essence (formulated in abstraction from the
incarnation), rather than determining God's essence on the basis of that
concrete existence grasped by faith: Jesus Christ. Indeed, in Jesus we
must think of God and the human together in a single existence, an
historical actuality. God's coming is the historical fact of the word
which awakens faith (GGW 257 [190]). Thus theology learns to think
God's existence as the "inclusion" (*Inbegriff*) of God's essence from its
reflection on faith in Christ. To think God, one must grasp the
connection between the thought of God and involvement in the co-
existence of God and humanity in Jesus, even if one does not personally
acknowledge that involvement or participate in it. For Jüngel, the

necessity of thinking God and faith together has nothing to do with piety. That necessity springs from the fact that faith acknowledges the ontological simplicity of God's being; it confesses that God's essence "takes place" (*sich vollzieht*) in God's existence with the human being Jesus (GGW 259 [191]).

These comments suggest that the concept of divine simplicity aims toward an ontology of God's trinitarian being. The study which follows is not an exposition of Jüngel's trinitarianism (itself essentially a development of Barth's), but a treatment of the way in which Jüngel develops a theistic conceptuality in critical dialog with theological and philosophical traditions, in order to serve faith's "thinking" of God. The discourse of divine simplicity represents an ontological elaboration of trinitarian doctrine in the service of that doctrine; it is emphatically not an attempt to demonstrate or "ground" the doctrine philosophically. The importance of this topic in Jüngel's thought will become clearer as this study proceeds. His theistic reflections are so complicated, so ramified, and so intimately linked with other areas of his thought, that it will be a worthwhile achievement simply to bring to light this basic idea driving his theistic reconstruction.

As for the importance of this study to contemporary theological problems, that must ultimately depend on the verdict rendered on Jüngel's thought itself. In particular, the plausibility and intelligibility of his fundamental ideas on revelation, faith and the trinity must be at issue in any assessment of his theistic reconstruction. This present work is undertaken in the conviction that this basic theological framework is intellectually viable and of potentially enormous significance for Christian proclamation and ecclesial life. The more specific interest in Jüngel's theistic reconstruction is an acknowledgement of the necessity of responsible and careful use of concepts in our attempts to apprehend God on the basis of the confession of Christian faith. Some intellectual procedure of the kind which Jüngel puts into motion must always be ingredient in theological reflection in order to preserve the clarity and integrity of faith.

It seems to me that the ideas brought to light by this study have scarcely even been grasped in discussions of Jüngel. This is disappointing, for in my opinion they should play a weighty part in any contemporary conversation on the God of Christian faith. Moreover, Jüngel's theistic project is so adventurous and encompassing that it could constitute an important intervention in some broader debates concerning the relationship of theistic discourse to questions of being and language. While he refuses to speak of a God "without being," his approach involves interrogating the priority of being as a master concept; "being" is irreparably fractured by the diastasis between God and humanity revealed on the cross.[24] The result is an irreducible pluralism in ontology. No longer can being be the great integrator of God and the world in the manner of an "onto-theo-logy," for the discourse of being itself can only be integrated analogically in the proclaimed unity of divine and human love in Jesus Christ. Here, too, Jüngel's stress on the historical-linguistic mediation of God's presence in ecclesial practice and the consequent priority of word over thought in constructing the concept of God is a potentially fruitful contribution to the formation of a post-liberal theology based in the praxis of lingually-shaped communities.

The study will proceed as follows. The first two chapters following this introduction frame the problem of the divine simplicity in a preliminary way. Chapter Two represents an overview of how Jüngel conceives the practice of theology, concentrating on the centrality of reflection on faith and the linguistic mediation of faith's originating event, the history of Jesus as Christ. Important implications will surface about the kind of God presupposed in this theological project. Chapter Three turns to the drama (or trauma) of modernity in which the classical formulation of divine simplicity fell to pieces as the self-grounding rationality of Descartes gained the ascendancy. Once this "necessary" God was revealed in its superfluity, its intellectual and cultural death had to follow.

It is on the ruins of the necessary God that Jüngel begins to reconstruct the unity of divine essence and existence in a new way. Chapter Four presents the initial, highly abstract gestures toward a "more than necessary" God; already at this stage Jüngel begins to bring out the implications for theistic thinking of a divine simplicity based on God's givenness as an historical fact in Jesus. This process of elaboration is further portrayed in Chapter Five as Jüngel's views on God the creator are shown to point toward love as the existence with which God's essence must be equated. Chapter Six then examines more closely the "ecstatic" procedures of language and faith as explications

---

[24] The phrase in quotes comes from Jean-Luc Marion, *God Without Being: Hors-Texte*, trans. Thomas A. Carlson (Chicago: University of Chicago Press, 1991).

of how God's being is identified with the crucified one. Finally, Chapter Seven concludes the study by summarizing its results in relation to Jüngel's trinitarianism, and by offering assessments of his theistic project, its strengths, weaknesses and potential significance.

CHAPTER TWO

FAITH AND *WISSENSCHAFT*: JÜNGEL ON THE STRUCTURE OF THEOLOGY

Eberhard Jüngel's theology is a *Glaubenslehre*. I use this term broadly to mean a formulation and explication of basic theological categories grounded in an analysis of the phenomenon of Christian faith. Unlike the key nineteenth-century proponents of this theological model, such as Schleiermacher and Troeltsch, Jüngel argues for a version of faith which interlocks completely with the proclamation of the crucified Christ as God's radical identification with an historical human person. One of the implications of this study will be that Jüngel's model of divine simplicity is an attempt to define God's being in such a way that justice is done to such an understanding of the Christ-event and the faith it calls forth.

As a prolegomenon to that project, it will be useful to provide a broad overview of the nature and tasks of theology as conceived by Jüngel. This would be a daunting proposition if one tried to determine principles or method based on his extraordinarily rich and complex major works, which often present considerable difficulties to the interpreter. An easier way is available, however, since Jüngel himself has provided some incisive reflections on the nature of theology, albeit in relatively obscure articles virtually ignored in discussions of his work. Indeed, it is surprising just how little of the secondary literature generated by his theology has been devoted to his own conception of the theologian's task.[1] Consequently, this chapter will have to provide

---

[1] The only exception with which I am familiar is Engelbert Paulus, *Liebe — das Geheimnis der Welt: Formale und materiale Aspekte der Theologie Eberhard Jüngels* (Würzburg: Echter, 1990). His study is relevant from the standpoint of this essay chiefly due to his intriguing attempt to integrate formally the theological reflections of the later Jüngel (especially *God as the Mystery of the World*) with the earlier methodological scheme under consideration here. For Paulus (p. 40), the concept of freedom is central to this task, insofar as Jüngel's article on the freedom of theology (see note 2 below) presents freedom as the content determining the form of theology, while *God as the Mystery of the World* thematizes freedom as the content determining the event of God's word.

what is lacking elsewhere: a synthetic presentation of Jüngel's programmatic statements concerning theology.[2]

The difficulty of Jüngel's German prose along with the subtlety and occasional obscurity of his thought have been often remarked. The task of clear summary is rendered even more difficult in the case of this topic, which touches the nerve-center of the tangled interrelations of the various theological *loci*. Nor can there be much more than a cursory attempt to indicate the web of influences behind his conception of the theological program, although the influences discussed in Chapter One (i.e. Barth, Bultmann, Fuchs and Ebeling) will be readily apparent to anyone familiar with German theology since the Second World War. But Jüngel's position cannot be reduced to a mere function or convergence of these influences; his ideas have their own internal connection and characteristic trajectory, which this chapter will seek to delineate.

The Nature of Christian Faith: A Preliminary Sketch

The difficulties of summary are peculiarly acute at the outset; to understand the nature of theology for Jüngel, the richness of his doctrine of faith must be given an inevitably cramped treatment.[3] To begin with one of his typically dense and lapidary formulations: the event of faith corresponds to the event of truth; the event of truth is the

---

2 The following articles by Jüngel will be utilized: [1] "'Theologische Wissenschaft und Glaube' im Blick auf die Armut Jesu," in Eberhard Jüngel, *Unterwegs zur Sache: Theologische Bemerkungen* (Munich: Christian Kaiser, 1972), 11-33. [2] "Die Freiheit der Theologie," in Eberhard Jüngel, *Entsprechungen: Gott — Wahrheit — Mensch. Theologische Erörterungen* (Munich: Christian Kaiser, 1980), 11-36. [3] "Das Verhältnis der theologischen Disziplinen untereinander," in *Unterwegs zur Sache*, 34-59. [4] "Theologie in der Spannung zwischen Wissenschaft und Bekenntnis," in *Entsprechungen*, 37-51.

3 The concept of faith outlined here is not delineated in detail in the programmatic articles of concern to this chapter, although they clearly presuppose it. Therefore, this opening section will resort to some more explicit remarks on the idea of faith contained in two later writings: Eberhard Jüngel, "Zur Lehre vom Heiligen Geist: Thesen" in *Die Mitte des Neuen Testaments*, ed. U. Luz and H. Weder (Göttingen: Vandenhoeck und Ruprecht, 1983), 97-118; Eberhard Jüngel, "Glauben und Verstehen: Zum Theologiebegriff Rudolf Bultmanns," in Eberhard Jüngel, *Wertlose Wahrheit: Zur Identität und Relevanz des christlichen Glaubens: Theologische Erörterungen III* (Munich: C. Kaiser, 1990), 16-77. For a useful critical analysis of Jüngel's understanding of faith see Walter Kern S.J., "Theologie des Glaubens, vorgestellt anhand von Eberhard Jüngel," *Zeitschrift für katholische Theologie* 104 (1982): 129-146.

event of God's coming to the world.[4] Jüngel speaks of the "truth" of the world as an event, that is, an occurrence, something that happens (or does not happen), to indicate that the truth of the world, the quintessence of what it is, the realization of its most genuine possibilities, is not immanent to the world.

The world's truth is not a metaphysical "attribute" or a "state" of the world, a static possession. The world only becomes true when God takes up a certain disposition to the world; then, the truth of the world "happens." Jüngel extends this complex of metaphors to the relation of God to individual human beings within the world. If God's interaction with creation is God's coming, then God's interaction with humanity is God's speaking. God speaks a "word" to humanity, and when people actually hear and respond to that word there then occurs that event which is analogous to the world's truth: faith.

It is crucial to see that for Jüngel "faith" in the Christian sense is simply not a general human possibility. The capacity for faith is not "built-in" to the structure of human existence, at least not in the sense that it could be actualized at will, or in the course of normal human interaction. It is a response to the concrete occurrence of the word from God, which is dependent on God's coming to the world. Hence the event of truth is the ground of the event of faith. And so it must be said that faith is not an anthropological category, nor is it an "expression" of the human subject; it is an occurrence in which the human person participates, not a thing possessed by the person.[5]

Faith comes *to* a person, it comes from God, and it comes in the form of the word (which, as the word of the one who comes to the world as the world's truth, can itself be called both the word of faith and the word of truth).[6] These expressions are admittedly abstract. Two questions in particular demand attention. Materially, what is the content of this word, what does it say? Formally, how is it

---

[4] Jüngel, "Lehre vom Heiligen Geist," 110.

[5] Jüngel, "Theologische Wissenschaft," 19. Herein lies the cogency for Jüngel of Barth's protest against Neo-Protestant "subjectivism." Nevertheless, Jüngel follows Bultmann in orienting Christian theology directly to the phenomenon of faith, Barth's sardonic comments about "pisteology" notwithstanding.

[6] See Jüngel, "Lehre vom Heiligen Geist," 115. Cf. idem, "Theologische Wissenschaft," 22.

communicated? What happens when a human being "hears" and responds to this word? The answer to both questions is implicit in Jüngel's affirmation that the word of God is none other than the man Jesus of Nazareth, a quite traditional statement but in this case deeply informed by the particular developments associated with Barth and Bultmann. As a living figure in the past this person is both a personal identity and a complex of events and actions, the subject of a narrative or history (*Geschichte*). The event of faith occurs when the word about this person is received as the story of God's own coming to the world, so that Jesus himself is apprehended as God's past and continuing word to humanity. A person hears the word about Jesus, and in accepting Jesus as God's decisive activity within the world, as God's "Christ," that person participates in the reality of faith.

Thus the answer to the first question as to the content of the word leads immediately to the second question about what it means to hear this word. This close connection of the subjective and objective poles in the event of faith is no accident; indeed, for Jüngel the peculiar unity of subject and object in faith touches on its deepest meaning. In fact, he follows Bultmann in holding that human participation in faith opens up a new self-understanding for the participant.[7] The term "understanding" (*Verstehen*) as used by Bultmann (following Heidegger) is laden with existential significance. It is not simply a kind of knowledge, but rather the permeation or conditioning of a person's entire existence by some determinate meaning. As a response of the total person it involves knowledge, to be sure, but extends beyond that to encompass all action in response to that knowledge.

Thus a person's response to the word in faith is an act of that person's entire existence, in which acts both of knowledge and of will are involved as essentially related moments.[8] And as self-understanding it means that one comes to a new understanding of one's own reality. But calling faith "self-understanding" seems to make the "object" of faith to be one's own self, whereas it has already been determined that faith is oriented to the word of Jesus Christ. How can faith be at once the unity of subject and object (the self coming to a new

---

[7] For what follows see Jüngel, "Glauben und Verstehen," 65ff.

[8] Ibid. 66.

understanding of itself) and also an opening, a response to a word from beyond the self?

The answer for Jüngel, again following Bultmann, can only be that in hearing and accepting the word about Jesus Christ one is *ipso facto* and at the same time accepting a new reality for one's self. In the word, Jesus is identified as the human being whose existence is in every way a perfect correspondence (*Entsprechung*) to God's reality. In accepting this word, one elects to receive this existence as one's own; in fact, in making this very decision one is already actually participating in this new existence, and in the new self-understanding which comes with it. In the word of Jesus one's very reality is revealed as something coming from beyond, from outside. The reality or the existence which had hitherto been accepted as one's own, or, put another way, the self painstakingly constructed from a lifetime of acts, is now revealed as a deadly self-deception. It is, to use Pauline language, a life according to "flesh" (*sarx*). This "natural" existence only becomes visible to a person in the act of faith; only when the new self-understanding is received is one's old existence revealed for what it was, a past which can be and is in fact done away with.

In the old self-understanding one exists in accordance with what one is or does; in the new self-understanding, one exists in accordance with what one has received from God.[9] Thus there is the closest connection in faith between the internal and the external: faith is "'a letting-be-determined by what is known' and thus 'a being-in-what is known.'"[10] The phrase "what is known" here refers of course to the word of Jesus Christ. It points to a central issue in Jüngel's conception of faith: the relation of faith to knowledge.

In several places in his writings Jüngel has striven to distinguish the genuine New Testament idea of faith (represented paradigmatically by Paul) from the influential definition by Plato of faith (*pistis*) as a species of mere opinion (*doxa*), to be distinguished from true knowledge, or *episteme*. True knowledge is knowledge of being, whereas faith is related to matters of becoming; it is a kind of

---

[9] Jüngel, "Theologische Wissenschaft," 21.

[10] Jüngel, "Glauben und Verstehen," 66. The phrases are cited from Rudolf Bultmann, *Theologie des Neuen Testaments*, ed. Otto Merk, 9th ed. (Tübingen: J.C.B. Mohr [Paul Siebeck], 1984), 431: "ein sich Bestimmenlassen durch das Erkannte"; "ein Sein im Erkannten."

knowing, but a deficient kind.[11] For Jüngel this makes the mistake of classifying faith as one among a set of anthropological possibilities, whereas faith conditions our total existence both in its cognitive and non-cognitive aspects. Faith is not a deficient mode of knowledge, but knowledge is an inherent moment of faith. And as a distinct moment it has a certain relative validity and independence.

Bultmann wants to subsume this moment completely within the praxis of Christian existence. But for Jüngel the knowledge which faith has of its object must be theoretical as well as practical, and this theoretical aspect "indeed can never be isolated from the practical character of this knowledge, but just as little can it be absorbed by it."[12] Hence he can say that faith as the human correspondence to God's word is not only the free act of "ex-centrically" grounding oneself outside oneself (trust in God, *Gottvertrauen*), but is also a knowledge directing itself to the ground of faith as its object, as the event of truth (knowledge of God, *Gotteserkenntnis*).[13] This knowledge does not represent the supercession of faith. For Jüngel the Anselmian *fides quaerens intellectum* cannot be understood to mean that faith finds its end or *telos* in knowledge. Faith does not pass over into knowledge; instead, faith's knowledge is for the sake of faith itself: *fides quaerens intellectum quaerentem fidem*.[14]

It was seen above that the object of faith (the event of God's word) is at the same time the ground of faith's possibility. This close coordination of ground (*Grund*) and object (*Gegenstand*) is central to the discussion of the cognitive dimension of faith. Jüngel agrees with Bultmann that God (in God's word) is only given along with the act of faith, but he argues that this means that God is also "given" for the element of knowledge implicit in faith. Indeed, the word must be known as something over against the individual (*ein Gegenüber*) in order for it to be the ground of belief.[15] In this way it could be said that

---

11 Jüngel, "Theologische Wissenschaft," 20. Jüngel refers specifically to Book VIII of the *Republic*.

12 Jüngel, "Glauben und Verstehen," 77.

13 Jüngel, "Lehre vom Heiligen Geist," 116-7.

14 Ibid.

15 Jüngel, "Glauben und Verstehen," 76. On Jesus Christ as the personal "*Gegenüber*" of faith see idem, "Lehre vom Heiligen Geist," 117.

the fact *that* faith knows is grounded in *what* faith knows. The theoretical moment witnesses to the grounding of faith from beyond the individual's existence (*ek-stasis*).[16]

Theology as the Thinking of Faith

Theology thinks faith. This is Jüngel's most succinct formulation of the nature and task of theology.[17] In and of itself, faith is not identical with thought; it cannot be self-reflective and still be faith, since by its very nature it is a correspondence to the word which comes to the individual. "Because faith in every respect points *away* from itself, the *believer* needs something like theology".[18] In other words, theology can reflect on faith and the event of faith because theology is not itself an act of faith — it is an act of thought. Faith does not, properly speaking, think; thought thinks. This compact formulation indicates the tension inherent in the theological endeavor, as well as the essence of its critical task vis-à-vis faith.

There is a constitutive tension in theology due to the fact that the individual is attempting to bring under discursive, reflective scrutiny the very power which determines and shapes his or her existence. Jüngel speaks of faith and thought as two powers which put existence into movement. Where there are two movements, there is the possibility of an encounter between them, or even a clash.[19] The potential for conflict, and thus the internal tension of theology, is heightened in the present time because theology as thought is part of the changing history of thought. Discursive rationality is not a fixed structure; it is part of the social and intellectual history of humanity,

---

[16] For more extended criticism of Bultmann, see Jüngel, "Glauben und Verstehen," 55. It should be noted that while Jüngel defends the relative independence of the theoretical moment of faith from the praxis of faithful existence, he is concerned that Pannenberg's approach attempts to secure a purely theoretical kind of knowledge of God. Jüngel agrees with Pannenberg that the content of faith is not a product of the pure act of faith, rather that the very possibility of the act is grounded in the content (i.e. in God as the object of faith). But Jüngel insists that the content which grounds the act of faith is nevertheless only given in the context of that act. See Eberhard Jüngel, "Nihil divinitatis, ubi non fides," *Zeitschrift für Theologie und Kirche* 86 (1989): 233-34.

[17] Jüngel, "Theologische Wissenschaft," 13.

[18] Jüngel, "Freiheit der Theologie," 25.

[19] Jüngel, "Theologische Wissenschaft," 12.

and assumes different forms over time. In the modern epoch thought has repeatedly aspired to an ideal thought-form, that of "science" (*Wissenschaft*); thought has been driven by responsibility to this scientific goal (even if this ideal has become increasingly disputed of late).[20] In short, theology must be a science, despite the fact that science in our day prescinds utterly from the question of God; it is a-theistic, at least with regard to its method.[21]

A more detailed examination of the scientific character of theology for Jüngel will be the task of the next section. But at this point a more basic question demands attention, namely, why faith needs theology at all, i.e. why it must be reflected upon in thought. According to Jüngel, faith stands in need of constant self-critique, a critique which only thought can undertake, and which therefore can only be accomplished for faith by theology. But what is the function of such a critique? The simplest way to approach this complex question is to take up Jüngel's language of a dual distinction. Granted that the event of faith is an event in which God and the human person come into the closest correspondence, then theology's task is to distinguish faith from God on the one hand, and from the believer on the other.[22]

This is by no means as straightforward as it may sound. For Jüngel knowledge of God is only given in the praxis of Christian existence; indeed it is true in a certain sense that God is only present where faith is present.[23] Because of this reciprocal relationship faith is constantly threatened with a "Feuerbachian" inversion, seeing itself as grounding God rather than vice-versa. Theology is the critique of faith; it thinks the event of faith in such a way as to elucidate the

---

20 Ibid. 12-3. We will continue to use the word "science" to translate the German "*Wissenschaft*," even though the ranges of meaning of the two words do not exactly coincide. The *Deutsches Universal-Wörterbuch* defines "*Wissenschaft*" as "research in a determinate area producing knowledge supported by argument" ("argumentativ gestütztes Wissen hervorbringende forschende Tätigkeit in einem bestimmten Bereich"). *DUDEN: Deutsches Universal-Wörterbuch* (Mannheim: Bibliographisches Institut, 1983).

21 Jüngel, "Theologische Wissenschaft," 12. Jüngel cites Max Weber's famous statement that science is a "power specifically foreign to [the idea of] God" ("spezifisch gottfremde Macht").

22 Jüngel, "Freiheit der Theologie," 25.

23 See Jüngel, "Nihil divinitatis," 234.

foundational role of God's act, and this means the concrete history of Jesus, his death and resurrection. Otherwise, faith might become so absorbed in its present existential reality as to turn the word "God" into a mere cipher for the actual grounding of faith within the structure of human existence itself. Were that to happen, the ultimate truth that God is the *"creator fidei in nobis"* would be displaced by the equally ultimate but perilously ambiguous insight of Luther that faith is the *"creatrix divinitatis in nobis."*24

The necessity of this act of dual differentiation is closely connected to the event-character of faith. It is an occurrence in which God and human beings enter into a determinate configuration, in fact into the closest communication; but precisely because of this intimate proximity thought takes care that the two "moments" of faith, the divine and the human, retain their respective identities. God and faith are not identical, even though the event of faith is the locus of God's very presence. Nor is faith simply identical to something given in and with the believer's existence, even though faith is an event radically conditioning that existence. "Were faith not distinguished from God, then 'God' would become a superfluous word. Were the believer not distinguished from faith, then faith would become a matter of course [*selbstverständlich*]."25

Another perspective on the same question of theology's critical task of thinking faith, one which more closely delineates the nature of concrete theological reflection, is provided by Jüngel's statement that theology involves properly relating the "richness" of faith to the "poverty" of Jesus.26 Jesus' poverty is the frailness of his utter humanity, the fragility of a public human history, terminating in the catastrophic exhaustion of crucifixion. This weakness of the man Jesus is his openness to God's act; the meaning of the resurrection for Jüngel is the open announcement to faith that this human history and death are God's history and death. Jesus' humanity, his poverty, is the holding open of a place in history for God; "precisely in his poverty Jesus stands

---

24 Jüngel, "Freiheit der Theologie," 25. Note the various citations in this article of figures from Bultmann's school, especially Ebeling, Käsemann, and Jüngel's own teacher Fuchs, all of whom have influenced his argument at this point.

25 Ibid.

26 Jüngel, "Theologische Wissenschaft," 27ff.

in God's place."[27]   Faith is the richness of God's presence as a power determining the believer's existence; but faith must not therefore forget that God's presence in history has been defined in the weakness of Jesus' history, culminating in the crucifixion.[28]

When theology thinks faith, it recalls it to its ground beyond itself. To be sure it is grounded in God; but God here can only mean the word of the crucified man Jesus as Christ. Jüngel's insistence, mentioned above, that the ground of faith must be brought into the closest relation to the object of faith holds true here as well. For Jüngel (in accord with Christian tradition) God's very Spirit is the ground of the believer's present faith. But the object of faith is the word of God, the history of Jesus Christ. To say that ground and object are one is another way of saying that God the Spirit and God in Christ are one; the Holy Spirit is the Spirit of Jesus Christ.

This construal of theology as a kind of basic rational reflection on faithful existence invites the question of its relation to philosophy, a question all the more relevant given Jüngel's constant probing of the philosophical tradition. Jüngel's relation to the theistic conceptions of philosophy will be a theme throughout this study, but here the question must be dealt with in a preliminary fashion.   Much of his later writing involves critical conversations with the standard "classical" categories of anthropology and metaphysics. Indeed, his careful and historically informed critiques of, for example, the traditional ontological privilege enjoyed by actuality over possibility, or of the metaphysical reading of God in terms of a "highest" or "most perfect" being, are central to his material theological project.   The revision and ad hoc utilization of philosophical motifs according to theological criteria points to a conscious eclecticism justly associated with the theology of Barth.   But this practical relationship of the theologian to philosophy is grounded in a strict formal delimitation of the two disciplines.

Already before the publication of the programmatic essays on theology, Jüngel was struggling against any attempts to conflate

---

27 Ibid. 28. "Denn gerade in seiner Armut ist Jesus der Statthalter Gottes." The term *"Statthalter"* literally means a satrap or viceroy, an official empowered to act with the authority of the sovereign.   As such he is the actual locus of the sovereign's executive presence in a province distant from the capital.

28 Ibid. 29.

theological and philosophical thinking, particularly certain arguments for a direct dependence of theological categories upon the kind of fundamental ontology propounded by Heidegger. In his first published work, Jüngel registered sharp disagreement with Heinrich Ott's demand for "a kind of personal union" of theology with philosophy in the person of the theologian.[29]

For Jüngel, even the most basic philosophical categories of being and existence must be radically reformulated under the decisive impact of the founding event of Christian faith and its historically mediated linguistic forms. "[T]he range of problems determining every theology [has] come to speech in the language-events characterizing the New Testament in a manner which binds theology to precisely these language-events."[30] The same concern surfaces at key points in his well-known book on Barth's doctrine of the trinity; Barth's language of God's "being" is not grounded in a conception of being in general, but arises from faith's reflection on God's revelation in Christ.[31]   For Jüngel, the independence of theology from any philosophical grounding demands the sharpest possible distinction between the two kinds of thinking.   This necessary distinction is touched on only briefly in the articles of chief concern here, most notably in "Die Freiheit der Theologie," where the same distinction is

---

[29] Eberhard Jüngel, "Der Schritt zurück: Eine Auseinandersetzung mit der Heidegger-Deutung Heinrich Otts," *Zeitschrift für Theologie und Kirche* 58 (1961): 104-22 at 113.   The citation is from Heinrich Ott, *Denken und Sein: Der Weg Martin Heideggers und der Weg der Theologie* (Zollikon: Evangelischer Verlag, 1959), 14. On a similar note, see also Eberhard Jüngel, review of *Sein und Existenz*, by Gerhard Noller, in *Evangelische Theologie* 23 (1963): 218-23.

[30] Ibid. 115.   "Ist nicht in den das Neue Testament auszeichnenden Sprachereignissen die jede Theologie bestimmende Problematik in einer die Theologie an eben diese Sprachereignisse bindenden Weise zur Sprache gekommen?" (I have translated this rhetorical question as an assertion.)

[31] Eberhard Jüngel, *Gottes Sein ist im Werden*, 4th ed. (Tübingen: J.C.B. Mohr, 1986) 75-6.   Werner Jeanrond has stressed this point in a recent article.   The hermeneutical element of Jüngel's theology is ontologically grounded, but only in the sense that it is grounded in the doctrine of the trinity as the "most adequate ontological approach to God's dynamic and singular being." See Werner Jeanrond, "The Problem of the Starting-point of Theological Thinking," in *The Possibilities of Theology: Studies in the Theology of Eberhard Jüngel in his Sixtieth Year*, ed. John Webster (Edinburgh: T&T Clark, 1994), 70-89 at 83.

made in a highly schematic way.[32] Theology "hands over" the word to thought, and does so in such a way that the "otherness" of the word over against thought is preserved.   That is, the word itself is linguistically mediated via the event of proclamation and is appropriated as word only in the actual situation of a faith response. It is not derived from the structure of thought itself as a general human possibility.   In contrast, Jüngel understands philosophy (formally speaking) to be thought's self-reflection, the "handing over" to thought of thought itself.   As such, philosophy is its own justification: it "posits itself absolutely," being grounded in the very nature of thought.[33] Theology cannot posit itself; it is parasitic, so to speak, upon the occurrence of the word in history.

Theology as *Wissenschaft* and the Theological Disciplines
It can be seen why theology, since it (critically) thinks faith for the sake of faith, is defined by a dual responsibility.   As critical thought it is caught up in the ongoing history of thought; it must be current, true to its time (*zeitgemäss*).   But as the self-criticism of faith it must measure faith by the word; it must be responsible to the event of the word as its object (*sachgemäss*).[34] Theology is actualized in the interaction of these two responsibilities and in the attempt to locate the ground of their unity.

In the modern period, theology repeatedly has been conceived as a scientific endeavor; this is part of what it means for theology to be true to its time.   It has long been a commonplace of German *Wissenschaftslehre* (theory of science) that the nature and unity of a science is determined by the object of that science.[35] As will be seen, the object of theology has a certain complexity which has resulted in the development of different sub-disciplines of theology arising within the academy, each coordinated to a different aspect of that object and each

---

32 Jüngel, "Freiheit der Theologie," 56-7.

33 Jüngel takes up this theme in the context of his discussion of the debate between Fichte and Schleiermacher over the "positive" (as opposed to "speculative") character of theology. Jüngel, "Verhältnis der theologischen Disziplinen," 43. See also Paulus, *Liebe — das Geheimnis der Welt*, 22-3.

34 Jüngel, "Freiheit der Theologie," 13.

35 Jüngel, "Theologische Wissenschaft," 33.

employing different methods. Each of these sub-disciplines has tended to have a "natural" alliance with its closest non-theological counterparts, looking to the latter for methodological clarity and scientific legitimation. Biblical studies might align itself with philology or ancient history, church history with secular world history, systematic theology with philosophy, etc. The obvious danger is that the unity of the former disciplines as part of a single (theological) enterprise might be eroded, and each might drift apart from the others, gradually becoming "naturalized," or even vanishing altogether as separate disciplines.

For Jüngel this problem of the unity of the theological disciplines is not merely an organizational difficulty; it is central to any configuration of theology as a science.[36] For the basis of his approach Jüngel recurs to Schleiermacher's dispute with Fichte on the propriety of theology as a distinct faculty within the university.[37] Jüngel claims that the aporia within theology exposed by Fichte (i.e. the tension between its claim to a place within the realm of science and its appeal to a particular revelation) was transformed by Schleiermacher into the very foundation of its scientific character.[38]

According to Schleiermacher's brilliant *Brief Outline of the Study of Theology*, theology's appeal to a particular revelation means that its realm of investigation is a particular historical complex, the living tradition of the Christian God-consciousness and its objectified forms over time. In addition, the unity of the various disciplines comprising theology is insured within the university not by the speculative construction of its object, nor by its place within a system of sciences derived from the nature of pure thought. The unity of theology lies in its being ordered to the practical function of training leaders of the Christian church. It is the "positivity" of theology, its direct

---

[36] Jüngel, "Verhältnis der theologischen Disziplinen," 54.

[37] These debates were occasioned by the formation of the new University of Berlin in 1809. For a detailed discussion which recognizes the significance of this occasion for later reflection on theology, see Hans Frei, *Types of Christian Theology* (New Haven: Yale University Press, 1992) 92-116.

[38] Jüngel, "Verhältnis der theologischen Disziplinen," 43.

connection with concrete praxis, which binds the various theological disciplines into a unity.[39]

Jüngel constructs his own conception of theological science on the two foundations laid by Schleiermacher: theology's fundamentally historical character (its *Geschichtlichkeit*), and its practical goal (its *Positivität*). "The historical nature of its scientific object brings theology *into* the realm of the sciences. — The historical nature of its practical aim grants theology the unity of a single science."[40] This statement shows what Jüngel appropriates from Schleiermacher and at the same time how he moves beyond him. Schleiermacher did not succeed in thinking the historical goal of theology (the praxis of Christian existence) and the historical object of theology in their unity as one history.

In other words, theology must show how Christian praxis, the historical task laid on the Church in the present, springs from the kind of historical object it is concerned with in the past. Indeed, that object must be capable in the present of calling forth faith and serving as its criterion.[41] The central integrating concept which allows the coalescence of historical praxis and historical object and determines the proper organizational scheme of the theological disciplines is that of the word-as-event, or word-event. The presupposition of theology as an historical science is that the event of the word of God is only properly historically elucidated (*historisch erklärt*) when it is "answered for" by activity in present history (*geschichtliche Verantwortung*).[42] To understand the past occurrence of the word is to

---

39 Ibid. 43-4. See also Friedrich Schleiermacher, *Kurze Darstellung des theologischen Studiums*, ed. Heinrich Scholz (Leipzig: A. Deichert, 1973, original ed. 1910); English translation: *Brief Outline of the Study of Theology*, trans. Terrence Tice (Richmond: John Knox Press, 1966).

40 Ibid. 50. "Die Geschichtlichkeit ihres wissenschaftlichen Gegenstandes bringt die Theologie *in* das Ganze der Wissenschaften. --- Die Geschichtlichkeit ihres praktischen Zweckes läßt die Theologie als ein Ganzes Wissenschaft sein."

41 Ibid.

42 Ibid. 51. The elegant precision and extreme compression of Jüngel's thoughts at this point completely unravel in translation. Two points are crucial for comprehension: 1. *Historie* and *historisch* tend to connote the scholarly practice of historical science, whereas *Geschichte* and *geschichtlich* indicate the actual temporal career of persons or social collectives whether in the past or the present. 2. The verb *verantworten* means to answer or account for; the noun *Verantwortung* means

recognize a word addressing the present as well, an event which seeks its own repetition, its own propagation as an ever renewed happening (*als erneut geschehendes*).

Theology must explicate and interpret the word of God historically, i.e. as an historical occurrence in the past, but it must do this only because it seeks to be responsible to that word in the present. The word-event conceptually and actually integrates theology's object and theology's purpose. In his own determination of the different theological disciplines, Jüngel's use of the historical "repeatibility" of the word-event provides a four-fold division in place of Schleiermacher's tripartite scheme.[43] This theological division of labor will only be briefly sketched here.[44]

The first two disciplines, exegesis and church history, are concerned with the past occurrence of the word-event. The one deals with the Biblical text, the other with the entire later history of Christian tradition. The need for two separate disciplines might seem problematic, especially since Jüngel has pointed out that the divine word is available to theology only in its human formulations; in other words, the past event of the word is always historically mediated via its theological interpretations by those concerned. Hence no strict historical distinction can be drawn between the words of the Bible and those of later tradition.

But the words of the Bible are the original linguistic articulation of the dimension of God's decisive act; they are witnesses,

---

responsibility. When Jüngel uses these words or others with the same root he seems to have simultaneously in mind the following shades of meaning: a) the activity of accounting for something, b) the activity of responding to something, and c) the state of being responsible or accountable to something. In this case the "something" is the same in all three meanings, namely the event of the word of God.

[43] For Jüngel the principle of Schleiermacher's division remains sound: a historical theology combining exegesis and dogmatics, a philosophical theology mediating the relation of theology to the other sciences, and a practical theology mediating theology to the practical task of church leadership. But both Schleiermacher and Jüngel stress that these divisions are not exclusive, as all theological work must participate in all three tasks, albeit in different degrees according to the context. Although Jüngel sometimes uses similar terms, the principle of division is different, so that no one discipline in his scheme precisely corresponds to any of Schleiermacher's.

[44] What follows synthesizes elements from the two detailed breakdowns of the theological disciplines offered in Jüngel, "Freiheit der Theologie," 33-4 and Jüngel, "Verhältnis der theologischen Disziplinen," 57-9.

born of the actual encounter with the reality of God's advent. They are thus "canonical," since it is only as shaped by these original theological decisions that the word is encountered by later generations.[45] Church history is concerned with the historically interpreted and "fixed" word-event, measuring the interpretations against the primal word-event mediated in the words of scripture. Exegesis, however, must engage in "*Sachkritik*"; it can only measure the scriptural interpretations against the reality which they themselves mediate.

The conception of the word-event and its repetition integrates the object of theology (the continual occurrence of the word in the past, its fixation in linguistic forms, springing from its original event) and the present goal of theology (to achieve a new formulation of the word from the canonical texts, a word for today). The latter is the specific task of practical theology. It is the science of the word of God as event, not in the sense of past event, but in the sense of something taking place now, in the present. In short, its particular province is the determination of church praxis, the responsibility of the believing community to respond to the word of Jesus Christ in the concrete situation. It seeks the possibility of proclaiming the present reality of Jesus Christ in thoughts, words, and actions.[46]

Exegesis inquires after the original event of the word to be repeated. The repetitions of the word occurring in the past are the concern of church history. The repetition of the word in the present is sought for by practical theology. But it is this very characteristic of the word, that it is repeatable, that it occurs again and again in history with unaltered power and validity, that is the concern of systematic theology.[47] It asks about the relationship between the three forms of

---

45 Jüngel, "Freiheit der Theologie," 20.

46 Jüngel, "Verhältnis der theologischen Disziplinen," 58.

47 Paulus devotes considerable attention to the notion of "systematicity" in theology. In fact, he goes so far as to describe Jüngel's own theology as a "system of freedom" (*Liebe — das Geheimnis der Welt*, 17). He admits that this represents a risky departure from Jüngel's own usage, and the specific justificatory citations he mentions are somewhat unconvincing. More helpful is his careful delimitation of the meaning of "system" in this context (ibid. 15). Theology can be called a system insofar as it is a "methodically presented doctrine of Christian faith" which, because of its character as discourse about God, concerns the structure of reality as a whole. Theology is also a system in another sense, as a unified interpretation of faith which

the word dealt with in the other disciplines, demonstrating their unity as modes of the one event of Jesus Christ.[48] Jüngel describes the inexhaustible reiteration of God's word in Jesus, its ability to enter into every new pattern of human self-understanding, as its truth. Systematic theology is the science of the word of God as truth.

Each discipline takes up a special responsibility vis-à-vis the word, thus achieving a partial "relieving" of the burden (*Entlastung*) which the others must bear. But the essential meaning of such "responsibility" is that God's word is the only object and goal of all theological activity. Neither the Biblical text, nor the ecclesial tradition, nor even the presently existing Church itself can be mistaken for an end in itself. Therefore each discipline has a critical function; exegesis, church history and practical theology are to be understood as critiques of the Biblical texts, tradition, and of present ecclesial praxis respectively. Because systematic theology considers all the disciplines in their unity, it must prevent their centrifugal drift toward purely secular status. It seeks to understand the nature of the theological by entering into a "a critical conversation of faith with unbelief," and therefore functions as the self-critique of theology.[49]

Wissenschaftlich Theology as Historical and as Dogmatic

It was seen above that Jüngel distinguishes two types of disposition toward the past. Historical explanation (*historisches Erklären*) involves application of the tools of historical science, the historical-critical method, in the reconstruction of past events and their causal interrelations. But there is also responsibility for or toward the past (*geschichtliche Verantwortung*) which implies understanding the human past as both a demand and a possibility for human activity in the present. It is characteristic of Christian theology for Jüngel that these normally separable dispositions must be closely interrelated; the event of God's word and its repetition is to be ascertained and delineated through historical research, but,

---

in its separate parts and as a whole claims the identity of a single science. These are justified insights, even if their relation to Jüngel's own sparse use of the term "systematic" remains obscure.

[48] Jüngel, "Verhältnis der theologischen Disziplinen," 58.

[49] Ibid. 59.

paradoxically, the event itself can only be recognized in faith, that is as the power determining Christian existence in the present.

The difficult feat of unifying these dispositions as single moments of one concrete task is the condition for the very possibility of theology. One of Jüngel's several definitions of theology describes it as discerning the freedom of Christian existence in the responsibility of thought. As pointed out above, theology is challenged both by its special object (*Sache*) and by its present time (*Zeit*). Jüngel tends to associate the "discerning of Christian existence" with theology's objective concern, and the "responsibility of thought" with the peculiar demand of the present.[50] The historical nature of theology which he insists upon is not just a function of its adopting the peculiarly modern form of historical understanding, i.e. historical-critical method. It also demands the recognition of the "historicity" of theology's object, which precisely means to take up responsibility to the word-event in faith. Historical-scientific explanation and historical-existential responsibility are the two poles which theology must unite: it must be "historical" in both senses.

The paradox indicated above which arises in the juxtaposition of explanation and responsibility is resolved for Jüngel by carefully distinguishing between "historical" and "dogmatic" perception (*Wahrnehmung*) of the past. Theology does not have direct access to the past event of God's word. Instead, it must reconstruct the shape of that event through the faith-testimony of those among whom the event occurred. In other words, the divine word is only available through the historical medium of human language, language in the form of theological interpretation. Looking back to the word, theological interpretation always encounters an earlier theological interpretation of that word.

That the event of Jesus is God's own advent is never directly visible from historical facts, and was not so visible even to contemporaries of the event.[51] But the linguistic and conceptual form in which these witnesses articulated their faith-perception, and

---

[50] Jüngel, "Freiheit der Theologie," 30.

[51] The Kierkegaardian influence here, perhaps mediated via Bultmann, is strikingly obvious. See Søren Kierkegaard, *Philosophical Fragments and Johannes Climacus,* ed. and trans. Howard V. Hong and Edna H. Hong (Princeton: Princeton University Press, 1985), 55-71.

therefore that perception itself, are both very much a function of the social and intellectual milieu or the symbolic universe within which they moved, and are thus subject to historical investigation. "Of course, all these claims [i.e. of faith] have entered into a necessary and close connection with a wealth of [historical] delimitations and completely determinate representations."[52] Faith must perceive the contours of the original word-event through the interpretation of past faith-confessions; the first step in accomplishing this must be the most rigorous historical examination of those testimonies which is possible.

Another way of grasping the task involved here is to say that the word of revelation is only given to theology "according to human reception" (*secundum recipientem hominem*). To move from the critical or purely historical moment to the dogmatic one means to grasp (in an historically informed way) the context of that human word of confession as an original revelatory event, the event to which it is the response and of which it is the linguistic articulation; the word of revelation received mirrors (albeit with inevitable distortion) the word as spoken by God (*secundum dicentem Deum*).[53]   The historical artifact of linguistically fixed confession is for theology an abstraction from an original concrete situation of correspondence between God and human beings, a faith-situation. The turn from historical to dogmatic perception is marked first of all by an act of faithful imaginative reconstruction of that faith-situation. It is interpreted as a situation in which historically-given acts of faith are responses to an act of divine revelation which is itself not historically given.   That such reconstruction is fraught with uncertainty and the potential for ideological deformation is manifest, but it is still the crux of theological interpretation.

The moment of historical explanation in theology is, so to speak, a "secular" enclave within theological understanding.   It "reckons with *the world* 'as if there were no God.'" But the act of theological understanding always involves a complementary act of dogmatic interpretation, which as the responsible answer in faith to the past word will not allow theology to "reckon with *God* 'as if there

52 Jüngel, "Theologie in der Spannung," 43:   "Zwar sind alle diese Behauptungen mit einer Fülle von Feststellungen und erst recht mit ganz bestimmten Vorstellungen eine notwendige und feste Verbindung eingegangen."

53 Jüngel, "Freiheit der Theologie," 19.

were no God.'"[54]   In this complementarity of historical perception and dogmatic perception, neither properly grounds the other, and yet dogmatic perception is dependent upon historical perception due to the linguisticality of Christian faith.   "Dogmatic perception is *interpretation* of historically perceived language as the language of past faith for the purpose of *uncovering* the language possible and necessary for faith today."[55]

Analysis of this last quotation might help to highlight what is characteristic of dogmatic perception. We inherit a set of documents from the past (in this case, the scriptural documents). Historical perception is concerned to interpret the language of these documents as a record of human belief, and so, too, is dogmatic perception. But the basic procedures or "ground rules" differ in accordance with the respective purposes of interpretation. At least initially, historical perception interprets these words with the intention of reconstructing a human situation within the horizon of typical human capacities and social interactions. The faith of the actors is of interest only insofar as it contributes to an understanding of that human situation. Dogmatic perception, however, refuses to stop with the fact of human witness; it attempts to discern the shape of that event of divine disclosure which is being pointed to, and which purely historical perception is content to leave as a mere blank or lacuna.

Why does dogmatic perception take this extra step? It is motivated to do so by the belief that the divine disclosure recorded in the scriptures can and does occur in the present as well, and that the language needed to mediate and witness to that disclosure now is always an interpretation of the historically-given language which witnessed to that disclosure in the original event of Christ, the pattern

---

[54] Jüngel, "Verhältnis der theologischen Disziplinen," 52. In both citations, the phrase in single quotation marks represents my translation from the Latin actually used in the text: "*etsi Deus non daretur.*" Although it appears there without attribution, the phrase ultimately springs from Grotius by way of Bonhoeffer (cf. GGW 76-7 [58-9]). Although *etsi* technically should be translated "even if" ("as if" more properly corresponds to *quasi* or *ut si*), and that is probably how to interpret the phrase as it appears both in Grotius and in Bonhoeffer, I think that my translation captures better Jüngel's meaning in this context. At any rate, Jüngel himself does not bother to provide a German translation.

[55] Eberhard Jüngel, "Thesen zur Grundlegung der Christologie," in *Unterwegs zur Sache*, 274-95 at 285.

for all later disclosures to Christian faith. This faith that the same revelatory event which shaped the response of faith in the past can and will occur in the present is what separates the dogmatic moment from the historical one.

Clearly, when Jüngel claims that "the historical-critical method is the way to the word of theology" he does not imply that the dogmatic method has been supplanted.[56] Against an interpretation of theological history such as that of Troeltsch, which sees the historical method as the legitimate successor of a now obsolete dogmatic method, Jungel asserts the integral relation of the dogmatic and historical in every act of theological understanding.[57] In this he again claims to follow the lead of Schleiermacher, who, by uniting exegesis and dogmatics under the one heading of historical theology, was at once opposing Fichte's demand for a strictly non-historical (i.e. non-confessional or philosophical) theology in the university, and rejecting the theological tradition (running back to Gabler) of a strict separation of exegetical and dogmatic theology.[58]

Jüngel's summary formula of his position shows his love for dialectically balanced assertions. "Because theology is historically [*geschichtlich*] responsible for nothing which it has not also historically [*historisch*] explicated, theology is in every respect historical. But because theology *is* historically responsible for what it

---

[56] Jüngel, "Freiheit der Theologie," 32. Cf. Gerhard Ebeling, *Theologie und Verkündigung: Ein Gespräch mit Rudolf Bultmann* (Tübingen: J. C. B. Mohr [Paul Siebeck], 1962), 14-5: "Dogmatic theology completes the task of interpretation not in the sense of a method competing with historical exegesis, but rather in the sense of a turn, called for by the subject matter itself, from the historical to the dogmatic way of understanding." Cited in James M. Robinson, "Hermeneutic since Barth," in *New Frontiers in Theology* vol. 2, *The New Hermeneutic*, ed. James M. Robinson and John B. Cobb, Jr. (New York: Harper & Row, 1964), 68.

[57] The classic statement of this position is Ernst Troeltsch, "Über historische und dogmatische Methode in der Theologie," in *Gesammelte Schriften*, 4 vols. (Aalen: Scientia, 1962; original editions 1913 and 1922), 2: 729-53. Now translated in Ernst Troeltsch, *Religion in History*, trans. J. L. Adams and W. Bense (Minneapolis: Fortress, 1991), 11-32. It should be pointed out, however, that Jüngel evidently understands "dogma" and "dogmatic" in a manner closer to Karl Barth's "historicized" conception than to Troeltsch's more traditional usage. See also Gerhard Ebeling, "Die Bedeutung der historischkritischen Methode für die protestantische Theologie und Kirche" in idem, *Wort und Glaube*, vol. 1 (Tübingen: J.C.B. Mohr, 1960), 1-49.

[58] Jüngel, "Verhältnis der theologischen Disziplinen," 47-50.

historically explicates, it is in every respect dogmatic."[59] With regard to this difficult relationship, so central to his vision of theology, Jüngel makes the remarkable claim that "[t]he tension between historical and dogmatic understanding is to be resolved in a critique of historical reason which has yet to be written."[60] Theology is still awaiting an analysis of the rational categories which determine both how past historical events are apprehended and how these events are integrated within the present historical trajectory of human understanding. Lacking such a categorial framework the theological integration of past history and present historicity outlined above will appear as a tenuous and tension-filled procedure.

Conclusion

This chapter has shown that there is a characteristically provocative approach implicit in Jüngel's formal reflections on the nature of theology. These early essays are an important part of his grand attempt to reconcile the divergent trajectories of the dialectical theology tradition. One matter not touched upon here is how his synthetic approach ultimately employs the material dogmatic category of the trinity (in a form appropriated from Barth) to provide the ontological framework for the formal structure of theology. But that structure, for its part, is largely couched in terms of a Bultmannian hermeneutic of the faith event.

Language is manifestly the key integrator here; the central category of "the word" is at once theological and supremely anthropological (human being as linguistic being).[61] Behind the schematism of the different forms of the word-event is discernible not only Barth's "threefold form of the word of God" (i.e. revealed,

---

59 Ibid. 51. Emphasis mine.

60 Jüngel, "Freiheit der Theologie," 34: "Die Spannung zwischen historischem und dogmatischem Verstehen ist auszutragen in einer noch ausstehenden Kritik der historischen Vernunft."

61 The move was made possible by the concept of "word-event" in Fuchs and Ebeling, who followed Bultmann in rejecting the old idealistic notion of a pre-linguistic faith-experience which is then objectified in linguistic form as confession. As response to God's word faith is linguistic primarily, at its very core; as a linguistic event it is integrated within the linguistic context of human culture, and as a tradition of confession it is linguistically mediated in human history.

written, preached) but also a linguistic figuring of the trinity (the Son as the word, the Father as speaker of the word, and the Spirit as the historical event of the word's reception). Much more research needs to be devoted to this issue, but at the very least these articles are a salutary attempt to recover the original concerns of dialectical theology in their contemporary relevance by reconceiving ossified polemical categories (Barth vs. Bultmann, "neo-orthodoxy" vs. "demythologization," etc.).

As a theology oriented strictly to God's self-revelation in Christ and its appropriation in faith it represents a continued vigorous protest against any attempt to provide a set of criteria for theological concepts which would "ground" them in some putatively more basic discourse, such as a general metaphysics or some normative socio-ethical praxis. That Jüngel is abundantly aware of the difficulties of this position and the dangers of theological isolationism is clear from many of his writings, particularly those on the problem of so-called "natural theology." At any rate, this insistent grounding of theological judgement within the interpretive circle of faith does not imply a rejection of dialog in favor of a cozily insulated dogmatism.[62] But these considerations raise all the more strongly the question as to what kind of "*theos*" is at issue if theology is conceived in this way.

Theology always exists in a symbiotic relationship with particular conceptions of God; the two feed off of each other and grow together. It was pointed out at the beginning of the chapter that as his career has progressed Jüngel has turned away from explicitly methodological treatments of the task of theology. This is not to say that the issue has lost importance for him, but rather that in his mature work the question as to how to do theology has been completely integrated into the question of the identity of the God of Jesus Christ. Reflections on the dogmatic task are almost inextricably woven into the actual performance of that task. Indeed, *God as the Mystery of the*

---

[62] Jüngel's complex and subtle appropriation of various strands of the theological tradition makes his theology rather difficult to "place" among the standard positions. For a brief but suggestive characterization utilizing Hans Frei's typology see John Webster, "Introduction" in *Possibilities of Theology*, ed. Webster, 1-6. A similar attempt by Jeanrond to situate Jüngel with respect to the so-called Chicago-Yale debate is less satisfactory, largely due to a sketchy and at points superficial portrayal of the opposed positions. See Werner Jeanrond, "The Problem of the Starting Point of Theological Thinking" in ibid. 70-89.

World, a profound exploration of the God apprehended in Christian faith, can also be seen as one massive treatise on theological method.

This being so, the earlier essays explored in this chapter have the advantage of relative abstraction; in helping to clarify Jüngel's understanding of theology they also proleptically suggest the basic theistic conception to be explored in the remainder of this study. First of all, the determination of divine being will obviously not be grounded in a general construal of being in the manner of a fundamental ontology or general metaphysics. But more than this, God's being will have to be understood in intimate connection to the human existence of Jesus and to the historical and linguistic mediation of the faith which confesses God's identification with that existence. What kind of God-concept results from thinking in accord with such demanding conditions? Clearly, it will be a concept at odds with many of the presuppositions concerning God's being which dominated theological and philosophical thinking until recent times. The story of how that dominance came to an end must be explored in order to understand the particular moves Jüngel makes in constructing an alternative theistic conceptuality.

CHAPTER THREE

THE MODERN DISCOVERY OF GOD'S NON-NECESSITY AND THE FATE OF THE DIVINE SIMPLICITY

The different articles which lay behind the just-completed sketch of Jüngel's conception of theology represent some of his earliest attempts at systematic theological reflection. They show a remarkable energy and a comprehensive view of the theological task; clearly their author has taken his essential framework from Bultmann and his successors in the hermeneutical theology tradition, but there is also evident a commitment to a more radically trinitarian vision of God reordering the emphases and reshaping the agenda. This trinitarian vision is the fruit of Jüngel's deep penetration of Barth's later theology. But for him this is not an artificial grafting onto the Bultmannian stem of an alien branch; Jüngel wishes to strike the common source of the divergent strands of the "dialectical theology" tradition by means of his explorations in the modern history of the concept of God in theology, in philosophy, and in culture in general.[1] The counterpart and presupposition of his program for an evangelical theology will be shown in the next chapter to be a God whose existence and essence are identical and which is thus "more than necessary."

Post-Cartesian Metaphysics as the Philosophy of the Death of God

Jüngel understands the modern notion of the "death of God" and thus the phenomenon of modern atheism to be closely linked with the concept of God's "non-necessity" within the worldly or human horizon. The first step on the path of understanding the demand for theistic reconstruction is to grasp the manner in which the necessary God of the Western metaphysical and theological traditions (in their mutual interpenetration) underwent a relentless disintegration in the course of the modern metaphysical development initiated by Descartes. In presenting Jüngel's interpretation of this process, the present chapter will

---

[1] For Jüngel the critique of metaphysical theism was an endeavour common to the various branches of the dialectical theology movement. See GGW 55-6 (43-4).

emphasize the more strictly intellectual or theoretical problems generated by the absolute or necessary God-concept in its modern metaphysical career; the practical and ethical dispute between the modern consciousness of autonomous freedom and the absolute Lord of the tradition can be for the most part laid aside.[2]

According to Jüngel the crisis of metaphysical theism arose when the idea of God, defined as a being in whom essence and existence are strictly identical, became philosophically inconceivable under the altered conditions of post-Cartesian rationality. Jüngel points out that this thesis of the identity of essence and existence was closely linked with the necessity of the divine being. The notion of God's necessity within the worldly horizon as the metaphysical cause or explanation of various phenomena (what might be called God's "instrumental" necessity) demanded as its counterpart an elimination of every trace of contingency in the divine being itself: "To the worldly necessity of a highest essence corresponded the ontological necessity of the existence of this essence" (GGW 136 [103]). It was precisely the God defined as necessary by means of the thesis of the unity of essence and existence which equipped Descartes for the task of grounding human thought in its own certainty. The irony of this development was that Descartes' demonstration of God's ontological necessity (his version of the "ontological argument") proved to be a turning point for the consciousness of God's worldly necessity; as Jüngel says, this proof of God's necessity was the "midwife" of modern atheism (GGW 23 [19]).

According to Jüngel, the modern discovery of God's worldly non-necessity is intimately linked to the dissolution of the idea of God in the course of post-Cartesian metaphysics. This intellectual trajectory and its corresponding cultural manifestations were eventually to issue in the "death of God" heralded by Nietzsche. To understand the nature of the resulting atheism it is important to recognize the concepts of divinity which were destined to be rejected.[3] Jüngel reiterates what

---

2 For this distinction see GGW 24 (20) and 135 (102).

3 The contribution to the rise of atheism in the early modern period made by theological apologetics in general, and of a metaphysically constructed theism in particular, has recently been the topic of some sensitive historical explorations. See Michael Buckley, *At the Origins of Modern Atheism* (New Haven: Yale University Press, 1987) and also Louis Dupre, *Passage to Modernity* (New Haven: Yale University Press, 1993). In the latter work note especially the summary on p. 181.

has also been remarked by others before and since: "The understanding about God which it disputes is always decisive for any sort of atheism; indeed it is that understanding which makes the dispute possible" (GGW 23 [19]).

Jüngel conceives of the historical dissolution of the idea of God in terms of a collision between a predominant traditional concept of divinity (as a being characterized by the identity of essence and existence) and a peculiarly modern notion of autonomous human thought. The initial site of this collision, as is coming to seem almost inevitable for anything characterizing the modern intellect, is the thought of Descartes, though he himself did not apprehend the difficulty. What were the peculiar characteristics of the God inherited by Descartes?

The Theistic Inheritance of Early Modernity

The two central postulates concerning divine being which modern metaphysics received from the theistic tradition were, first, that God is absolute perfection, superior to all worldly being, and, second, that in God there can be no real distinction of essence and existence (GGW 275-6 [203]). It is the task of thinking both these postulates together in their unity which was to be rendered all but impossible after the revolution initiated by Descartes. The two will be discussed in turn to bring out their implications.

The first postulate is God's superiority to the world and all that is in it. The varied expressions for this superiority in turn spring from some prior evaluation of the characteristics of worldy beings. That is, what is decried as weakness and inferiority within the world, must be expunged from God; what seems to be of superior value will then naturally be located in God in some intensified form. Thus, different expressions arise for formulating divine superiority.

One of the more general formulations is "absolute perfection"; indeed God can be said to be "perfection entirely perfected" (*perfectio omnino perfecta*). Because this means that God is complete and entire, lacking any defect, it follows, temporally speaking, that "God can always already look back upon his own completion (*ganz und gar auf sich zurückblicken*); his being is free from becoming" (GGW 7 [7]). As that which surpasses everything, divine becoming would have no "direction" in which to move toward something better or more complete. For Anselm, this superiority becomes in itself a definition of

God. His formula has, of course, become classic: God is "that than which nothing greater can be conceived."[4] God, then, is absolute being; becoming, understood as opposed to being, must be utterly foreign to divinity. It follows, granting the metaphysical concepts developed by classical Greek thought and largely perpetuated by late antiquity and the scholastics, that God's being is pure act or actuality (*actus purus*). As becoming was banished from the idea of God, so must any taint of potentiality or possibility (GGW 71 [54]). The conceptual dichotomies implicit in these definitions are crucial; pure actuality excludes all possibility just as surely as pure being excludes all becoming.

In addition to these metaphysical categories, concepts taken from social relations, properly modified, were also invoked for the construction of deity. The traditional God must be conceived of as a "Lord" in the most fundamental sense, indeed as *the* Lord. God is first and foremost the possessor of absolute power. Of course, sincere protests were raised against any notion of lordship which would make of God a tyrant. Even so, Jüngel claims, the ultimate subordination of God's love and mercy to God's omnipotence proved all but irresistible. The former characteristics tended to devolve into subsidiaries; God's power was conceivable in and of itself, quite apart from God's love. God is "free to love or not to love" (GGW 26 [21]). As Jüngel dryly remarks: "This is indeed the way one thinks here below of a lord: first of all he has power and then perhaps he can be merciful — but then again, perhaps not" (GGW 25 [21]).

So much for the postulate of divine superiority, which is the key to what Jüngel refers to as the "axiom of absoluteness" (GGW 51 [42]). The fundamental procedures of a metaphysical theism are here manifest: reality in general is analyzed in terms of basic categories, which are then projected into the concept of God on the basis of their hierarchical organiza on in terms of value. The second postulate important for Jüngel's argument, that of the identity of essence and existence in God, will exemplify this kind of thinking as well. In fact, his initial discussion of this postulate of identity attempts to link it to the postulate of superiority as a kind of natural outgrowth of the latter. As a genetic account of the idea this seems hardly satisfactory;

---

4 This, possibly the most awkward phrase in English to become famous, is found at the beginning of the second chapter of Anselm's *Proslogion* (and passim).

here as occasionally elsewhere the historical currents and counter-currents of the tradition are oversimplified in Jüngel's hasty overview. However, I do not believe his intention is really to determine the historical or even the logical origin of the identity postulate. It is rather to suggest that there is a structural kinship between these classic theistic claims.

The treatment in question is found in the context of Jüngel's discussion of modern atheism in terms of God's "location" (GGW 136 [103]). The question "Where is God?" in the modern context is understood not as a response to the absence of a deity whose nature is presupposed, as in the Bible. Quite the contrary, it expresses a dispute over the very definition of God.

As has already been indicated, God's essence was defined as superiority to the world and to humanity; more positive characteristics were then needed to clarify this superiority, which is itself seen as the question of God's essence. Jüngel points to the particular importance of the notions of omnipotence and omnipresence. In the context of sophisticated reflections on the unity of the divine attributes, these two notions came to define one another reciprocally: "One thinks of omnipotence itself as omnipresent . . . and of omnipresence as constantly active omnipotence . . ." (GGW 136 [103]). The conjunction of these two must mean that the divine essence is actively present at every point in space and time; absence is utterly excluded by the very nature of God's essence. It is at this point that Jüngel sees the affinity of the identity postulate to the superiority postulate. It is the essence of divine superiority to be everywhere present, actively and absolutely. But what is this conclusion but another way of saying that God's essence implies a necessary and superlative mode of existence?

Jüngel's rather labored attempt to relate the two postulates in this way is, then, more an interpretive than a historical endeavor; one suggestion of this is the lack of any cited precedent in the tradition for just this kind of link. Indeed, he is elsewhere capable of approaching the thesis of identity from a completely different direction. In the European metaphysical tradition at least since Aristotle, the idea of God has served as the guarantor not only of the interconnection of all things, but also of the coherence of thought and being. More precisely, it was the idea of God as a thinking being, of the *intellectus divinus*, which functioned in this way. According to Jüngel, the interconnection (*Zusammenhang*) of thought and being was identified by Aristotle with the interconnection of thought with itself. God as the thinking of thought or thought thinking itself (*noeseos noesis*), is that in which everything coherently "hangs together" (GGW 139 [105-6]). Thus divine self-identity grounds the unity of the cosmos.

This conceptuality found its corresponding expression in scholastic theology. The ability of the human intellect to attain truth in the knowledge of things was due ultimately to the common creator of both intellect and objects. Insofar as truth is the proper relation of the thought to the object of thought (*adaequatio intellectus et rei*), then God the creator is the original and absolute instance of truth. All things are perfectly "equated" to the divine intellect because of the preexistence there of their ideas. In other words, God's intellect as the interconnection (*Zusammenhang*) of all things can be identified with God's creative power which "holds them together" (*zusammenhält*) in being. God's knowledge creates its object (Kant's *intuitus originarius*).[5] What is essential here, though, is the idea that it is again God's self-identity which is the coherence of the universe. God knows all things in God's self, as the forms of things to be created (*res creandae*). This perfect creative knowledge is in turn grounded in God's perfect self-knowledge, God's knowledge of God's own necessary essence. Absolute unity and simplicity, with no distinction between God's existence and essence, are again presupposed; God's being is "essential being" (*ens per essentiam*) (GGW 139 [106]).

In the mainstream metaphysical tradition both of the postulates we have looked at contributed to an understanding of God as necessary being (*ens necessarium*). In the case of what we have been calling the identity postulate this is more or less easy to grasp. As a being which exists essentially, God cannot be conceived apart from God's existence, unlike created things, the ultimate contingency of which always allows a strict distinction of some sort between their essence and their existence.[6] That necessary existence follows from the

---

5 Jüngel reformulates this concept in an intriguing way, more indebted to Luther than to Kant. See Eberhard Jüngel, *The Freedom of a Christian*, tr. Roy Harrisville (Minneapolis: Augsburg Press, 1988), 35-7.

6 Actually, Jüngel admits that where finite beings were concerned, a considerable controversy was carried on through the tradition with regard to the precise determinations of essence and existence. But whether existence was considered a kind of "thing" (*res*) which can be added to essence, or rather (with

notion of God's absoluteness and superiority which we discussed earlier is perhaps not so obvious, but the train of thought is similar. The perfect being is free of all becoming; the act of pure reality is the exclusion of all potentiality. Becoming and potentiality are the hallmarks of contingent existence, of the realm of possibility, and the devaluation of these categories by the tradition assured that they would be characteristics of the created world alone. God is rather the absolute necessity grounding all worldly being and preventing the infinite regress of contingent causes. According to Jüngel, what I have been calling the identity thesis and the absoluteness thesis have operated in tandem, as it were, mutually reinforcing one another. We return to the statement quoted earlier: "To the worldly necessity of a highest essence corresponded the ontological necessity of the existence of this essence" (GGW 136 [103]).

Before leaving this discussion of the traditional concept of God two implications which will be important to the later discussion must be noted. The first was already outlined in discussing how the traditional concept of the divine attributes involved a conjunction of omnipotence and omnipresence. Jüngel shows how God is rendered essentially incapable of being absent. Equating existence with the notion of "absolute presence," and making God into the locus of that absolute presence would together present a peculiar problem for the modern tradition following Descartes.

The second implication, also to have weighty consequences, was the necessity of a *conceptual* distinction between God's essence and existence combined with a rejection of the *reality* of the distinction. The tradition of metaphysical thought found the distinction of essence/existence quite indispensible for thought in general. If thought about the divine being was not to be blocked by the bald assertion of the identity of essence and existence, then in God's case it had to entertain the distinction precisely for the purpose of annulling it. Typically, scholastic terminology formulated this difficult task by a distinction of terms. The distinction of essence and existence required by thought is an artificial distinction; it finds nothing real corresponding to it in the utter simplicity of the divine being. It is a *distinctio rationis*, not a

---

Suarez) this notion of "*compositio*" was rejected in favor of a merely abstract distinction of essence and existence in things, the tradition remained essentially in agreement with regard to the peculiar status of God's unity of essence and existence. See GGW 141 note 5 (107).

distinctio realis. In order to think their unity, essence and existence must be conceptually distinguished; the *distinctio rationalis* is for the sake of, not in spite of, the unity (GGW 140-1 [106-7]). Jüngel's exposition of the course of modern metaphysics will attempt to show how this tiny, seemingly innocuous distinction will, under the impact of the Cartesian reconfiguration of human thought, grow into a rift eventually disintegrating the very concept of God.

Descartes: God as the Accomplice to the Ego's Self-Grounding

Descartes is crucial for the modern problem of conceiving God, but not because of some innovation he made in the traditional doctrine of God. Indeed, the whole thrust of Jüngel's argument is precisely that Descartes was not an innovator at this point, that he took up central aspects of traditional metaphysical theism largely intact. His crucial significance lies in his new conception of "the relationship between the essence of God which is thought as ultimately unthinkable and the human ego which thinks it" (GGW 136 [103]). Jüngel's investigation is therefore "not so much interested in repeating the sufficiently well-known Cartesian ideas but rather in grasping as acutely as possible the cluster of theological problems contained in them" (GGW 144 [109]).

The basic accomplishment of Cartesian thinking was the establishment or "securing" of the human ego as the "unshakeable foundation of truth" (*inconcussum fundamentum veritatis*) and, indeed, of all existence.[7] The procedure involved is of course the famous method of universal doubt. Methodological doubt is like a corrosive bath in which every representation, every thought, must be submerged; that which survives merits the status of absolute certainty. And what in fact survives this treatment turns out to be the represented existence of the doubter: *cogito ergo sum.* Jüngel emphasizes two features of this procedure. The first is the driving concern for utter certainty which throws the thinking self back onto its own resources; in fact the individual is withdrawn into a zone of absolute contemporaneity, and therefore of absolute self-presence. In this position, the self makes a

---

[7] The phrase "unshakeable foundation of truth" is found in GGW 148 (112). The language of "securing" (*sicherstellen*) is taken over from Heidegger and plays an important role throughout Jüngel's discussion of post-Cartesian metaphysics. See GGW 153 (116) citing Martin Heidegger, *Nietzsche*, Vol. 2 (Pfullingen: Neske, 1961), 152.

virtue of necessity: the fragility of its knowledge, its capacity for doubt, becomes the instrument for the eventual overcoming of doubt (GGW 149-50 [113-4]).

The second feature, one that has been often remarked (and often bewailed), is that Descartes equates this discovery of the existence of the self in the act of thinking with the discovery of the essence of the self. Jüngel's formulation ironically echoes the traditional discourse of the divine unity: "Descartes has . . . determined the *existence* and the *essence* of the *human person* as identical (*ein einziges*). . . . 'I think, I am' (*Cogito sum*) means 'I am a thinking thing' (*sum res cogitans*)" (GGW 151 [115]). But the procedure of doubt means that the unity over time of that secured existence, that is its continuity through successive moments, has not been secured. To ground certainty of the persistence of the ego and therefore of the world in general something else is needed.

Once again, the ego must make use of its own deficiency. As is well known, the paradigm case for truthful cognition in Descartes turns out to be "clear and distinct perception," the prototype for which is the self's perception of its own existence, the *cogito*. But the path to insuring the truthfulness of clear and distinct perception involves necessarily the invocation of God as the guarantor. For Jüngel everything at this point turns on seeing how this does not supplant the ego's self-grounding, but rather confirms it. He accurately perceives that the God invoked to secure the thinking ego is itself secured through methodological doubt.

Since doubting has proven to be the method for rendering things certain, then doubting must be the way to insure that a clear and distinct perception is never wrong. But the only way to doubt our clear and distinct ideas is to invoke something with a superhuman power of deception; this is the famous "deceiver god" (*deus deceptor*). Jüngel argues that to postulate the existence of an omnipotent deceiver is in fact to put the very essence of God into doubt, since that essence is to be "the highest form of the good" (GGW 155 [118]). Only the good, true God is capable of banishing the deceiving god. In other words, the fundamental category of divinity which is relevant to the Cartesian project is that of necessity. God is what is necessary to secure the "thinking thing," the individual human self.

An interesting fact which Jüngel remarked upon with regard to the "ontological argument," namely that in Descartes' version the fundamental premise is that of a necessary being, not (as with Anselm) an absolutely perfect one, now assumes unexpected importance.[8] The idea of God which the human ego finds within itself is that of a more perfect being than the human self, one which is capable of validating the self-perception of the ego as less than perfect. In other words, the innate idea of God is granted only that kind of perfection which is sensed as a lack by the ego evaluating its own cognitive processes. Of course, Descartes goes on to identify God with absolute perfection, that is as the unity of all perfections formally speaking. But Jüngel's point is that for Descartes the idea of God's perfection derives from what the imperfect human ego perceives to be its own deficiency.

    The necessary being is thus necessary precisely because it must be invoked first to validate doubt as an imperfection, and then to banish the spectre of doubt inflated to infinite size as the "deceiver God." In short, the "deceiver God" is the threat posed by the method of doubt to its own triumphant progress. The "God who is good" is the only recourse for eliminating the deceiver, and that good God's existence is then proven on the basis of the presence in the mind of ideas putatively beyond the capacity of human production. At every point, God is called upon to verify the grounding of the self actually achieved by methodological doubt. Indeed Descartes' proofs for God all begin (as they must) from an idea already present to the thinking ego. This makes them in fact paths of self-discovery for the ego! Jüngel summarizes:

> Without *dubitare* there is no *cogito sum*, without *cogito sum* there is no certainty of a *res cogitans*, without a *res cogitans* there are no *modi cogitationes* and thus no *ideae*, and thus no idea of God! Without an idea of God there is no proof of God, and without a proof of God there is no certainty of God! Without the certainty of God there is still the self-certainty which was arrived at through doubt, but there is no assurance of this self-certainty beyond the present moment . . . God is necessary as the back-up insurance against my own doubt (GGW 158 [120]).

We are now in a position to see why this new configuration of the relation between the traditionally understood concept of God and the thinking ego must in Jüngel's opinion result in a potentially fatal rupture in that concept. He believes the implication of Descartes'

---

[8] See GGW 147 note 1 (112).

thought to be that the human ego has now become "*the location of presence.*"[9] What he means is that for Descartes representation by some thinking ego has become the determinant or paradigm case of the very meaning of existence. It was seen that what is most originally and absolutely present to the ego, present clearly and distinctly, is the ego itself in the act of thought. Jüngel wants to argue that by linking the certainty of an existent thing to the clarity of its perception by the ego, Descartes has radically redefined the very notion of existence to mean "presence with the thinking ego." And the presence of everything outside the self is measured against the absolute presence of the self to itself as its original criterion. To exist means to be present, and to be present means to be located before and with the knowing ego; all objective presence is, as it were, an adjunct to subjective self-presence.

But this privileged position of the human subject was secured only with the aid of God, a God whose particular perfection was conceived as the necessary condition for the possibility of compensating for the defects of the human self. From the presence of the idea of God to the ego the existence of God is demonstrated. However, this God's essence must be defined in terms of lack of defect and of absolute power (GGW 162 [123]). This is the case both because the logic of proving God's existence demands an idea of perfection beyond the originative capacity of the human intellect, and because the very reason for invoking a divine presence in the first place was to secure the continued self-identity of the self through its derivation from an all-powerful creator. Essentially, God must be thought of as something transcending the self.

It therefore seems that the concepts of the divine essence and of the divine existence are moving in opposite directions, so to speak; and this is in spite of the traditional assurance that they are in fact identical. Jüngel defines the resulting "aporia" or difficulty this way:

> (a) Because the essence of God is represented by me, the existence of God is secured through me.
>
> (b) With regard to his *essence* God is the almighty Creator, who is necessary through himself and through whom I am. . .

---

[9] GGW 164 (124), italics in original.

(c) In terms of his *existence*, however, God is through
me, in that *his* existence can be understood as representedness
through and for the subject, which "I" am.[10]

Note the parallelism of the final two statements, which indicates why
the task of securing the thinking ego as the unshakeable
epistemological foundation assigned contrary valences to God's essence
and existence. The divine essence, through which I have being, is
beyond comprehension; but what of the divine existence, if existence
means being represented by a subject? Would not then the human subject
be that through which God has being?

Of course, Descartes did not conceive of matters this way.
Jüngel claims that the problem was concealed for him as such by the
scholastic conceptuality he had inherited. Jüngel points not only to
Descartes' affirmation of the standard notion of the identity of essence
and existence in God, but also to his insistence that there is no common
notion of being or of substance applicable univocally to God and to finite
beings (GGW 165 [125]). Jüngel assumes that Descartes can ignore the
problem he is raising because the philosopher presupposes that the
finite self never really comprehends the infinite spiritual substance
which is God. That "existence," therefore, which is accorded to the
divine essence on the basis of its representative presence in the human
subject is not identical with the genuine divine existence (which is
identical with the divine essence).

The later parts of this chapter will discuss how Jüngel traces
the ensuing evolution of modern metaphysics and the inevitable
working out of the rupture in the concept of God, which had merely been
repressed but not at all neutralized by repeating the old formulae. For

---

10 GGW 165 (125). The parenthetical addition of "imagined" after
"represented" in Guder's translation (both here and two paragraphs later) has no basis
in the German original; it seems best to avoid this interpretive addition, even though
Jüngel in discussing Fichte (GGW 184) does use "imagination" in apposition with
"sensuous faculty of representation." "To represent" is the standard and adequate
translation of the German verb "*vorstellen*"; it is only the reflexive use of this verb
("*sich vorstellen*") which connotes imagination. In any case, in German
philosophical terminology the faculty of representation is often distinct from that of
imagination, the latter being rendered by terms such as "*Einbildungskraft*" or
"*Phantasie.*"

now, I will briefly sum up the nature of the difficulty which Descartes handed on to philosophical theism.

It will be recalled that the unity of the divine being in the metaphysical tradition was conceived as the identity of essence and existence in God. The paradox always latent in this conception was that the distinction had first to be made precisely in order to be nullified. Everything turned on the ability to maintain the dichotomy of a "real distinction" and a (merely) "rational distinction," especially because in this case the rational distinction (essence/existence) was one of the most fundamental to human reason. It denoted the dialectic of persistence and change: the essence is that which remains self-identical in every transformation. What made this distinction so dangerous was that on this basis it was difficult not to associate existence with being under the conditions of space and time, with being "in the world." Were that so, surely the eternal and absolute God could not be said to "exist"!

Such a conclusion, however, would be absurd; some sort of existence must be attributed to the God who creates the world, space and time. The solution to this problem lay in grounding human reason in a more ultimate, divine reason. It is only the imperfect, human intellect which cannot dispense with the distinction of essence and existence. The divine intellect, however, in its perfect self-knowledge perceives no distinction between "*what* God is" and "*that* God is." Not only is God the perfect unity of essence and existence, but God is also that act of perfect rational intellection in which that unity is grasped. It was pointed out above that what human reason perceives as true is only really true insofar as it is grounded in the absolute unity of thought and being which is the divine intellect. For this reason the seemingly unavoidable distinction of essence and existence could be seen as a distinction required by the inferior human intellect but not a true or real distinction because on the level of divine intellection it disappears (GGW 142 [108]).

However, it is the peculiar characteristic of the movement of thought intitiated by Descartes that the superiority of the divine being is now invoked to secure the *self*-grounding of the human intellect. The metaphysical apparatus which allowed the dangerous "rational distinction" to be quarantined disappears as a result. "Henceforth, whatever human reason deemed it necessary to distinguish could not then also pass for something already abolished *a priori* for some

higher intellect."[11]   The fateful consequence of this turn for the
metaphysical idea of God was the disintegration of the idea of God in
the very act of conceiving of God. But this only surfaced in later
philosophy, climaxing in the discovery of the "death of God" in the
nineteenth century. We must now turn to Jüngel's analysis of this final
intellectual development.

Tracing the Breakup: Kant, Fichte, Feuerbach, Nietzsche

Jüngel chooses three representative assertions of 19th century
philosophical figures to illustrate the various modes of dissolution of
the metaphysical concept of God. He nowhere suggests that these
particular developments were inevitable, only that the general result
of a destructive hiatus between God's essence and existence had to
follow given the application of Cartesian self-grounding thought to the
traditional idea of God. As with his analysis of Descartes, Jüngel is
concerned solely to interrogate these "texts" with regard to their
position on the problem under investigation, namely that of the
relation of human thought to the concept of God. He is interested
neither in portraying the overall development of the thought of each
of these figures, nor even in placing them in some kind of genetic or
developmental relationship to each other. With these reservations in
mind, our task in this section is not to repeat Jüngel's treatment so much
as to indicate briefly how each analysis uncovers the same pattern: the
failure to hold together an essence conceived in absolute terms with an
existence conceived in human terms.

The first examination of this rupture centers on the documents
produced by Johann Gottlieb Fichte during the so-called "Atheism
Controversy." Jüngel's basic argument in this section is that Fichte

---

[11] GGW 142 (108): "Denn was die menschliche Vernunft zu unterscheiden
für notwendig erachtete, das konnte hinfort auch für keine höhere Vernunft mehr im
nachhinein als doch schon a priori aufgehoben gelten." Guder's English translation
of this sentence seems thoroughly confused. Part of the difficulty of this admittedly
obscure sentence is the relation of the temporal adverb "*hinfort*" to the nearby
adverbial phrase "*im nachhinein*", which is very similar in meaning. I take the first
("henceforth") to refer to all intellectual developments taking place *after* the
Cartesian self-grounding of thought. On the other hand, the adverbial phrase
("afterwards, after that, then") refers to the impossibility of asserting the *a priori*
abolishment (at a higher level) of a distinction *after* it has been determined as
fundamental for human reason.

arrived at the conclusion of the absolute impossibility of thinking the absolute essence by means of his development of the Kantian epistemological doctrine which itself, in turn, represents a continuation of the Cartesian grounding of thought in the "*cogito.*" The Fichtean development was possible, Jüngel claims, because of the ambivalence of the Kantian epistemology which demanded but at the same time threatened a distinction between thought (*Denken*) and theoretical knowledge or cognition (*Erkenntnis, Erkennen*).

It is well known that Kant disputed the theoretical knowability of God, freedom and immortality; these are not objects, and by definition cannot be subordinated either to the forms of sensible intuition (i.e. time and space) or to the categories. Theoretical knowledge, cognition, demands sensible intuition. Kant did, however, claim that these ideas could be and indeed are legitimate objects of thought. Nor can this thinking be construed as the mere entertainment of a logical possibility. The very structure of practical reason gives to the concept of God, for example, an "objective validity." To think God is not to cognize God, since there is no possible sensible intuition by means of which God could be given as an object. But to think God as a necessary postulate of practical reason is to think something real. The complex arguments whereby Kant tries to establish the concepts of God, freedom and immortality as postulates absolutely necessary to the exercise of rational moral deliberation need not concern us here. The point Jüngel is making is simply that Kant places great weight on the distinction of thinking and knowing (theoretical cognition of a given object). Kant insists that part of the positive significance of the *Critique of Pure Reason* is to prevent an equating of the bounds of the real with the bounds of the sensible. The claim to *know* God as an object is a contradiction which threatens the very *thinkability* of God as a rational idea.[12]

However, Jüngel shows how this distinction between cognition and thought, which opens up the possibility of a legitimate thinking of God apart from the demands of theoretical knowledge, was undercut by Kant's way of grounding the possibility of thought in the thinking ego. The result was a liaison between thought and sensible intuition so close

---

[12] GGW 172-3 (130-1). The Kant citation can be found in a note on page xxvi of the second edition of the *Critique of Pure Reason* (B XXVI). I follow Norman Kemp Smith's translation.

that the distinction of thought and theoretical cognition could come into question, which is precisely what occurred with Fichte. How did this ambivalence in Kant arise?

According to the *Critique of Pure Reason*, the "synthetic unity of apperception" is "the first pure cognition of understanding . . . upon which is founded all its [i.e. the understanding's] other exercise." But Jüngel finds a curious tension hidden within this principle.[13] For Kant, the very possibility of knowledge implies a bringing together of the flux of sensible inputs (the "manifold of intuition") with the awareness of their mental coordination and organization by a single, self-identical self or ego. Kant describes this capacity to connect the manifold to a single subject in terms of an implied "I think . . ." attached to every act of thought and making it possible. But if this is the case, then the "I" of the "I think" cannot possibly be an object of perception: distinct awareness of it arises *with* every perception and unifies a purely intellectual consciousness of self (the Cartesian *cogito sum* again!) with an empirical self-consciousness, which arises by contrasting the flux of representations determining consciousness with the stability of the self through time as that which undergoes that changing determination.

Herein lies the ambivalence within Kant's notion of thought which Fichte used to undermine the distinction of thinking and knowing so important to Kant. Although Kant claims that thought is not bound to the limits of sensible intuition, the unity of apperception which must accompany all thought seems to bind thought in just that way, since it demands the unification of the purely intellectual "I" with the empirical "I" which only becomes conscious over against the sensible objects given to it. In fact, Jüngel seems to imply that Kant's entire mode of "transcendental" argumentation in the first critique (whereby thought is understood in terms of the necessary condition for the possibility of the knowledge of objects) reveals within the "I think" a coordination (*Zuordnung*) with the manifold of intuition. [14]

Undoubtedly, Kant did assert the possibility of thinking God on the basis of the practical reason, quite apart from theoretical

---

[13] For what follows see GGW 174-9 (131-5).

[14] GGW 177 (134). Jüngel's phrase is "dem sich auf das gegebene Mannigfaltige hin entwerfende 'Ich denke.'"

cognition. This in itself requires a relative independence of thought from the categories of sensible intuition. But Jüngel regards it as especially telling that Kant's construction of a concept of God on the basis of the practical reason must utilize the representations of theoretical cognition in an analogical manner (GGW 179 [135]). In short, in the thinking of God reason seems reduced to complex maneuvers to free itself from utter dependence on objective intuition. In his attempt to render Kant more consistent, Fichte found it both necessary and suspiciously easy to dispense with these gymnastics entirely. He developed Kant's epistemology in the direction of an unambivalent dependence of thought upon the capacity of sensible representation which drives him to the consistent conclusion: "God cannot be thought at all."

In the "Atheism Controversy", Fichte had asserted the impossibility both of conceiving God as a substance possessing "being" (because thought can conceive of substance only in terms of extended matter in space) and of conceiving of God as "outside" the world (since such a location *ipso facto* robs God of infinity). Has thought no resources for thinking beyond these worldly terms? Could not God be thought as Kant does, in terms of the "noumenal" realm of spontaneous freedom? Fichte replies that God simply must not be "thought" at all (GGW 180-1 [136-7]). It is not the actuality of God that Fichte disputes, but the possiblity of any concept of God. Unlike Kant, he refuses even analogical understandings of God, but he does this because he accepts the close connection Kant discerned between thinking something and "realizing" it, i.e. rendering it in terms of space and time. Jüngel shows this in his discussion of Fichte's understanding of the "schematism" of all human thought.

Both Kant and Fichte understand thought as a schematizing activity: because cognitive judgements must unite a spatio-temporal intuition with a category which has no essential relation to space or time, the mind produces "schemata" (perhaps "diagrams" most closely suggests the meaning here) which adapt the category to the spatio-temporal form of intuition. For Fichte, there are two basic kinds of schema corresponding to the two basic kinds of experience: that of external objects in space, and that of the self as a source of spontaneous actions. The first schema is that of extended matter, the second is that of pure activity. The key is that for Fichte, all thought is *ipso facto* a schematizing procedure. Obviously God cannot be thought of as extended matter, but why not under the concept of pure active freedom? Is not this alternative schema suitable for thinking a being both infinite and beyond time and space? Indeed, the idea of God as *actus purus* is one of the oldest in the Western metaphysical tradition.[15] And Fichte does assert that it is in activity that the human ego encounters God. "*As an actor* the human ego is certain of itself as pure activity and at the same time certain of God as pure activity: of itself as the one who is obliged to act through freedom, of God as the one who obligates to freedom through activity" (GGW 184 [139]).

If God is thus encountered as pure activity, why cannot God be thought as pure activity? The answer for Fichte is that the schematism of pure activity is by definition an act of "limiting" and "grasping" (*begreifen*), and as such always falls short of the purity and infinity demanded of its own "supersensible" (*übersinnlich*) schema. A person's spontaneous act of freedom is apprehended as a primal, absolute demand (i.e. that of the command to act, a transformation of Kant's categorical imperative), but this consciousness of involvement in a "supersensible moral order" transcending time and space can only be thought (made into a concept) by bringing it under the schema of activity. The turn from the act to thinking the act is, as it were, a fall from grace (metaphysically speaking).

The reason is traced by Jüngel to Fichte's appropriation of Kant's ambivalent epistemology:

> The paradox that the supersensuous schema for its part falls short of the truth which it conceives is connected with the fact that fundamentally we apprehend (*auffassen*) everything which is grasped *in* the first supersensuous schema only *through* our sensuous faculty of representation (imagination) (GGW 184 [138]).

Fichte explicitly asserts that the perception of the schema of activity by the power of imagination transforms it into the "second schema," that is, the schema of extended matter in space. Jüngel sees this orientation of the first schema to sensuous representation as directly analogous to the implied dependence in Kant of thought upon the given manifold. Fichte simply resolves what is ambiguous in Kant and draws

---

[15] See Aristotle's *Metaphysics*, bk. XII, ch. 6ff.

the proper conclusion: the God encountered in action is ultimately inaccessible to conceptual thought.

There remains only the God "revealed" to human beings in their inner selves, in the execution of their moral activity. In Jüngel's wonderful phrase, "Man, who lifts himself up to pure activity, is compensated for the unthinkability of God with the immediacy of God" (GGW 185 [139]). What has in fact happened is that, confronted with the irreconcilable claims of the traditional metaphysics of divine being and the new conception of thought as grounded in and bound to the temporal, finite, indeed perishing subject, Fichte has opted to eliminate representation of God's essence in thought in order to preserve the pure actuality, uncontaminated by temporality, accorded to that essence by the tradition. The diastasis of essence and existence concealed in the Cartesian project has surfaced, demanding the resolution of the dilemma; in this case that resolution takes the form of a rejection of existential predicates for God, precisely for the sake of God's deity. "The concept of God cannot under any circumstances be defined through existential statements."[16] Forbidding the thought of God and denying God's existence are two expressions of the same movement of thought.

As Jüngel sees it, the path upon which thought had been set by Descartes had to result in the dissolution of the concept of God as a being whose essence and existence are a unity. In his treatment of Fichte (and Kant) Jüngel has uncovered this breakup at the genesis of classical German idealism. But his next move is to analyze a statement, this time from a representative of post-idealist, "left-wing" Hegelianism (Feuerbach) which seems to contradict Fichte's ban on thinking God. In fact, Feuerbach claims, in the act of thinking God thought comes to its essence: "Only when you think *God*, are you *thinking*, rigorously speaking."[17]

In Feuerbach, the Anselmian definition of God becomes an instrument in the transformation of theology into anthropology, or rather in the discovery that all along the deepest meaning and essence

---

[16] J. G. Fichte, "Rückerinnerungen, Antworten, Fragen", in *Sämmtliche Werke*, ed. I. H. Fichte (Berlin: Veit & Company, 1845 [=1971]), 5: 371. Cited by Jüngel, GGW 186 (140). This kind of denial of existence to God, as mediated by Schelling, found its characteristic theological representative in Tillich.

[17] GGW 167 (127) citing Ludwig Feuerbach, *Das Wesen des Christentums*.

of theology was the divinity of humanity. The key to the Feuerbach citation is his transformation of the famous Anselmian formula already mentioned (which names God "that than which nothing greater can be conceived" [*id quo maius cogitari nequit*]) into an expression of the essential limit of human understanding. He begins from the Hegelian premise that self-expression and self-objectification are essential moments of the realization of human spirit. In the case of human reason (one member of Feuerbach's tripartite anthropology of reason-will-heart), self-objectification reaches its pinnacle in the form of a highest thought. The idea of God is that thought in which reason expresses itself as the highest essence (GGW 192-3 [145]).

It is the essence of thought to intensify, to magnify itself, although it cannot transcend itself. Indeed, in the highest thought reason does transcend the empirical self; but it does not transcend the self insofar as the self is conscious of its own highest essence. As conscious of its own essential distinctiveness from every other kind of being the human self is called a "species-being ."[18] The human being as species-being represents the limit, the highest rational value, the point at which reason in its self-magnification runs out of steam, so to speak. At this point of exhaustion, reason utters its highest thought, the thought of God as the highest idea, than which no greater is possible. With the thought of God, reason consummates itself; hence Feuerbach's assertion that the thought of God is reason's most authentic activity, its very essence. Reason creates the thought of divinity, its *pièce de résistance*.

But if the idea of divinity is simply a massive reflection of human reason, the represented essence of its infinite capabilities, then what has become of God as a separately existing being? Of course, it is the idea of a God as separate, as over against humanity which Feuerbach is trying to replace with the notion of divinity as in fact the proper attribute of humanity. This replacement is effected by appeal to the other members of the tripartite anthropology. It is reason or understanding which mistakenly clings to the "abstract opposition" of divinity to humanity. As the essence of the will, however, God

---

18 Guder's translation of this discussion by Jüngel offers "genus of existence" for Feuerbach's technical term "*Gattungswesen*". This is confusing and probably betrays a lack of familiarity with Feuerbach's terminology. This word is usually rendered "species-being" or "species-essence" in English.

becomes the demand for humanity to realize this projected, alienated perfection, i.e. the law. But fulfillment of this law demands the final member of the triad, the heart; here God's essence is seen to be love, and it is love which meets the demand for perfection by dissolving the opposition of God and humanity.[19]

At this point Jüngel's characteristic concern in this all-too-brief analysis returns to the fore; indeed, he argues that in spite of the seeming opposition between the statements of Fichte and Feuerbach, they are ultimately at one in ratifying the disruption of divine being. Both take up central strands of the tradition of metaphysical theism in order to identify and preserve the notion of a divine essence: Fichte prefers the notion of God as infinite, pure act, while Feuerbach appropriates the Anselmian highest being. And in both cases, the outcome is the denial of divine existence: for Fichte, existence as a predicate clashes with divine infinity, while for Feuerbach divine existence is that illusion of self-alienated reason which locks the essence of divinity into abstract independence, and which is overcome by the Christian definition of God as love. "Therefore, like Fichte, Feuerbach had to declare God's essence and God's existence as incompatible with each other, so that the concept of God as the highest and infinite being which combines all perfections and lacks every deficiency could be preserved" (GGW 201 [151]).

Whereas Fichte had denied that the notion of God was even thinkable, Feuerbach's statement implies that the idea of God is precisely the quintessential achievement of thought. But the contextual analysis of these statements betrays a hidden analogy. The idea of God is preserved here solely in its role as the necessary objectification of human reason. The cost of this preservation is very high; the essence of the divine is only salvaged when it is reappropriated by humanity as its own essence. "To be sure, like Fichte, Feuerbach was interested in preserving the metaphysically determined 'divine.' But it is not the divinity of God which is supposed to be preserved, but the divinity of humanity" (GGW 201 [151]). For

---

[19] GGW 190 (143). Jüngel is concerned elsewhere to combat the enmity which Feuerbach sets up between faith (that which preserves the being of God as something separate over against me) and love (which abrogates this separation). See "Gott ist Liebe: Zur Unterscheidung von Glaube und Liebe," in *Festschrift für Ernst Fuchs*, ed. G. Ebeling, E. Jüngel and G. Schunack (Tübingen: J.C.B. Mohr, 1973), 193-202. Also GGW 430-70 (314-343).

Feuerbach talk of the "existence" of God endangers God's essence, but not, as with Fichte, because it reduces God to the status of a worldly object. Rather, it is God's "existence" as an objective being which hinders an understanding of God's true worldliness; it is a relic of a self-objectification process which has fixed God into an alien "other." Dissolve God's existence, and God's essence is free to migrate back into thought as a new human self-consciousness.

Jüngel's brief investigations of these thinkers are intended to present different historical trajectories and therefore not devoted to criticism of the positions portrayed. However he does point out what he thinks is a tension or contradiction within Feuerbach's position. Feuerbach has taken up the Anselmian definition of God to shore up his argument but has failed to grasp its inherent logic, which is precisely the strict connection of the divine essence thought by the mind with its necessary existence independent of that mind (GGW 194-5 [146]). To the extent that Feuerbach relies on this traditional metaphysical definition of God his demand to think God without an assertion of existence (i.e. to think God as the essence of humanity) is strictly self-contradictory. Metaphysically speaking, "a God which is permitted not to exist is not thought as God at all" (GGW 201 [151]). This inconsistency is used by Jüngel not as a refutation of Feuerbach, but as a further indication of the way in which the traditional metaphysical God has become quite inconceivable for modern (post-Cartesian) metaphysics. Feuerbach may have been unaware that the concept of divinity which he wishes to appropriate cannot stand up to the abuse; theology cannot become anthropology without shattering the integrity of the very concept of the *theos*. A thinker who was far more sensitive to this necessary disintegration was Nietzsche.

As was true for the relation of Fichte to Feuerbach, so too for the relation of Feuerbach to Nietzsche it is the case that a seemingly contradictory stance actually conceals a shared position. Nietzsche's opposition to traditional theism culminates in Zarathustra's pointed question: "Could you *think* a God?" (GGW 167 [127]) This rhetorical question implies a negative answer because of the limitations to thought which Nietzsche strives to set up. Nietzsche's endeavor is ultimately bound up with his attempt to banish a "bad" notion of infinity from human thought in favor of a "good" infinity. The idea of God is representative of "bad" infinity because it fixes infinity over against human finitude rather than conceiving of infinity as precisely the limitless creative thrust of the human will.

For Nietzsche the human will, though finite, is capable of a creative surpassing of itself (*Über-sich-hinaus*), a kind of self-intensification which Nietzsche roots in "thinking one's senses to the end" (GGW 197 [148]). Creative thought is tied to the sensuous nature (*Sinnlichkeit*) of human being. What falls within the realm of the senses is for Nietzsche capable of transformation by the creative will of human beings. Nietzsche, in the persona of Zarathustra, urges his hearers to limit their conjectures to what is truly capable of being thought, always implying that the thinkable (*denkbar*) must coincide with what the human will can achieve (*machbar*). Thought is the passage to the creative self-surpassing of human finitude in the direction of the "Superman" (*Übermensch*). So the question "Could you *think* a God?" must be answered in the negative because the question "Could you *create* a God?" must also receive a negative reply. In refashioning thought in this way Nietzsche also rehabilitates the notion of the infinite. "The *infinite* is now transformed into the dimension of the Superman's *becoming*, that is into the dimension of a finitude which is not limited from the outside" (GGW 199 [150]). If infinity is the creative self-intensification of finitude, which is in principle limitless, then the conjecture of God (the "bad" infinity) must give way to that of the Superman; "the death of God according to this understanding is the removal of the fixed opposition between finitude and infinity" (GGW 196 [147]).

What binds Nietzsche to Feuerbach is their common acceptance of the metaphysically understood God; indeed the basic concept of divinity operative in both thinkers is the Anselmian "that than which nothing greater can be thought." And, according to Jüngel, both thinkers follow a similar procedure in removing the scandal of this pinnacle of thought. "In each case an alien height which is superior to human thought is reduced to that height which belongs to human thought (*die dem menschlichen Denken eigene Höhe*)" (GGW 199 [150]). The main difference is that Nietzsche has grasped the logic of the Anselmian definition in a way Feuerbach has not. Since "that than which nothing greater can be thought" must be thought of as actually existing (i.e. as independent of our thought of it) then the attempt to appropriate the concept of God as a projection of thought's own essence destroys that concept. Nietzsche sees that the intolerable superiority of an alien infinite is inextricably bound up with the very idea of God; when humanity truly comes to itself, the divine must die. Feuerbach, intent on salvaging theology by demonstrating its anthropological secret, wants to make the human species divine; he does not see that an idea whose very essence is its superiority to the human cannot, even if it is a mere projection, be made an attribute of the human — at least not without violence.

Conclusion: The Misconceived Unity of Essence and Existence

In summary, the historical developments reveal a complex of basic problems, which turns on two factors: first, the way God's unity of essence and existence (simplicity) was conceived; second, the way the notion of existence came to be transformed under the impact of the post-Cartesian understanding of the nature of human thought. This two-fold way of determining the problem is in line with Jüngel's constant insistence on the inseparability of noetic concerns and ontic ones, of problems of thought on the one hand and problems of being or objects to be thought on the other.

It will become more and more evident as this study progresses that Jüngel is committed to defending a notion of divine simplicity. His critique of the traditional notion is not centered on its goal of thinking God's essence and existence as a unity; his own theological project is fully in accord with this aim. What he objects to, and indeed what in his opinion was disastrous for the fate of the God-concept in the modern period, was the definition of God's essence in terms of absolute superiority. This axiom, when combined with the unity of essence and existence in God, demanded a mode of existence for God which proved increasingly difficult for post-Cartesian thought to accept.

This move took place in more than one way. As indicated above, it could be a construction based on the absolute superiority of the divine essence; existence could be extrapolated from particular divine predicates such as omnipresence. Or it could involve one of several modes of "ontological argument," incorporating a notion of necessary existence directly into the very idea of divinity. The path chosen was ultimately less important than the intolerable strain to which the unity of essence and existence so conceived was subjected after the Cartesian turn to the subject began to take hold.

More than one solution to this dilemma was and is possible. One could simply ignore the problem, continuing to insist on the existence of an absolute and necessary being at the cost of the increasing disdain and finally indifference of modern culture. Or one could dispute the way in which existence came to be exclusively linked with the finitude and transitoriness of human subjectivity; but for Jüngel this latter move would be both unnecessary and, given the deep hold of the subjective turn on modern culture, a further contribution to theology's self-imposed isolation.

Jüngel's own path out of the cul-de-sac of the metaphysical death of God involves a reconstruction of that divine absoluteness and simplicity which was accepted at the genesis of modern thought without undergoing any thorough interrogation. The fact that it then remained lodged in modern culture as a foreign body until the increasingly alien environment could support it no longer has provided Christian theology the opportunity to subject it to radical revision. As the remainder of this study will attempt to make clear, that revision involves questioning the way in which an abstractly conceived divine essence is allowed to dictate the terms of divine existence. The proper way of conceiving the simplicity of God's being will in turn allow God's existence to call decisively into question the absoluteness of God's essence. It remains to explore how this complex theistic reconstruction is played out at different levels of Jüngel's thought.

CHAPTER FOUR

GOD AS MORE THAN NECESSARY

Jüngel believes that the modern discovery of God's non-necessity is in fact a valid insight if understood properly. God is not necessary; rather God is "more than necessary." Indeed, he introduces his first volume of collective essays with the claim that virtually everything he wants to say can be summed up in this statement.[1] He is aware of the awkwardness of the phrase "more than necessary," and admits that it only gestures toward the position he wishes to establish.[2] But he uses it anyway, perhaps with the sly awareness that its very strangeness might serve to bring the reader up short, and thereby signal the distance Jüngel wishes to maintain from traditional ideas about God's being. What, then, is the meaning of "more than necessary"?

We have already examined the notion of God's non-necessity as Jüngel sees this played out in the genesis of modernity; but as it stands the statement of God's non-necessity bears only a negative relation to the concept of God. It is more precisely a formula for the consciousness modern humanity has of itself and of the world; as such, it indicates an important cultural insight which he has no wish to dispute. But in order for the concept to be "processed" theologically, it must be transformed into a positive determination of the divine being. If God's being is, properly speaking, not necessary with respect to that kind of being characterizing humanity and indeed all worldly objects, then what kind of category best indicates its uniqueness? Jüngel answers this question with the formula "God is more than necessary in the world."

This chapter will attempt a schematic presentation of the cluster of ideas lurking behind this phrase. In particular, it must offer a careful examination of the second section of the introductory chapter of *God as the Mystery of the World*, entitled "Is God Necessary?", where Jüngel discusses the phrase at some length (GGW 16-44 [14-35]). At this point in Jüngel's argument only an abstract structure will emerge;

---

[1] Jüngel, *Unterwegs zur Sache*, 7.

[2] GGW 42 (43). Cf. GGW 30 note 15 (24): the phrase is "admittedly unusual and logically difficult."

69

the idea of the peculiar modality of divine being is posited as a possible framework for conceiving of God, one which borrows critically from some reflections of absolute idealism. However, only the concrete, theological representation of the divine being (which ultimately derives from analysis of the fact of revelation and its apprehension in the act of faith) gives a determinate content to these abstractions; in fact, by the end of this chapter it will be clearer how the God of faith is directing the argument from "behind the scenes."

Necessity, Contingency and Grounding

If Jüngel seeks, in effect, to carve out an independent conceptuality for God's being, the first step is an attempt to locate his conceptions with respect to more familiar categories. The uniqueness of divine being cannot without further ado be inserted into one of the generally established and accepted modal categories; it might well be that God's being is neither "necessary" nor "contingent", at least not in the accustomed meanings of those words. At any rate, as will soon be seen, Jüngel is suspicious of the often hidden ontological prejudices involved in our putatively "logical" use of modal categories (GGW 30 [24]). The first such tendency he wishes to dispute is a conflation of the contingent with the arbitrary.

The necessary is that which cannot (within a given context) be otherwise. But the mere fact that something need not be the way it is (i.e. contingent) does not mean it could have been or could be simply any way at all (i.e. arbitrary). Jüngel's initial point is simply that there is no necessary connection between accidence and contingency; there is nothing in the meaning of the words themselves to prevent something contingent from being essential. In this rather innocuous context the "unusual" phrase makes a subdued entrance. If the phrase "less than necessary" delimits the realm of the arbitrary, then "more than necessary" indicates initially nothing more than a "supra-necessary" realm defined by a kind of non-arbitrary contingency. Of course, the precise relationship to necessity has yet to be indicated.

This ordering of the "more than necessary" to the realm of contingency clearly indicates that the phrase cannot be construed simple-mindedly as an "intensification" of necessity, which would make little sense. In these very schematic initial comments the "more than necessary" gains its first determinations negatively; it is defined over against the concept of necessity. As a result, Jüngel wishes to highlight those characteristics of necessity which are (negatively) significant for the "more than necessary." But first he brackets any notion of an absolute necessity, claiming that only necessity with respect to the world (*weltlich Notwendigkeit*) is of concern here. Indeed Jüngel claims flatly that the notion of an absolute necessity of God (which abstracts completely from God's relation to the world) is simply incoherent and meaningless (GGW 30 [24]). The reason for this is in itself by no means clear, but can be fruitfully illuminated by his discussion of the contextual or relational character of any and every notion of necessity.

For purposes of clarification, Jüngel utilizes a philosophical treatise on the modal categories from an ontological (as opposed to purely logical) perspective, a work by the once well-known but now (at least in English-speaking contexts) somewhat neglected Nicolai Hartmann.[3] He uses Hartmann's two categorizations of types of necessity to point to what every kind of necessity has in common: what is defined or determined as necessary is always *ipso facto* put in relation to something else. In other words, the necessary is always necessary in relation to something else. Hence Jüngel's comment that "necessity always and only appears as the characteristic of a context" (GGW 32 [26]). That is, necessity specifies a peculiar relation of one thing to another thing or set of things; in this sense the necessity of a thing is, to use Jüngel's language, "grounded" outside the thing itself. But the relationship need not be reciprocal; that thing or set of things which grounds the necessity of the other need not itself be necessary.

Some further clarification is in order. Hartmann provides a philosophical typology of four kinds of necessity, to which Jüngel adds a fifth. "Logical" necessity involves the rigorous entailment of one proposition on the ground of some previously posited proposition, as in the hypothetical form of logical implication (if A, then [necessarily] B). "Epistemic" necessity is introduced as a necessary reservation in light of Hartmann's ontological realism. The fact of something's

---

[3] Nicolai Hartmann, *Möglichkeit und Wirklichkeit*, 3rd ed. (Berlin: Walter de Gruyter, 1966). Jüngel is manifestly uninterested in any rigorous logical or semantic study of the concept "necessity" in isolation from his particular theological interests. For an exploration in the context of recent modal logic and Anglo-American philosophy of religion, one which attempts an updating of the "ontological argument," see Alvin Plantinga, *The Nature of Necessity* (Oxford: Oxford University Press, 1974).

necessity, i.e. of its being strictly grounded in and implied by another (its *Gegründetheit*) is not identical with our knowledge of that fact.[4] Something is epistemically necessary if a knower can link it to its proper ground; this means moving beyond determining *what* something is to stating *why* it is so and not otherwise, submitting it to a "grounding" procedure (*Begründung*). The final two forms then indicate the two kinds of necessity or "groundedness" which might obtain for real entities (as opposed to propositions, where logical necessity is at issue). "Essential" (or inner) necessity refers to those properties which a thing possesses as a function of its very identity, those properties without which it would not be what it is. The essential properties of a thing are grounded in its essence, and are therefore necessary. Finally, "real" (or outer) necessity "signifies the determination of one really existing thing through another." Here again, as in each case, the phrase "A is necessary" implies "A is necessary *with respect to B*" and is thus convertible with the phrase "A is grounded in B."[5]

The relational pattern revealed within the various concepts of necessity is clear. It should also now be clear why Jüngel would be suspicious of a putative claim to necessity which attempted to abstract from every context, a notion, that is, of absolute or unconditioned necessity. In particular, the idea of God as an absolutely necessary being, abstracted from every external (in this case, every worldly or creaturely) context is dismissed as a "logical game." On the one hand, Jüngel believes that Kant has shown with sufficient rigor the purely heuristic function of the idea of a final, necessary ground of all things. This ultimate, absolute ground of the world, a pillar of classical natural theology, collapses upon strict examination; it must be relegated to the role of a regulative ideal of reason, not a proper concept to which a real object might correspond.[6] Besides, Jüngel will argue that God's being is "more than necessary" within the context of the world; the attempt to bestow some kind of absolute necessity on

---

[4] One might recall here the analogous point Aquinas makes about things which are self-evident in themselves (*per se*) but which are not thereby necessarily self-evident to us.

[5] The fifth type of necessity is added by Jüngel: "hermeneutical" necessity. It is not significant at this point.

[6] GGW 52-3 (40-41). Cf. GGW 23-4 (19-20).

that being as a kind of added endowment would seem superfluous. As indicated earlier, "more than necessary" does not mean "necessity to the n-th degree"; it points instead to another modal realm entirely.

There does indeed seem to be a category of necessity which might render meaningful a notion of absolute necessity. Unlike the other types, essential necessity, although at its heart no less relational than the other kinds, does seem to involve a single, potentially isolable being. The grounding relationship is internalized; the necessary presence of certain properties of a being is grounded in the essential identity of that being. Is this not precisely the kind of absolute necessity associated with the ontological argument? Traditionally, necessary existence is premissed as an essential property of divine being. Jüngel is unimpressed. As far as he is concerned, to apply this kind of necessity to God depends upon a confused analogy between worldy beings (from analysis of which the distinction of essential and nonessential attributes is derived and so for which the notion has some meaning) and God's being (GGW 30 [24]). The analogy is confused precisely because it misinterprets that identity of essence and existence which characterizes God's being as opposed to things in the world. As for the attempt to prove God's absolute necessity in some formal logical manner — Jüngel relegates his sardonic dismissal of this possibility to a single footnote (GGW 31 n. 17 [25]). At any rate, Jüngel draws the conclusion that the relevant kind of necessity ascribed to God, the kind which he is concerned to discuss and dispute (by means of the concept of "more than necessary") is necessity for or with respect to the world or humanity, worldly necessity.

The Principle of Sufficient Reason and the Experience with Experience

This still leaves somewhat unclear what "worldly necessity" means in this context. Again his procedure affirms that "the explication of what is meant by 'more than necessary' must involve a reflection upon what is necessary" (GGW 35 [28]). He chooses to highlight those aspects of God's worldly necessity under dispute by examining the "principle of sufficient reason." Although often associated with Leibniz it has in fact undergone a long development and numerous formulations.[7] As a fundamental principle or axiom, it

---

[7] GGW 36 note 38 (29). Jüngel finds ancient antecedants of the principle in Aristotle and even in Lucretius.

states that every being has a ground, a reason why it is so and not otherwise, indeed a reason why it is at all (*nihil est sine ratione*). But insofar as a "ground" is merely the logical role played by some thing or other, that thing too needs a reason why it is so and not otherwise, and so on, running the risk of infinite regress unless some end to the grounding process can be found. It is a commonplace of the history of natural theology that Leibniz postulates for this purpose a last or ultimate ground, which he calls God. On this basis, God is the "necessary being" (*ens necessarium, notwendige Seiende*).

Jüngel cites this principle negatively in order to clarify the notion of worldly necessity he is trying to dismiss as an inadequate category for God, but also positively in order to locate the category of the "more than necessary" which, as he points out, has a "point of relation" to the necessary. On the first point, Jüngel once again makes use of Hartmann, relying on an alternative analysis of necessity, this time based on its usages in ordinary language. When God's necessity is invoked on the basis of the principle of sufficient reason, Jüngel believes that two different meanings of "necessary" as commonly used are immediately involved:

> [T]his conception on the one hand understands God as the indispensible condition for the being of beings, and on the other understands every being (*alles Seiende*) as determined through grounds which find their last ground, their *ultima ratio* in God (GGW 37 [30]).

In the first instance, God's necessity is that of a condition for the existence of something else. In the second, the necessity is that of the conditioned, that which follows necessarily from the nature of its previous determination by something else, in this case its ground. There is still a third type of necessity at work here, one which follows from the first two and which Jüngel calls "hermeneutical necessity."[8] This derives from the interpretive relationship involved in understanding something *as* something. Jüngel postulates a reference to an other implied in every act of understanding something, an other which "constitutes" the hermeneutical "as", as when a mother is only

---

[8] As was already pointed out, this is not one of Hartmann's categories, but comes to Jüngel from Heidegger via Fuchs. See GGW 33 note 29 (27).

identifiable and understandable as such based on the existence of her child. In effect, this kind of necessity overlaps with and is implied by the other modes of necessity identified by Hartmann (epistemic, essential and real). In the specific case under examination, the world is only understandable as world from the concept of God. As the realm of grounded and grounding beings it is unintelligible apart from the ground of all grounds, God.

The "necessity" which is at work in the classical conceptions of the *ens necessarium* and the principle of sufficient reason is multivalent; Jüngel refers to a "composite" (*Verbund*) of different kinds of necessity. These can be shown to interlock, as it were. God and world are mutually implicated because of the putatively universal and axiomatic metaphysical function of "grounding," insuring that the meaning of "God" is only derived from the meaning of "world," and vice versa. When Jüngel declares that the category of "more than necessary" as applied to God is concerned to dispute just this complex of necessities, he has succeeded in a further negative delimitation of the proper conception of God's being (GGW 37 [30]). The reciprocally conditioning relationship of what is necessary as ground to what is necessary as grounded means that a God which grounds worldly beings is for that very reason a grounded being as well, functionally determined by what it grounds. To say that God is "necessary" vis-à-vis the world is a "shabby" proposition, unworthy of the unique modality of divine being (GGW 31 [25]). The assertion that God is more than necessary is concerned to dispute each of the kinds of necessity implied by the principle of sufficient reason, dissolving at a stroke the whole complex.

The denial of the relevant modes of necessity with respect to God is *ipso facto* the denial of the principle of sufficient reason, or at least of its universal validity, its axiomatic claim. But its usefulness as a negative determinant of Jüngel's conception is not, of course, thereby impaired. The conclusion reached so far is that the concept that God is more than necessary implies at the very least a refusal to define God's being as a ground of other beings (i.e. as the ultimate determinant of the rationally conditioned nature of things, their "groundedness") since that is tantamount to grounding God's being in worldly being (i.e. as a being whose basic ontological identity is determined from the peculiar grounding role whose universal validity it is invoked to secure). Thus for the statement that God is not necessary can be exchanged the statement that God is groundless; God neither is a rationally transparent ground nor has such a ground, at least not in the metaphysical sense formulated in the principle of sufficient reason.

But Jüngel's interrogation of the principle is by no means exhausted in this negative result. There is a more positive role that it can play in helping to indicate God's ontological character: it is used to delineate how God's "groundlessness" is not that of an arbitrary (i. e. "less than necessary") being, but that of a more than necessary being. Leibniz already had recognized that the kind of question generated by this axiom pushes toward an ultimate question. If it is possible to ask why something is the way it is, it is also possible to ask why it exists at all. Nor does there appear any logically compelling reason to restrict such questioning to individual beings. What happens when the question is directed to the existence of all that is? The result, for Jüngel, is to move the process of questioning to an entirely new level. The question "Why is there something rather than nothing at all?" has a way of turning on the one who seriously contemplates it, opening up a new realm of experience; for the first time, the concept of the possibility of non-being looms on the horizon of beings, of those things which are. Every being is seen to bear a mark, the stigma of its possible absence (GGW 38-9 [30-1]).

Jüngel immediately insists on the ambiguity of this new experience of things. The factual presence of beings can be interpreted both as permanently threatened by non-being, or as gifted with being, as preserved from non-being. If the word "God" is to have a meaningful location within the context of our experience of worldly beings, of those things which exist, then the assertion that God is more than necessary in the world intends to force God's ontological role onto another level. God must no longer be rationally construed as the implied necessary ground of conditioned beings, but must rather be experienced as "the one who decides between being and non-being (and to that extent as the one who first distinguishes being from non-being)," in short as creator of what is (GGW 41 [33]).

The principle of sufficient reason generates an interrogative dynamic; the process of interrogating the ground of beings, continually extrapolated, discloses (or at least brings into clear resolution) a peculiar realm of experience. That realm might be more precisely designated "meta-experiential," since it involves not the presentation of a new object to experience, but rather a new experiential disposition towards one's ordinary experiences, indeed toward experience itself. But this kind of second-order experience is not simply to be identified with the rational reflection associated with its emergence. Jüngel is firm in classifying this new disposition toward the whole of one's experience (including all particular experiences) as itself experiential in character, a mode of concrete receptive apprehension and not of reflective abstraction. Hence he calls it "an experience with [i.e. of] experience" (*Erfahrung mit Erfahrung*).[9] Indeed, he insists that the experience itself is neither reducible to nor rationally derivative of simple reflection on ordinary experience.

It is only in the new situation ushered in by the principled interrogation of beings that what can be called ordinary or first-order experience is revealed for what it is: the experience of beings (*Seienden*) as such. That which characterizes beings as such is precisely the recognition of their possible non-being. The being (*Sein*) of beings (*Seienden*) is precisely that being which is viewed as a coordinate of non-being. The revelation of the being of beings is only possible in terms of the experienced crisis of being; with worldly being there is simultaneously revealed non-being as correlative, in fact as the horizon or limit of worldly beings.

In these comments Jüngel is obviously mining a rich vein of existential and phenomenological psychology; he is dealing in general anthropological possibilities, and has yet to introduce his own theological twist into this well-known material.[10] The philosophical tradition whose trajectory Jüngel is following here (Schelling, Scheler, Heidegger) had recognized the basic ambiguity of this experience of being within the sphere of possible non-being. The nature of the experience itself shifts fundamentally depending on how the precarious position of being is apprehended. If perception of the reality of the threat of non-being gains the upper hand, then a fundamental anxiety (*Angst*) is provoked; however, if the persistence of being in face of that threat comes into focus, then fundamental gratitude is the result. These basic existential moods are in themselves equally "valid," and Jüngel claims that oscillation between these two dispositions toward being,

---

[9] GGW 40 (32). According to note 49, the expression is borrowed from Gerhard Ebeling.

[10] Note the roll call of thinkers invoked in GGW 39-40 (31-2).

indeed even moments of simultaneity, is characteristic of human experience once this level of awareness has been exposed. Each position is as authentically human as the other. One cannot be abandoned in favor of the other on the basis of a decision. Only at this point does Jüngel indicate a theological possibility in the strict sense, one in which the moment of gratitude is permanently and unambiguously affirmed (GGW 41 [33]).

For Jüngel, this possibility does not appear within the horizon of philosophical analysis. It is neither demanded as a component of human authenticity, nor is it a rational implication of any analysis of worldly structure or processes. It is, in short, strictly gratuitous; it is the unanticipatable concomitant of an experienced contingent event.[11] Jüngel's description of this possibility as "miraculous," and of the event which grounds it as "the revelation of God," indicate clearly enough that the threshold of properly theological discourse (as Jüngel understands it) has been reached. But it is congruent with his aims at this point that he is satisfied merely to indicate this as a bare possibility, not to engage in further analysis or argue for it as something actually realized. All is subordinated to evoking the category of the "more than necessary." With the disclosure of this possibility, which can be described as the experience of worldly being as gifted or created being, the transition is finally begun from the groundless as not necessary to the groundless as more than necessary. A more decisive position is reached on the kind of groundlessness characterizing the more than necessary as opposed to that of a merely arbitrary event.

---

[11] The fact that theological reflection operates within the awareness and acceptance of this contingent and historically mediated experience, namely the confessed presence of God in the history of Jesus Christ, distinguishes it from philosophical reflection, even when theology must (unavoidably) utilize philosophical terms and concepts. Similar to the distinction above between historical and dogmatic perception, this distinction is less one of terminology or methods and more one of intention and use. In short, philosophical reflection is "general" or "abstract" when compared with theology because it can understand events only within that broad framework of capacities understood to accrue to nature and the human being as such. Theology, then, is more "concrete" by contrast in that it reshapes understandings of nature and the human in light of a particular configuration of historical events ("revelation"). Of course, as liberation theologies remind us, theology itself is a "general" category which abstracts in turn from the various concrete human and socio-historical contexts within which theological reflection must take place.

This special event in which all experience of worldly being is now conditioned unambiguously by a sense of its radical giftedness is simultaneously the revelation of a creator; "God" or "the creator" here comes into view solely as the decision underlying the preservation and affirmation of being, hence as that which has disposal over being.[12] This divine "nature" or "reality" is understood as enacting the basic decision concerning being and non-being, or, what amounts to the same thing, distinguishing being and non-being from each other.[13] With this, a decisive concept begins to emerge as a correlate of the more than necessary: freedom.

On the basis of what was said earlier, it is of course true that the groundlessness of the contingent in general can be characterized as "freedom" in purely negative terms, as the lack of conditioning by some necessity in which it is grounded.[14] Insofar as the "more than necessary" shares this attribute of contingency, a more than necessary creator could not be grounded in beings individually or even in the being of worldly beings in general and is therefore "free." But the shape of the experience with experience (which affirms gratitude as an ultimate) points beyond these negative determinations; it gestures toward something like a will determining being and non-being. A more positive notion of freedom is thus implicated in the category of the "more than necessary."

---

[12] It is important to avoid misunderstanding at this point. Jüngel is indicating the mere possibility of this affirmation, and therefore is attempting to describe in terms provided by philosophical reflection what it might mean to experience the world as creation. He is certainly not offering a kind of deduction of divine existence from analysis of these anthropological categories; as is clear, the emergence of the new category of "creation" is linked with a particular event which at this point remains undefined. In my opinion, careful reading of these passages would exclude the astonishing accusation that the experience with experience is the product of an "abstraction" from "general experience," or even that Jüngel is equating experience of God with the existential experience of nothingness. See Garrett Green, "The Mystery of Eberhard Jüngel: A Review of his Theological Program," *Religious Studies Review* 5 (1979): 38-9.

[13] Jüngel speaks here of a "*Wesen*," a word which in this study will usually be translated as "essence" but which sometimes (as here) has the more general meaning of "entity" or "being." I have chosen the terms "nature" and "reality" in order to register the proper note of vagueness and especially to avoid the term "being" which will generally be reserved for translating "*das Seiende*."

[14] GGW 29 (24): "The contingent cannot be deduced, cannot be grounded in another."

To argue for the equal primordiality and authenticity of gratitude and anxiety is to imply that worldly being presents itself as an ultimate actuality, impenetrable to rational analysis in its sheer givenness. Despite the ambiguity of its relation to non-being, it cannot be said rationally to point beyond itself; God, therefore, is groundless as neither grounded in nor grounding worldly being in any sense transparent to reason. But if on the basis of a special contingent experience God is revealed as the free decision or enactment behind the giftedness of worldly being, then God's groundlessness cannot be that of the utterly indeterminate, the random, the arbitrary. It is simply impossible to draw conclusions about God based on general analysis of the structure of the world or of being; but the concrete experience outlined here points beyond any purely negative freedom of God from the world. Even so, in this context Jüngel only gestures toward the truly theological content; by indicating this as a possibility, a further step has been taken, but more is needed to elucidate the category of the "more than necessary."

It should be recalled that Jüngel entered upon a discussion of the principle of sufficient reason with the intention of clarifying the idea of the "more than necessary" in its relation to necessity. The radical application of the idea of necessity to reality as a whole has been shown to issue in the disclosure of a unique region of experience defined by the non-necessity of the being of beings, its ambiguity or, better, its contingency. For Jüngel, neither ordinary experience nor rational thought is capable of pushing beyond this fundamental contingency; the fact of worldly being appears as a blank wall, impenetrable to meaning. The experience of worldly being as sheer arbitrariness (less than necessary) could in theory only succumb to the revelation of a radical creative decision, even though no such resolution is demanded by that experience as such.

The locus of such a decision is precisely for Jüngel an instance of the more than necessary. It meets the basic criteria of being essential, even foundational, within a given context without that logical transparency to the grounding intellect characteristic of necessity. As instanced by the possibility (and so far it is still just that) of a divine creative gesture underlying the facticity of being, the more than necessary may be described as radically founding gratuity or gift. We can now move from this particular instance to see if this category acquires a more definite conceptual shape.

Hegel and 'Absolute Necessity'

In spite of his love for striking or even bizarre turns of phrase, there are some indications that Jüngel wishes to immunize the reader from the initial strangeness of the idea "more than necessary"; he is especially aware of its peculiarity from the standpoint of the more traditional logic of modalities. As will be seen in Chapter Five, part of the logical difficulty is dissolved in light of the fundamental reconception of modal categories he wishes to initiate on a theological basis. In this context however, what Jüngel provides is a tantalizing set of historical resonances for the peculiar complex of ideas he has so sketchily delineated.

Is there any precedent in philosophical thinking for the idea of a contingency which transcends the necessary, whose presence remains unsuspected to the rational analysis of being in its static structure and is only revealed in a contingent event? If so, is there any historical echo of associating God with this strange category? The answer to these questions can be found in some specific references to Hegel and Schelling; although they might seem incidental to the main course of his argument, upon closer examination their importance as spurs to Jüngel's theological conception of the more than necessary should become evident.

The most illuminating example is Hegel's attempt to resurrect a notion of "absolute necessity" (after its relegation to a purely heuristic function by Kant); it highlights precisely those elements required by Jüngel for the articulation of "a being (*ein Sein*) which surpasses the concept of the necessary" (GGW 35 [28]). Hegel's discussion of "absolute necessity" is a short and extremely dense section of his massive *Science of Logic*. It would be beyond the scope of this study to provide a detailed analysis of the passages involved, even assuming that could be done apart from a full scale interpretation of Hegelian logic as a whole. Fortunately, all that is required is to examine Jüngel's selective appropriation of the Hegelian conceptuality, providing only as much background commentary as is sufficient to illuminate how the different concepts fit together in their original context. A bit of conceptual dissection must be performed on the difficult but very significant passage where Jüngel lays out Hegel's ideas; it will be divided into three parts and each will be discussed individually.

Jüngel understands Hegel's concept of absolute necessity as a kind of reprise of that notion of "necessary being" or final causal ground which, as already mentioned, had been expressly rejected by Kant as a reality beyond human subjectivity. But Hegel's "absolutely necessary" presents the old idea in a radically different light.

> Hegel, in conscious opposition to Kant, explicitly affirmed anew the being of an "absolutely necessary" (*schlechthin Notwendigem*) which in its "absolute necessity" (*absoluten Notwendigkeit*) depends upon no other. "The absolutely necessary *is* only because it *is*; otherwise it has neither condition nor ground." To that extent it is "simple immediacy or *pure being*." However, in that it has always already grounded itself, and so is simultaneously "simple reflection-in-itself" — "it is *because* it is" — the "absolutely necessary" is for Hegel not only "*pure being*" but just as equally "*pure essence*" (GGW 34 [27-8]).

To anyone familiar with basic Hegelian terminology this passage need not present any special difficulty. That which is given, simply and immediately, is "being" (*Sein*). It appears as completely undifferentiated and undetermined; that is, it has not yet been mediated or penetrated by thought. It has no depth, so to speak. However, the sphere of essence (*Wesen*) is the sphere of a differentiation of being, specifically of a stratification of being into an external level of mere appearance and a deeper, internal level of essential being. Thought no longer simply accepts the immediately given as true; "everything is regarded in a double aspect."[15] In short, being is now conceptually mediated by the concept of essence, which serves as the ground of being.

Hegel's point, then, in the passages cited by Jüngel must be that with the notion of the simply or absolutely necessary logic has achieved a new determination in which being and essence are unified. The immediate in fact is always already mediated; relationality in the form of reflection has penetrated even the immediacy of being. What first appeared as immediately given to reflection and thus external to it, now is revealed as a relation of reflection to itself. As one commentator puts it: "Reflection has no origin in the sense of

---

[15] W. T. Stace, *The Philosophy of Hegel: A Systematic Exposition* (New York: Dover Publications, 1955), 176.

something prior to reflection from which the relation of reflection first gets going. Any pretended origin is always already reflection."[16] The same phrase repeated with shifting emphases presents the differentiated unity of being and essence in the absolutely necessary. It is not mediated by anything external: it *is* (only) because it *is*. It has no ground, and thus is pure being. However, it is *self*-mediated, since it is in fact grounded and conditioned — by itself.[17] It is *because* it is. As self-grounded, it is pure essence.

In the following section of the passage, Jüngel begins by relating this concept of absolute necessity to what he has already said about the inescapable relationality of the notion of necessity.

> Through his determination of "absolute necessity" Hegel thus attempts to maintain the relationality-structure of the concept "necessity" by locating [the verb is *ansiedeln*, literally "to settle"] the relation so to speak inside the "absolutely necessary". Appropriately, the "absolutely necessary" appears as contingent over against another, indeed "pure being" appears as contingent over against "pure essence". "But this contingency is rather absolute necessity; it is the essence of these free actualities which are necessary in themselves."[18]

After the first sentence serious interpretational difficulties arise, largely due to Jüngel's selective quotation from an already complex and highly compressed source.

That the "absolutely necessary" would appear as contingent over against all others is simply the result of locating the relation implied by necessity *within* the "absolutely necessary" itself. As self-grounded, it appears completely ungrounded with regard to everything outside itself. That is, the determinations of its existence are not dependent on any outside condition, and thus appear as contingent; as Stace says, "It is thus an existence for which no reason can be given why

---

16 John F. Hoffmeyer, *The Advent of Freedom: The Presence of the Future in Hegel's Logic* (Rutherford, NJ: Fairleigh Dickinson University Press, 1994), 46.

17 Cf. G. W. F. Hegel, *The Science of Logic*, trans. W. H. Johnston and L. G. Struthers (London: Allen & Unwin, 1929), 2: 185: "As Reflection it has Ground and condition, but it has for Ground and condition only itself."

18 GGW 34-5 (28). The final sentence cites Hegel, *Science of Logic*, 2: 185.

it must be so."[19] But what does it mean for "pure being" to be contingent over against "pure essence," and what are the "free actualities" mentioned in the last sentence? As was seen, pure being and pure essence are the two aspects or moments of absolute necessity. The claim is that because of the internalization of the grounding relation, these two moments do not appear in their essential unity but "fall apart" as it were into an accidental relationship to each other. This represents an interpretation on Jüngel's part, for what Hegel actually says is that it is "actuality" and "possibility" which fall into a contingent relationship to each other.

For Hegel, possibility represents sheer lack of self-contradiction; it is "abstract self-relation" or "identity."[20] As a simple "reflection-into-self" (that is as sheer identity which needs nothing external to be represented as itself) it corresponds to "pure essence." This is because pure essence is abstract self-mediation, a being grounded in its own being, and hence a tautological or empty achievement of identity. On the other hand, "actuality" for Hegel represents the unity of inner and outer, of essence and appearance or manifestation.[21] The moment of essence always stresses the disjunction (at least in thought) of inner and outer. As mentioned above, for Hegel the realm of being normally abstracts completely from all inner/outer distinctions, and would seem a curious candidate to represent the moment of actuality in absolute necessity. But recall that it is precisely "*pure* being" which is at stake here. Its immediacy is grounded in the mediation of itself (it *is* because it *is*) and hence represents the perfect unity of inner and outer. Necessity in Hegel is the unity of possibility and actuality.[22]   In the case of absolute necessity, this unity of possibility and actuality is the unity of pure essence and pure being. This shows the legitimacy of Jüngel's interpretive substitution of vocabulary, but it does not yet touch on what this contingency of pure being versus pure essence (i.e. actuality versus possibility) is supposed to mean.

---

[19] Stace, *Philosophy of Hegel*, 214. Note that this statement implies the rejection of the "Principle of Sufficient Reason."

[20] Ibid. 213.

[21] Ibid. 211.

[22] Hoffmeyer, *Advent*, 47.

It must seem odd that within the absolutely necessary there appears to be an accidental relation between actuality and possibility ; after all, necessity in general is supposed to represent precisely their unity, and absolute necessity is the "truth" of both actuality and possibility. Although Hegel's reasoning is quite tortuous here, it will suffice to point out his insistence that in absolute necessity the two moments of actuality and possibility have the apparent status of "free actualities." They are actual because they are no longer simply reflective determinations but represent the form of the absolute itself.[23] They are free in the limited sense of free from each other. Each appears independent, self-grounded, necessary in itself and hence merely accidental or externally related to the other.[24] Recall that absolute necessity is both pure essence (utterly and perfectly grounded, unity of inner reality and outward manifestation) and pure being (utterly lacking external ground or mediation). But this unity is not apparent; instead the moment of being eclipses the moment of essence.[25] Absolute necessity is differentiated as actuality and possibility. The aspect of pure being in absolute necessity lends to the two differentiations the appearance of "free" beings; their essences which comprise their unity in absolute necessity are hidden.

But this cannot be the last word since, as the last sentence quoted by Jüngel indicates, this contingency of relation between the free actualities is in fact a manifestation precisely of their essence. Their appearance as distinct actualities contradicts their true relation: absolute identity.[26] Jüngel summarizes the problem and the manner of its solution in the last part of the passage.

> Therefore Hegel also calls "absolute necessity" "blind", and its essence, which is determined as contingency, [he calls] "that which shuns the light" (*das Lichtscheue*), because the "absolutely necessary" is precisely "only grounded purely in itself." There is need of a particular occurrence, so that the essence of absolute necessity must "burst out and reveal" specially in the "necessary actualities" "what *it* is and what *they* are" (GGW 35 [28]).

---

23 Hegel, *Science of Logic*, 182.

24 On Hegel's use of "freedom" here, cf. Hoffmeyer, *Advent*, 47.

25 Ibid.

26 Hegel, *Science of Logic*, 182.

Absolute necessity is a blind necessity because, like all necessity, it unites the possible and the actual, and yet the peculiarly absolute character of that unity in the special case of this kind of necessity renders that unity opaque to thought. Absolute necessity, foiled by its own radicality, can be viewed indifferently as pure being or pure essence; thought oscillates between these freestanding moments without discerning their connection. But for Hegel, of course, mind can never be ultimately thwarted upon its path toward the utter conceptual transparency of reality.

Hegel speaks of a kind of epiphany or manifestation of the essence of absolute necessity in or at (he uses the preposition "*an*") the free actualities to emphasize that their essential unity cannot be penetrated from outside, as it were. Rather, there must be a decisive breakthrough which for Hegel takes place in the transition from the notion of substance to that of subject, and from the illusory (because merely one sided and abstract) freedom of the "free actualities" to true concrete freedom. This indication of a breakthrough in the chapter on absolute necessity is actually an anticipation of the later parts of the *Logic*; no venture into that difficult terrain is required to divine Jüngel's particular interest in this "breakthrough."[27] The insular, self-grounded nature of absolute necessity was shown to invest its sublated moments with complete opacity. The movement of thought grinds to a halt in the static opposition of pure being to pure essence. Only a new movement of thought, initiated from the direction of absolute necessity itself in its essence, enables a manifestation of its own true nature.

For all its obscurity, the basic thrust of Hegel's discussion of absolute necessity is clear within the context of the *Science of Logic*. On the one hand an ever intensified penetration to the heart of the concept of necessity leads to the "demand for self-necessitating actual fact," that is to absolute necessity as a perfectly essential self-mediation of being.[28] On the other, the cost of this achievement is an opacity to the grounding reason which can no longer be resolved by following out the

---

[27] On Hegel's use of the "breakthrough" language see Hoffmeyer, *Advent*, 48.

[28] G. R. G. Mure, *A Study of Hegel's Logic* (Oxford: Oxford University Press, 1950; reprint, Westport, CT: Greenwood Press, 1984), 142.

logic of necessity but is only overcome in the transition to a radically new level where the logic of substance is sublimated into the logic of the subject. Jüngel is clearly fascinated by the dynamic of a transcendence of necessity which issues precisely into the realm of subjectivity, indeed of freedom.[29] But just as clearly he has no wish to grant a blanket endorsement to Hegel's totalizing idealism whereby the contingent is revealed to be the medium of the absolute's passage to self-consciousness. After all, that is precisely to grant necessity the last word, and corresponds to the ultimate *Aufhebung* of all finite subjectivity into the absolute. Hegel's attempt to combine the absolutization of necessity with its inherently relational character is thus fraught with "difficulties." Jüngel desires to appropriate only those elements suggestive of a kind of being surpassing necessity "without justifying the notion of the 'absolutely necessary' itself."[30]

What are these elements? Jüngel lists three of them, and this enumeration of characteristics implies that he has found within the philosophical tradition a set of problems intriguingly close to those characterizing the "more than necessary" in theology. The basic ideas he associates with the phrase also gain a certain structured configuration from their proximity to Hegel's thought which helps to dispel the impression of randomness which is a residue of his phenomenological approach to the idea in his analysis of the "experience with experience." The three elements selected by Jüngel from Hegel's discussion as the keys to the notion of the more than necessary are "groundlessness" (*Grundlosigkeit*), "event-character" (*Ereignishaftigkeit*) and "freedom". How each of these concepts is linked to the Hegelian discussion requires a bit more elucidation.

The "being" (*Sein*) of the more than necessary is groundless, but this lack of a ground "nevertheless does not allow this [being] to be taken for arbitrary" (GGW 35 [28]). Jüngel's meaning should be immediately evident on the basis of the preceding discussion; the

---

[29] Cf. Harald Knudsen, *Gottesbeweise im Deutschen Idealismus* (Berlin / New York: Walter de Gruyter, 1972), 166: "Die Substanz ist Subjekt geworden und Notwendigkeit Freiheit."

[30] GGW 35 (28). The ambiguity of Hegel's "absolute necessity" is due to the fact that it combines necessity with contingency. Jüngel's wish to emphasize the latter component over the former is precisely why he prefers the phrase "more than necessary" to "absolutely necessary." Hegel's terminology would inevitably lead to confusion. See GGW 42 (33).

notion of "groundlessness" is now supplied with a more positive significance than was apparent in the earlier part of this chapter. In particular, it illuminates the peculiar ontological constitution of a being which resists inclusion in a structure of universal grounding. This being is a self-grounded or self-mediated being. It cannot be called arbitrary because it is grounded, indeed thoroughly determined — by itself.   Nevertheless, its self-mediated character insures its appearance as contingent and ungrounded with regard to any other being. Herein lies the basic justification for a "third way" beyond the necessary and the arbitrary: not necessary because not externally grounded (or grounding), not arbitrary because self-grounded.

This more-than-necessary being also has the character of an event, and according to Jüngel this "allows it to be understood in its contingency which surpasses necessity" (GGW 35 [28]). It was seen that for Hegel the peculiar structure of self-grounded being rendered its true nature completely obscure; the manifestation of its essence is tied up with the transition to an entirely new level of reflection. Jüngel is perhaps influenced both by Hegel's somewhat violent language ("break-out") and by the indication of a definite occurrence in which the "free actualities" or moments are undermined from within by the revelation of the ground of their unity and as a result of which they "perish" (i.e. lose their illusory freedom).[31] In any case, he regards Hegel's insistence upon a revelatory manifestation of the essence of "absolute necessity" as justifying talk of the more than necessary in terms of an event or occurrence. Implicit in this is the rejection of any notion of the more than necessary as a static category or fixed structural element of reality. Only this dynamism of manifestation discloses that contingency which exceeds the illusory necessity or self-groundedness of the "free actualities", exceeds it because it is their very essence as moments of "absolute necessity."

Upon closer inspection, this disclosive event must be seen as the very mode of being of the absolutely necessary, and not an accidental occurrence which might very well not have occurred, leaving the absolutely necessary essentially untouched. This is, after all, the realm of the Hegelian logic; the movement of reality is understood as

---

[31] Cf. Hegel, *Science of Logic*, 186: "To this mark Necessity appeals as to the witness of its cause, and, touched by it, the Actualities now perish."

the dialectical development of the concept. The manifestation of the essential unity of pure being and pure essence is the very being of that unity. The logic is the itinerary of the *logos*; the realities it treats of are the stages of the absolute spirit in its coming to know itself. Hence, the *ordo essendi* cannot be separated from the *ordo cognoscendi*. It is possible to see in Jüngel's reference to the "event-character" of the more than necessary an appropriation of this aspect of Hegel's conceptuality. For if the more than necessary is defined by its status as a disclosive event, then its being must in fact be the event of its own disclosure. Like Hegel's "absolute necessity," Jüngel's more than necessary simply *is* the event of its self-revelation; its being is fundamentally self-disclosive.

The third and final characteristic singled out for appropriation is that of the "freedom" of absolute necessity. Jüngel is again calling attention to the revelatory character of Hegel's conception which was just outlined, only from a slightly different angle. If the event-character of the absolute necessity indicates its self-*revelatory* aspect then its freedom stresses that this is indeed a *self*-revelation. Of concern here is the tension between the opacity of pure being in the "free actualities" and the "breaking-out" (disclosure) of their essential unity. Jüngel's point is precisely this movement from within outwards. Essence in Hegel always refers to the inner, the mediated, what lies behind or underneath immediate appearance. In speaking of the apprehension of the essential one might well speak of a penetration or an unmasking of illusory appearance from the outside. What is intriguing to Jüngel here is that Hegel does not speak in this way, but instead speaks of the disclosure of absolute necessity as a breaking-out from within, from the side of essence. Hence Jüngel feels justified in speaking of a "being revealing itself from itself" (*ein sich von sich aus offenbarendes Sein*) (GGW 35 [28]). Freedom here refers to what might be called this centrifugal character of disclosure. The capacity for disclosure here resides entirely in that which discloses itself, not in the one to whom it is disclosed. This is the freedom Jüngel speaks of, a clear analogue to the "groundlessness" already discussed.

The Contribution of Schelling

These, then, are the structural features of the Hegelian "absolute necessity" which Jüngel has chosen for "the determination of the expression 'more than necessary'" (GGW 35 [28]). Clearly, Hegel is not being invoked as some kind of philosophical authority to justify Jüngel's theological conception; there is no attempt to defend Hegel's metaphysical scheme in its entirety, and the Hegelian terminology is appropriated with considerable freedom. In fact, Jüngel even disavows any interest in exploring the connections between Hegel's absolute necessity and the philosopher's concept of God (GGW 35 n. 32 [28]). He does, however, make reference to Schelling for a philosophical anticipation of the odd terminology of "more than necessary" which explicitly connects modal concerns similar to Hegel's to a reformulation of the concept of God. In fact, Schelling's later philosophy should probably be considered an important influence on Jüngel at this point, even if explicit references to it in this work are confined mainly to a few intriguing footnotes.[32]

The key passage cited by Jüngel is: "Are God and necessarily existing being identical concepts? In what way is He *more* than just this?"[33] The context is Schelling's discussion of Descartes, specifically of the Cartesian version of the ontological argument. Schelling has shown how Descartes argues for the notion of necessary existence as unavoidably implied in the concept of a most perfect being. But the Cartesian position ends up simply identifying the notion of God (i.e. the most perfect being) with that of the necessarily existing being. Schelling suspects this position of involving an aporia or contradiction; as a result, God must be somehow more than merely the necessary existent. The questions relevant to an understanding of Jüngel's interest in this passage are first, what is unsatisfactory in the identification of God and necessary existence, and second, what is Schelling's intention in granting God a status beyond this identification.

For Schelling, the necessarily existing being is precisely being itself, that is, the "pure concept," the subject already presupposed in

---

32 For a summary of Schelling's "philosophy of revelation" based on recently published materials, see Klaus Bannach, "Schellings Philosophie der Offenbarung: Gehalt und theologiegeschichtliche Bedeutung," *Neue Zeitschrift für Systematische Theologie und Religionsphilosophie* 37 (1995): 57-74. At points the similarity to themes in Jüngel's theology is striking. See especially 61-74.

33 GGW 30 note 15 (24). Jüngel cites F. W. J. Schelling, "Zur Geschichte der neueren Philosophie," in *Sämmtliche Werke*, division 1, vol. 10 (Stuttgart: J. S. Cotta'scher Verlag, 1861), 17. English translation: F. W. J. Schelling, *On the History of Modern Philosophy*, ed. and trans. Andrew Bowie (Cambridge: Cambridge University Press, 1994), 52. My citations will be from this translation.

every act of predication. Before the "is" of predication, there must be a "what," a "something"; understood most generally or abstractly, this is simply the being of any and every subject prior to assignment to it of any particular mode of being. This abstraction cannot be maintained, however, since "it is impossible that what is the entitlement, the precondition, the beginning of all being should not also be — this 'be' taken in the sense of existence, i.e. of being also outside the *concept*."[34] The mind simply cannot avoid assigning to being itself an objective existence. But for Schelling to exist necessarily is to exist blindly. This necessity is that of the absolute *"prius"*; it is not the actualization of preceding possibility. As that being which precedes all possibility it is blind, since for Schelling "the action which rushes ahead of the *concept* of the action . . . is a blind action."[35]

Schelling moves on to identify the difficulty in conceiving of God in terms of a necessarily existing being, as he claims Descartes does. The idea of God comes to philosophy from outside, from the realm of general religious belief. On the one hand, that idea certainly involves a notion of an absolute existent, of God as *ipsum ens*. On the other hand it is precisely this notion which must appear as a contradiction of "what we really *want* if we want God."[36]

> For the first thing about the concept of that which exists blindly (*des blindlings Seyenden*) is, of course, that it is devoid of freedom in relation to its being (*Seyn*); it can neither negate (*aufheben*), nor change, nor modify it. That which has no freedom in relation to its own being has no freedom at all — is *absolutely* unfree. If, then, God were the necessarily existing being (*Wesen*), He could only be defined at the same time as that which was rigid, immovable, absolutely unfree, incapable of any free action, progression or going out of himself.[37]

We have quoted this passage at length because it concisely presents a theme of utterly central importance to Jüngel's thinking about God, a theme which it is the purpose of this entire study to elucidate. The

---

34 Schelling, *History*, 53.

35 Ibid.

36 Ibid. 55.

37 Ibid. 54.

idea of God's freedom must include a freedom with respect to God's own being or ontological locus. To ground and secure this freedom as an implication of a trinitarian theology of the cross is Jüngel's basic theological achievement.

Schelling's suggestive comments on how this freedom is to be conceived provide the final conceptual element for the "more than necessary." Schelling's concept of true divinity (which goes beyond the "necessary existent") demands that God have the freedom to transform God's own being into something self-posited. This procedure is dialectical in the classical sense of that word as used in absolute idealism. In itself or immediately, God's being as such is necessary. To appropriate this being as a free act is precisely to negate its necessity, to make it contingent, something which is now posited by God. True to the well-known multivalence of the term "negation" (*Aufhebung*), Schelling insists that in this process the necessity of the divine being is not simply destroyed. It persists basically or fundamentally (*im Grund*) even as it is effectively or actually (*in der Tat*) converted into something different. It follows from the dialectical conceptuality of the *Aufhebung* that God's being must have a twofold structure, or rather must contain at least two moments. The immediacy of necessary being is first posited independently of God, but is appropriated in a gesture of freedom and hence, as effective being or being "in act" is now self-posited and contingent. For Schelling this free mediation marks the passage from the "dead" God (i.e. the God identified with the blindness of necessary existence) to the living God. "Life [*Lebendigkeit*] consists precisely in the freedom to negate its own being as immediate, posited independently of itself, and to be able to transform it into a being posited by itself."[38]

Conclusion

Jüngel's own comments suggest that his reference to Schelling has the goal of providing a philosophical precedent for the "admittedly unusual and logically difficult expression 'more than necessary'" (GGW 30 n. 15 [24]). The immediate context suggests it is not really a particular way of conceiving the more than necessary which is here in question, but merely the phrase itself. For Schelling,

---

[38] Ibid. 55.

in contrast to Jüngel, is not concerned to deny necessity as a proper attribute of divine being; in this case "more than necessary" seems to mean that identifying God as the necessary existent is one sided. God is the necessary existent — but God is more than this. At first glance this seems to clash with the previous discussion of Jüngel's position, which implied that the more than necessary should not properly be called necessary at all. If this were the whole story, Jüngel's invocation of Schelling as an early witness to the language of the more than necessary would look rather artificial.

That this is not the whole story is shown by the natural way in which Schelling's ideas seem to mesh with Jüngel's conception as already outlined. Although Jüngel eschews the language of absolute necessity, Schelling's notion of necessary existence as the absolute *prius* does in fact accord well with Jüngel's assertion of the utter groundlessness of God. As was the case with Hegel, Jüngel is willing to appropriate for his own conception ideas which in their original context involve some notion of necessity, as long as that notion avoids the particular elements of the ordinary concept of necessity which he seeks to overcome. Neither Hegel's "absolute necessity" nor Schelling's "necessary existence" involve that aspect of necessity dear to "Leibniz and the metaphysical tradition," namely the dialectic of grounding/grounded which when applied to God ontologically "fixes" the divine being as a function of worldly being, enmeshing it in a set of rationally determined reciprocal grounding relations (GGW 42 [33]). Both Hegel and Schelling are concerned to define a realm of necessity which keeps open a space of contingency and freedom. Jüngel, however, in light of the continuing influence of the metaphysical tradition of divine necessity and due to the paradoxical predominance of the moment of contingency in Hegel's and Schelling's discussions of necessity, prefers to dispense with the language of necessity entirely. "More than necessary" is "indeed only a suggestive expression, but one which suggests the issue intended better than the . . . concept of absolute necessity" (GGW 42 [33]).

Looking back on the manifold reflections of this chapter from the perspective of Schelling's suggestive comments, there is a clear convergence of the different strands of the discussion upon the central issue of freedom. The issue involved in the first part of the chapter, which culminated in the denial of the complex of necessary relations implied by the principle of sufficient reason, was the delineation of ungrounded being. The result of the second section turned on the disclosure within experience of the juncture of worldly being with non-being, a juncture which in turn became the possible location of a radically founding decision, a freedom revealed in a self-disclosive event. The discussion of Hegel in turn clarified the positive content of the more than necessary in terms of the ideas surfacing in these previous discussions: groundlessness, event-character, freedom. Schelling's God can now be seen as a clear foreshadowing of the more-than-necessary God which Jüngel is conceptually outlining.

In the Hegelian explication of "groundlessness," it was seen that a self-mediation or self-determination of being is at stake. Schelling's notion of God further illuminates this idea by presenting this self-mediation in terms of an act of appropriation of God's own being. This in turn demands an understanding of God's being as an event. It is not the particular actualization of a given category which could be abstracted from it. God's being is the free determination of that being as an ever new creative act. The most explicit point of contact between Hegel and Schelling is the idea of freedom, which clearly underlies and integrates the first two concepts. Especially of concern to Jüngel is the notion of freedom as absolute self-origination, and as self-diffusion outward from that center of origin, which will be formulated theologically by the central figures of "word" and "love."

As the invocation of these more theologically-oriented figures of speech suggests, the basic ideas which have been examined in this chapter are actually derived from Jüngel's material or dogmatic theological position. This is clear in spite of the formal dependance upon philosophical reflection which characterizes Jüngel's discourse in these sections. (As has been said more than once, it is not only legitimate but necessary in Jüngel's view to utilize philosophical concepts, suitably modified, in the articulation of theological ideas.) At its heart that theological position, according to the model of evangelical theology already outlined, must be an interpretation of the event of Jesus Christ as God's self-disclosure. The relation of God as "more than necessary" to that theological position becomes clear when the idea of the more than necessary as developed in this chapter is revealed to be a development or construal of Jüngel's basic position on God's simplicity.

In the traditional scheme of divine simplicity, God's existence was derived from God's essence in such a way that God was declared to be necessarily existent. The more than necessary God is precisely the refutation of this scheme.

> [F]aith must assert that the divine essence which derives from the unanticipatable existence of God, and which is thought of *as* this [existence], teaches one to think of God as one who simply cannot (for logical reasons) be understood as necessary in identity with the particular historical actuality of the human being Jesus (GGW 260 [192]).

God's essence cannot be determined as necessary because it identifies itself in and with a contingent historical event.

Indeed, the conceptual connection of the more than necessary and the ontologically simple goes deeper than this, because a being capable of such a radically free self-actualization of its essence or ontological identity renders meaningless the very distinction between identity or essence and the act of being or existence. The concept of the "more than necessary" developed in this chapter in terms of a self-grounding, self-revealing event is really an outgrowth of that equation of identity and act, of essence and existence which for Jüngel is the unavoidable result of God's radically free identification of God's being with the concrete human existence of Jesus. That historical existence is determinative of the divine essence, and that essence in turn must be described as more than necessary precisely because it is capable of that act of ontological self-identification in historical existence.

CHAPTER FIVE

CREATIO EX NIHILO AND GOD'S EXISTENCE AS LOVE

The highly schematic discussion of God's mode of being undertaken in the previous chapters must be theologically augmented or "fleshed out" in the chapters which follow. Jüngel is a thinker highly suspicious of abstraction, especially where the thought of God is concerned; it is the concrete role of God in dogmatic thinking which is of prime importance. The present chapter and the one which follows endeavor to show both how the abstract idea of God as more than necessary connects with God's being as creator and redeemer respectively, and also how these ideas can be interpreted as variations on the fundamental theme of divine simplicity. This current chapter centers on Jüngel's understanding of the doctrine of creation, and consists of three parts. A first section deals with the basic concepts needed to understand Jüngel's conception, particularly the Barthian motifs of creation as analogical and the creation/covenant relationship. The second part deals with Jüngel's treatment of the basic categories of "actuality" and "possibility," while the last section discerns an intersection of the concerns of the first two sections in a new and more precise definition of God's being.

Barth's Heritage: Reading Creation from the Cross

Properly speaking, Jüngel has no specific theology of creation, or at least he has not devoted any of his writing to an extended systematic exposition of the topic. There are enough scattered references, however, to indicate broadly the main lines of his thinking. The first step in understanding Jüngel's views on creation is to recognize his Barthian insistence on reading creation entirely in terms of God's revelation in Christ. Barth's conception of the relation of creation and covenant elaborated in the third volume of the *Church Dogmatics* provides the framework for Jüngel's own reflections on creation. This has a number of immediate consequences which must be highlighted to prevent confusion. The foundations of Barth's doctrine, and hence also of Jüngel's, are contained in the twin ideas of creation as an analogical act on the one hand, and creation as an irreducibly trinitarian act on the other. But before turning to these central motifs, some peculiarities of this kind of theology of creation must be brought into the foreground.

Jüngel follows Barth in understanding the general relationship of creator to creature from the specific relationship of God to humanity revealed in Jesus Christ. This will be explicated in more detail later in this section, but among the immediate consequences of this position for Jüngel is what might be called a "theo-anthropocentrism" in his thinking about creation. The absence of any kind of theological cosmology in his whole body of writing is quite striking when compared either to the classical theological tradition or to such contemporary theological movements as have been influenced by process thought or ecological reflection. This cosmological lacuna is quite deliberate; for Jüngel the really essential things are said when God is humanly experienced *as* creator and the human person experiences him- or herself *as* a creature, both experiences being aspects of faith in Jesus Christ. Only on this basis is it then possible to reflect on and experience the non-human world as God's creature as well.

In this context theological cosmology simply cannot arise as an independent theme, much less a foundational one. Indeed, throughout his writings Jüngel's preferred concept when dealing with the total context within which human beings are situated is "the world." The incidence of this word can cause confusion if one tries to interpret it in terms of a cosmology, since "the world" for Jüngel is actually a thoroughly anthropocentric notion; it refers to the human experience of reality as a meaningful whole (GGW 214 [160]). The world is always a constructed world, an interpreted or linguistically structured reality. In contrast, the notion of cosmos in "cosmology," at least as I have just been using that term, includes humanity to be sure, but refers to the whole of reality as independent of human experience, bearing any meaning or order it might have within itself. Jüngel, following Barth (and Bultmann as well), prefers to focus on human reality; any extrapolation to the nature of non-human phenomena must move outward from that reality, rather than bracketing it in a search for supposedly more basic or general cosmological principles.[1]

A second result of Jüngel's Christological concentration on creation is that the experience of reality as creation is properly a result of Christian faith. To know oneself and the world as created is not a basic postulate of human experience nor a logical inference therefrom. To "acknowledge God as the sovereign of being" is an act of faith, and not only in the pious sense that it is no indifferent assertion but implies joyful trust and gratitude (GGW 523-4 [382]). It is also an act of faith in that it is a response to God's revelation in Christ. The revelation of the creator in creation of which Paul speaks in Romans 1 cannot be received by human beings due to sin; Jüngel speaks of this as a "forfeited form of revelation."[2] The revelation of God as creator must occur in the event of Jesus Christ, and in those events in the history of Israel which form the preparation and context of that event. Even in the Old Testament, the creation story is just that, a story; it is not scientific or philosophical speculation, but an integral part of "God's history with Israel" (GGW 414 [303]).[3] Interpreting the doctrine of creation from the Christ-event, from the achieved reconciliation of Creator and creature, is possible because in Barth's understanding "the relation of sinful man and justifying God is not a special aspect within a larger situation but is rather the most general, actual situation."[4]

This close connection of the idea of creation with that of redemption is not without its difficulties. It is certainly the case that

---

[1] Barth's reasons for eschewing theological cosmology are contained in *Church Dogmatics* III/2, §43 ("Man as a Problem of Dogmatics").

[2] Eberhard Jüngel, "Zum Begriff der Offenbarung," in *Glaube - Bekenntnis - Kirchenrecht*, ed. G. Besier (Hannover: Lutherisches Verlagshaus, 1989), 215.

[3] This raises the interesting problem of Israel's experience of creation: was it, too, "Christological" in orientation? Although he does not say so explicitly, I presume Jüngel would claim (as Luther did) that the Old Testament teaching of creation was oriented toward Christ in a "prophetic" manner, understanding God's act of creation as the context within which dealings with the covenant people occur, and therefore as pointing ahead to the advent of God's messiah as the restorer and perfecter of that covenant. Insofar as it identified God the creator with the saving covenant God of Israel, the creation-faith of the ancient Jews was in its own way just as soteriological and Christological as that which Barth and Jüngel are advocating.

[4] Eberhard Jüngel, "Das Dilemma der natürlichen Theologie und die Wahrheit ihres Problems," in *Entsprechungen*, 169.

Jüngel's language is confusing at times; the ideas of God's overcoming of non-being in creation and of God's overcoming of sin in reconciliation are, as we will see, so closely related that they threaten simply to coalesce. Jüngel interprets both creation and reconciliation in an ontological fashion, that is, in terms of a struggle between being and non-being. The problem for Barth as well as Jüngel lies in how properly to relate the chaotic non-being against which God creates (*creatio ex nihilo*) with the annihilating non-being of sin which God overcomes in the event of the cross. That Jüngel wishes to maintain a distinction here is evident. For example, he says that the "well-being" of the world and its "salvation" are two different things; elsewhere he states that though creation is dependent on reconciliation, reconciliation is not yet "settled" in creation.[5] But the precise relation of God the creator to God the reconciler remains problematic, as some commentators have pointed out.[6]

At any rate, this problem need not be resolved here; it has been alluded to in order to introduce the basic scheme by which Barth and Jüngel attempt to understand creation in its relation to the Christ-event: creation and covenant. As is well-known, Barth spoke of creation (or "nature") as the "outer ground" of the covenant, and the covenant (or "grace") as the "inner ground" of creation. In a penetrating exposition of Barth's ideas, Jüngel expounds this reciprocal grounding relationship in terms of a "possibility-rendering-possible" and a "possibility-rendered-possible."[7] To put it briefly, the inner ground of creation is God's eternal election of humanity; that eternal act of election became an historical event in Jesus Christ. Creation exists for the sake of this covenant with humanity in history. Hence, paradoxically, the very created world, which in one sense makes all history possible, is itself only possible as the presupposition of God's covenant-history. It is the

---

[5] Eberhard Jüngel, "Thesen zur Grundlegung der Christologie," 275. Idem., "Begriff der Offenbarung," 220.

[6] Kern, "Theologie des Glaubens," 144. L. J. O'Donovan, "The Mystery of God as a History of Love: Eberhard Jüngel's Doctrine of God," *Theological Studies* 42 (1981): 251-71 at 260, note 24. To be fair it should be pointed out that Jüngel is aware of the problem. One purpose of natural theology is the proper relation of God the justifier to God the creator. Eberhard Jüngel, "Gelegentliche Thesen zum Problem der Natürlichen Theologie," in *Entsprechungen*, 198-200.

[7] Jüngel, "Möglichkeit theologischer Anthropologie," 218-9.

external ground of possibility for Jesus Christ, while Jesus Christ is the *internal* ground of the possibility of creation, *enabling* it to be that *external* ground of possibility! Hence creation is possibility-rendered-possible, while the covenant is the possibility-rendering-possible.

Flowing from this creation-covenant scheme are consequences vital to understanding the nature of God as creator. Jüngel claims that any adequate theology of creation must reject out of hand the idea that humanity is the result of an arbitrary creative decision. "A theology of creation which does not lead this possibility *ad absurdum* does not deserve the name." Barth's doctrine of eternal election (his so-called revised supralapsarianism) does just that by attributing the inner possibility and motive of creation to God's election of humanity as his covenant-partner in eternity, that is prior to creation. In a striking phrase, Jüngel interprets this to mean that "the creator is *moved* in his being by the being of man," that is the humanity which God freely chooses to create (GGW 48 [38]). But how can God, who has free disposal over God's own being (as was seen in the previous chapter), be "moved" or affected in that being by a creature? The twofold answer is that, first, God's very being is love and manifests itself in a freely-posited eternal otherness; God's being is eternally a "being moved" by an "other" in that God *is* or subsists in a reciprocity of relations of love. Secondly, God's eternal affirmation of God's self as "other" is freely mirrored by the affirmation of humanity, that is the creature, as other. This latter statement reflects the analogical structure of God's creative act, while the former statement points to God's trinitarian being as the ground of possibility of creation. I will take up each statement in turn, beginning with the issue of analogy.

Jüngel follows Barth in defining creation as a participation in God's act of free, loving self-affirmation. Once again, everything focuses anthropocentrically on God's election of humanity as the central presupposition of creation. God chooses humanity as a partner in love. But if it is truly to be a counterpart in *love* for which God elects, and therefore creates, humanity, then God is freely conceding God's own self-sufficiency. God opens God's own being to another being which must be free in order to love God in return (and therefore also free to reject God's love and turn away). As Jüngel puts it, as potential love-partner, humanity has been created for its own sake since someone can only be loved for his or her own sake. Indeed, it is the very mark of God's omnipotence to create something which could then be loved for its own sake (GGW 48 [38]). Now the claim that God is "moved in his own being" by the being of humanity can be clarified.

Jüngel has said that love means not wishing to be oneself without another; in love, one's path to oneself flows through another person, so that one must in effect receive one's self from that other (GGW 443-4 [324]). If God in electing and creating humanity (and this is the proper ordering of the two acts) is committed to a loving relationship with humanity (the covenant), then God's very being is "at stake" in some sense. It has already been shown to be axiomatic for Jüngel that God's being is grounded in God's free act of self-affirmation. Therefore creation must be seen as part of God's self-determination, indeed as a part of God's very identity.[8] And the point of saying that creation is an analogical act is that there is an analogy or correspondence between God's act of self-determination and the act of creating another. Although Jüngel does not put it precisely this way, it may be said that there is a formal similarity between God's self-election, and God's election-creation of humanity, and indeed that the latter consists in a participation in the former.[9]

This is Jüngel's exposition of the structure of Barth's analogy of relation (*analogia relationis*). The importance of this understanding of analogy is that it undercuts a certain way of conceptualizing metaphysically God's relation to the world which Barth associates with the traditional analogy of being (*analogia entis*). We cannot enter into the extremely complex territory of this dispute. But Jüngel's understanding of the important ontological consequences of the analogy of relation must be indicated. From what has been said above, it is manifest that the two relations between which the analogy subsists are the relation of God's being to itself on the one hand, and the relation of God's being to human being on the other. In each case, the relation consists of an act of fundamental affirmation grounding the being of that which is affirmed. In the first case, God's trinitarian being is understood as a free, loving self-affirmation: God's "Yes" to God's self. In the second case, God's creative act (grounded in the eternal covenant)

---

[8] GGW 48 (38). Cf. GGW 213 (159): "That other which has been taken along by God on his way [i.e. to himself] is called in the Bible *creation* . . ."

[9] Cf. Jüngel, "Schritt Zurück," 120, where he speaks of God's "Yes" to creation as a participation in God's "Yes" to God's self.

is understood as a free, loving affirmation of human being: God's "Yes" to us. The point of similarity, the formal basis of the analogy, is the utter freedom of God's being, the freedom in which the "Yes" is spoken.[10] And Jesus Christ is both of these affirmations in one person; for this reason, he is the "ground of both the being and the knowledge of all analogy."[11]

The crucial consequence of this understanding of creative analogy is that there is no metaphysical participation of creaturely being (*qua* being) in God's being. It is Barth's understanding of the analogy of being that it implies just such a participation, and hence justifies the application of the same basic metaphysical attributes to divine and to created being. God is thus envisioned as the ultimate instantiation of being and its so-called "transcendental" attributes (unity, truth, goodness). Jüngel is less concerned with the fairness of Barth's interpretation of the analogy of being than he is with this connection of the doctrine to a conception of God as the "highest being" (*summum ens*). In adopting the analogy of relation as the scheme for understanding the relation of the creator to the creature, Jüngel breaks decisively with the metaphysics of divinity as the highest being. The mode of creaturely participation has been displaced; instead of a metaphysical participation of creaturely being in God's being, there is now an analogical participation of God's affirmation of creaturely being in God's trinitarian self-affirmation. At one stroke, the possibility of describing God in terms of a categorial framework derived from the being of the world as generally given to experience is rendered acutely problematic (GGW 48 [38]).

This analogical framework is still no doubt "worldly" in the sense that it is a product of human thought, utilizing human categories. To make analogies is a human, and therefore a worldly activity. The point is that the experiential basis of the analogy has changed. The basic terms used in interpreting God's relationship to worldly being are no longer extrapolated from a "general" human experience or analysis of that being. Indeed, God and the world are not said to share "being" in common. Far from being a self-evident basis from which to

---

[10] Jüngel, "Möglichkeit theologischer Anthropologie," 220.

[11] Ibid. 212 (". . .Seins- und Erkenntnisgrund aller Analogie. . ."). Cf. ibid. 223.

understand God's relation to creation and humanity, worldly being is experienced as such and understood only through the experience of being creatively called into relation to God through participation in the unity of God and humanity in the Christ-event.

An understanding of the creative act as analogous to the inner movement or act of the divine being illuminates Jüngel's difficult statement that "historicity is constitutive of being."[12] This is the point at which, he claims, Barth's theological approach connects with Heidegger's ontological approach.[13] Nonetheless, no recourse to *Being and Time* is required to understand Jüngel's intention. On the one hand, the "more-than-necessary" God has been shown to have a being grounded in, or better, identical with, a free event of will or choice. Thus, God's being is identical with the history of God's self-positing; God's being is in coming or becoming. On the other hand, God's "Yes" to creation does not grant creation a participation in God's being, but grants it its own (created) being which is a participation in God's "Yes" to God's self, that is in God's history or self-enactment. In short, both divine being and created or worldly being are posterior to the divine act, the history which is God's being.

The structure of the creation-covenant relation, that of "possibility-rendered-possible" and "possibility-rendering-possible," is once again relevant here. Because God's free being is an event of love, and therefore, as said above, the election of the creature as love-partner is simultaneously a self-determination of God's very being, then the creative "Yes" to humanity participates in the eternal "Yes" to God's self. Their analogical point of contact is Jesus Christ, who is at the same time a divine affirmation of humanity and a divine self-affirmation. This person, this history is the history which grounds both God's being and worldly being! It is by this understanding of Jesus Christ that Jüngel can say that "historicity is constitutive of being," and that "history is constitutive of creation."

> To understand that is only possible, however, because historicity is rendered possible by the history of Jesus Christ, because created

---

12 Jüngel, "Möglichkeit theologischer Anthropologie," 218. See also idem., "Schritt Zurück," 120 and idem., *Gottes Sein*, 110.

13 Jüngel, "Möglichkeit theologischer Anthropologie," 218 note 12.

time is rendered possible by the *archetype of all time*, by the archetypal time of grace in the lifetime of Jesus Christ; rendered possible precisely in the sense that it is itself the possibility of the time of grace rendered possible by the time of grace.[14]

The event of Jesus Christ has emerged as central for understanding the analogical character of God's relation to created being. This is because the act of divine self-affirmation to which God's creative act analogically corresponds is understood by Jüngel in trinitarian terms.[15] Jüngel's penetrating and ramified reflections on God as triune form one of the pillars of his theological achievement. Nothing like a summary of his teaching in this area is possible or necessary here; the sole problem to be treated is that of the understanding of God's triune being as the basis for the doctrine of God the creator. More substantial indications of Jüngel's trinitarian accomplishment must await the final chapter.

That what we have called God's "self-election" (i.e. God's mode of being as self-positing freedom) provides the basis and pattern for God's creative act is clearly affirmed by Jüngel; in this he closely follows Barth. He cites the *Church Dogmatics* decisively:

> The freedom in which God posits himself as Father and through himself is posited as the Son and confirms himself as the Holy Spirit, is the same freedom in which he is creator of man, in which man may be his creature, in which this relation creator - creature is grounded by the creator.[16]

This quote stresses the trinitarian structure of God's self-election; it also highlights the divine freedom as the point of correspondence

---

14 Jüngel, "Möglichkeit theologischer Anthropologie," 218-9: "Das zu verstehen ist jedoch nur möglich, weil die Geschichtlichkeit von der Geschichte Jesu Christi, weil die Schöpfungszeit von dem *Urbild aller Zeit*, von der in der Lebenszeit Jesu Christi urbildlichen Gnadenzeit her ermöglicht ist; ermöglicht eben in dem Sinne, daß sie selbst die durch diese Gnadenzeit ermöglichte Möglichkeit für diese ist."

15 Cf. Jüngel, *Gottes Sein*, 110. There Jüngel speaks of God's saying "Yes" to Godself as "constituting" God's triune being.

16 Jüngel, "Möglichkeit theologischer Anthropologie," 215, citing Karl Barth, *Kirchliche Dogmatik* III / 2 (Zollikon: Evangelischer Verlag, 1945), 262.

between the trinitarian relations and the creator/creature relation. Jüngel's attempt to understand God's creation from a trinitarian standpoint has two important consequences: first, time itself is seen as an analogical phenomenon, and second, Jesus Christ as the eternal Son receives a central ontological and epistemological role in the creation story.

The idea that time is analogical is closely related to the analogical relation between God's being and created being; indeed, Jüngel often insists on a close conjunction of being and time, revealing once again the Heideggerian orientation of his philosophical background.[17] One of the basic ideas underlying contemporary doctrines of the trinity is that God is an eternal history, that eternity itself is not static but dynamic. The trinity is the story of God's eternal self-departure and self-arrival. For that reason, time or temporality cannot be linked exclusively to the created world; the trinity means that it is not meaningless to distinguish "God's time" and "worldly time." In fact, the analogical key to the temporality of created being lies in God's trinitarian self-relation, to which corresponds the relation between God and created being.

Far from being static, God's eternity is defined as a continual "conceding" of time.[18] The trinitarian history grounds all history. In short, to speak of the act of creation as a trinitarian act is another way of saying that a divine history is prior to divine being and therefore to created being as well. It is also on this basis that Jüngel can speak of God as the source of all true novelty and possibility in the world, a theme to be dealt with explicitly in the next section of this chapter. Here, too, it is a matter of a trinitarian understanding of God's being. The fact that God's path *to* God's self as the Son is not a path *away* from God's self is due to the Holy Spirit. God's reaching of this goal is always a new beginning because the Spirit binds God's goal and God's origin into a unity. God's ability to concede worldly, created time is

---

17 E. g. Eberhard Jüngel, "Grenzen des Menschseins," in *Entsprechungen*, 355-61 and GGW 542 (395).

18 Jüngel, *Gottes Sein*, 110. For an important exposition and critique of Karl Barth's theological understanding of time see R. H. Roberts, "Barth's Doctrine of Time: Its Nature and Implications," in *Karl Barth: Studies of his Theological Method*, ed. S. W. Sykes (Oxford: Clarendon Press, 1979), 88-146.

grounded in the fact that eternity is God's eternally new beginning with God's self.[19]

The central role of the second person of the trinity in creation has been implicitly thematic throughout the discussion. As Hans-Georg Geyer formulates the matter: "Systematically speaking, [for Jüngel] the trinitarian explication of God's being from Jesus' history precedes every other, such as God's being in relation to created being."[20] The crucial role of the Son in creation is a logical outcome of assertions already made: on the one hand, that God's affirmation of the creature corresponds to and participates in God's self-affirmation, and on the other hand, that God's self-affirmation is identical with God's being as trinity. As God's Son, Jesus Christ is the image or archetype of creation since he is the union in one person of God's self-election and God's election of humanity. The creation of an other is deeply implicated in God's very being-as-other; Jesus Christ as human and as the eternal Son is the witness to the fact that God's election of the creature is an election based on love, and hence the allowed intrusion of God's other into God's own path to God's self.

> If one wants to escape the fatal proposition "God is in and for himself," then one must confess (against the Arians) that God in his own becoming is aiming at the becoming of creation, that Jesus Christ is not (only) the *creative* instrument of the Creator-God, but that Jesus Christ as eternal God is himself the *original image*, the divine original image of the creation which is eternally distinct from him.[21]

God and the Primacy of Possibility

The trinitarian and analogical understanding of creation in Jüngel is an example of how he attempts to derive a new understanding of divine being from a reading of the Christ-event; it is clear why he

---

[19] Eberhard Jüngel, "Das Entstehen von Neuem," in *Wertlose Wahrheit*, 148.

[20] Hans-Georg Geyer, "Gottes Sein als Thema der Theologie," *Verkündigung und Forschung* 11 (1966): 3-37 at 30.

[21] GGW 526 (384). Cf. Jüngel, *Gottes Sein*, 121: The "incarnation of God" is identical with the "event" of the "affirmation of his creation."

can even define theology as "consequent exegesis."[22] What might be called the "extrapolative" logic of this procedure has already been pointed out; it begins from Christ and the reconciliation apprehended by faith as its center point, and works outwards to fashion the conceptuality necessary to interpret and frame this event. This method informs not only Jüngel's doctrine of God but also his understanding of general metaphysical and anthropological categories as well. These reformulated categories are not unrelated to the doctrine of God; they are intended to link up with Jüngel's reformulated theism in a harmonious way, whereby the members of the standard triad of world, humanity and God, now recast in the light of the Christ-event, mutually inform one another. The prime example of the close connection between Jüngel's doctrine of God and his conception of the processes of the world (and hence another motif in his understanding of God the creator) is his exposition of the proper relation of possibility and actuality.

The intention of this section is limited to summarizing some of Jüngel's provocative and rather sweeping statements in this area. Even the combination of a lengthy essay and a section of *God as the Mystery of the World* devoted to this question provide only the sketchy beginnings of the kind of full-scale revision of metaphysical categories which Jüngel claims is demanded by reflection on the gospel.[23] His treatment offers a mixture of very abstract theorizing and highly metaphorical, not to say poetic, language; for those accustomed to a certain kind of technical precision in the use of concepts such a mixture will be quite disconcerting. Fortunately, no attempt to construct a systematic position from Jüngel's pronouncements is required here, even if it were possible. Only the basics of his understanding of actuality and possibility will be indicated: its theological origins, the dominant philosophical tradition that it is positioned against, and a final word concerning its connections with Jüngel's understanding of language.

It is important to stress the theological roots of these reflections to combat the easy supposition that this is simply a new

---

[22] Jüngel, "Freiheit der Theologie," 19.

[23] Eberhard Jüngel, "Die Welt als Möglichkeit und Wirklichkeit: Zum ontologischen Ansatz der Rechtfertigungslehre," in *Unterwegs zur Sache*, 206-33; GGW 270-306 (199-225).

metaphysics called forth in response to the philosophical inadequacies of the tradition. Jüngel insists that "it is a material (*sachlich*) consideration of eschatology which overthrows the primacy of actuality."[24] Eschatology refers here not to a doctrine of "last things" but to the decisive intervention of God in the world of created being and history, embodied in Jesus Christ and issuing in the justification of human beings. The doctrine of justification is the real key to Jüngel's position; in line with his methodological concentration on the Christ-event as the interpretive context for the doctrine of God, he claims that "justification is a constitutive moment of God's lordship." As such, it is not merely a psychological or existential doctrine; it has ontological implications which serve a critical function with regard to certain constants of worldly self-understanding which find expression in the philosophical tradition.[25]

In this case, the result is a critique of an entrenched philosophical bias of the Western tradition: the priority of actuality (*Wirklichkeit*) over possibility.[26] Jüngel finds the classic exponent of this position in Aristotle. The distinction of possibility (*dynamis, potentia*) from actuality (*energeia, actus*) is necessary because Aristotle wishes to affirm the reality and validity of becoming and temporal change. Against the Megarian paradoxes, which insisted that the actual is identical with the possible and that what is not actual is therefore impossible, Aristotle argued that on this basis nothing could come to be, or that something not actually in motion could move at all. Hence he separated possibility or potentiality as an ability or capacity to be actualized. But one result of this separation is the identification of being with actuality, and the corresponding definition of the possible as a member of the class of things which are not (namely, "that part of the class of nonexistents which if actualized would result in nothing impossible").[27]

---

[24] Jüngel, "Welt als Möglichkeit," 215.

[25] Ibid. 220.

[26] Ulrich Barth interprets Jüngel's position as moving towards a "theological doctrine of categories." See Ulrich Barth, "Zur Barth-Deutung Eberhard Jüngels," *Theologische Zeitschrift* 40 (1984): 296-320, 394-415 at 410-11.

[27] Jüngel, "Welt als Möglichkeit," 210.

Not only does the actual possess being to the exclusion of possibility, but possibility is defined and understood completely in terms of the actual. In Aristotle, the primacy of actuality is interpretive as well as ontic; indeed, these two kinds of primacy are closely connected. After all, for Aristotle the possible is exhausted in its actualization; the actual is the precise actualization of its corresponding possibility. Indeed, the possible is precisely the "not-yet-actual," and thus can be said to strive towards its own actualization. Hence, Jüngel characterizes the relation of possibility to actuality in Aristotle as "teleological." Just as important, however, is the fact that, paradoxically, the ground of possibility for the actualization of the possible lies always in the actual, that is in something already actualized. The possibility of actualizing something always rests in a previous actuality of some kind. Possibility is a kind of ghostly mediator between actualities, without any independent ontological status. In effect, for Aristotle the actual is both origin and end, *arche* and *telos* of the possible.[28]

A final implication of Aristotle's position is the close connection of actuality with the idea of "work," both in the sense of the actualizing act (*kinesis, poiesis*) and in the sense of the final goal inherent in the act (*praxis, chresis*). Not only does the possible exist for the sake, as it were, of the actual, but the actual exists for the sake of work; every actualization exists for the sake of further actualization. This fundamental orientation shapes Aristotle's conceptions of the divine and the human. The famous ideas of the divine as "unmoved mover" and as "self-thinking thought" are traced by Jüngel directly to the ideal of perfection implied by Aristotle's scheme: an "actualizing act" which is "pure actuality devoid of possibility" because it is the "perfected unity of work and actualization."[29]

It is the function of Aristotle's scheme in anthropology, however, which first discloses a sharp disjunction with the

---

28 Ibid.

29 Ibid. 211.

implications of Christian soteriology.[30] Jüngel adverts to Luther's rejection of Aristotle's doctrine of virtue. For the latter, the presence of virtue (in the form of a *habitus*) in the soul, and therefore the capacity to act virtuously, is based on the previous performance of virtuous acts. In other words, the possibility of the ethical virtues does not preexist their actuality in the soul. A person creates realities in him- or herself which then serve as possibilities for new, increased effects. But for Luther, of course, actually being virtuous must precede any virtuous acts. No actions of the sinner can make the sinner virtuous since the being of the sinner can only be the ground for sinful acts. It is only the justifying decree of God which grants a righteous being to the sinner and on that basis enables righteous acts.[31] The key here is that the possibility of righteousness is not preceded by its actuality in the person; a possibility *ab extra* is granted to the person instead of being built up from previous acts. Possibility grounds actuality, not vice versa.

Much of the ontological suggestiveness for Jüngel of Luther's soteriology stems from its very radicality. The being of the sinner cannot ground just acts because it is the total negation of righteous being. There is nothing in the "old man" upon which God builds; the justification of the sinner is precisely analogous to the *creatio ex nihilo*.[32] Several motifs appear in this connection which will prove to be important for Jüngel's concept of God. When discussing Luther's notion that the nothingness (*nihilum*) from which God creates the new, justified person is in fact the nothingness (in the sense of death or destruction) into which God drives the old, sinful person, Jüngel hastens to clarify that this is no metaphysical destruction. It is rather the absence of relation which is characteristic of sinful being and which is aptly described as the death, the wage of sin. Sinful being is nothingness in that it lacks relation to God and indeed indicates a lack of true relation even to the self.[33] This understanding of nothingness

---

[30] Ibid. 213. According to Jüngel, only Fuchs and Moltmann have grasped this disjunction and rejected the "ontological priority of actuality," while Ebeling, Gogarten and even (to some extent) Barth remain within the traditional framework.

[31] Ibid. 217.

[32] Ibid. 218. Kern, not surprisingly, criticizes this position from a Roman Catholic perspective as threatening a disjunction between the God of creation and the God of grace. Kern, "Theologie des Glaubens," 144.

[33] Ibid.

and death in terms of relationlessness is an important theme in Jüngel's writings. The true character of the world as God's creation (including the ultimate priority of possibility over actuality) cannot be understood without thinking about the *nihilum* from which God creates and justifies.[34]

What, then, are the so-called ontological implications of the Christian doctrine of justification? To put it briefly and formulaically, taking seriously the nothingness from which God creates the world and justifies the sinner drives theology to claim possibility as the ultimate horizon of actuality, and to reject actuality as the ultimate horizon of possibility. For the latter is Aristotle's position as well as, according to Jüngel, the dominant position in the Western philosophical tradition; it is naturally also dominant in those strands of theological reflection which depend on that philosophical tradition.[35] The actual is the ontological horizon of the possible in that it is the ultimate context, the locus of being, the origin and *telos* of the possible. The actual is also the interpretive horizon of the possible in that possibility is defined in terms of actuality, defined in such a way that the possible is merely the "not yet actual." And thus the distinction real/not-yet-real becomes an ultimate ontological dichotomy.

But if possibility is the ultimate horizon of actuality, then according to Jüngel a new dichotomy is seen to surpass in ultimacy the old one: the distinction possible/impossible.[36] Impossibility here must mean that nothingness or utter lack of relation out of which God creates and redeems. If the cross and resurrection of Jesus Christ are the keys to our knowledge of both the justifying God and the creator, then these events are also the keys to conceiving of possibilities which come to the world and to human beings "from outside," in other words, from God. The world cannot actualize itself in its totality, nor can the person actualize his or her own justification on the basis of previous actualizations. Ultimate possibility comes from God.

---

34 Ibid. 220.

35 Ibid. 212-3. Conversely, Fuchs and Moltmann have freed themselves from this tradition at least partly through their reliance on philosophical critiques of it, by Heidegger and Bloch, respectively.

36 Ibid. 221.

As the origin of the world's ultimate possibility, God is also the source of the fundamental distinction between possibility and impossibility. It is precisely as the source of this distinction that God at one and the same time differentiates God's self from the world and yet relates to the world as God. On the one hand, as the creator God is not a "secondary phenomenon"; that is, as the determiner of the possibile/impossibile distinction God's being is not itself determined by it. Indeed God's role as creator, and therefore God's very divinity is "carried out" or accomplished in the making of this distinction. But this differentiation of God over against the world is not to be understood as a lack or deficiency in the world. For "in that he distinguishes himself from the world, God lets the world be actual."[37] Thus God creates the possibility which in turn the world actualizes. This means that God's self-distantiation from the world is simultaneously the closest and most vital relation to the world. Jüngel sees this truth expressed in the unity of Christ's death and resurrection; the nothingness or impossibility of the world is precisely the locus of God's life-giving creation, a creation "out of" death.

The creator and redeemer is active where the immanent possibilities of the world and humanity (those possibilities grounded only in the presently actual) are exhausted. This obviously has implications for understanding not only God as creator but also the world as creation. This opens up yet another difficult area in Jüngel's thought, full of suggestive but often cryptic statements: the world as history. Another of Jüngel's presuppositions comes to light in the discussion of history. His anthropocentrism was mentioned earlier; here a related interpretive presupposition comes to light: a basic dualism of human and non-human reality. This orientation is nowhere explicitly discussed but everywhere implied. It emerges in this context in the strict distinction between history as freedom grounded in possibility over against what can be called mere "process," which is actualization grounded in present and past actualities.

Consider for example Jüngel's statement: "The world's being as history occurs not in the distinction of real and not-yet-real, but is constituted by the difference of possible/impossible."[38] This should be

---

37 Ibid. 222.

38 Ibid. 223.

compared with the statement a few pages later: "It is God's love which makes the possible possible, apart from God's omnipotence, which makes the real real (through *our* works)."[39] These two claims lay out the basic outline of his idea of history. First of all, the phrase "being as history" is not an equating of being with history but refers to an aspect of the world's being; the dualism in the second sentence points to a duality within worldly being. The realm of history lives from the possibilities granted by God's love, while what is here being called the realm of mere process is a function of divine omnipotence, operating through "works." Recall that "works" for Jüngel means actualization on the basis of already possessed actualities. When human beings engage in "work" they are not really operating in the historical realm at all. This kind of actualizing process (which presumably encompasses the realm of non-human process as well) is grounded in God's power, God's "working all in all" through secondary causes. It is a genuine aspect of worldly and human being and, within its limits, legitimate. But it is not what Jüngel means by history.[40]

History is the more basic category of worldly being because it operates from the more basic dichotomy. It is God's creative love which distinguishes the possible from the impossible. And it is God's word coming to human beings which, by revealing and granting possibility, enables transformative action which transcends self-actualization. God grants possibility from the future, whereas mere self-actualization is grounded in the past.[41] History properly speaking occurs only where human beings act in freedom to transcend the capacities bequeathed to them from past actualizations. They act, as it were, from the nothingness of their own capacities. Hence the striking phrase: "Every step within history is a step . . . out of nothing into history."[42] Clearly the understanding of history at work here

---

39 Ibid. 226.

40 The Lutheran distinction of law and gospel is lurking behind these dichotomies, as well as the "two kingdoms" doctrine. Cf. ibid. 225: "The actuality of the world is the indispensible 'vita activa,' without which we would not be actual. But as creation the world is also the irreplaceable 'vita passiva,' without which we would not be possible."

41 Ibid. 226.

42 Ibid. 224. Cf. ibid. 221, where Jüngel speaks of nothingness as the world's "other dimension."

presupposes human, that is rational and purposive, agency; history is no natural process but is deliberately enacted.

The possibilities which enable true human freedom and thus history come from God to the present, actual moment. But then these possibilities are external, not ingredient to the actual. "The actual lives from arrivals of possibility from outside."[43] With the actualization of every possibility God creates "still more possibilities" for the resulting actuality; this is at least part of what creation means (GGW 464-5 [339]). But how is the juncture of possibility and actuality achieved if the possible is assumed to approach the actual from outside? How can a possibility unconditioned by the actual ever "meet" the actual? Jüngel identifies this as a central theological difficulty.[44] The external possibility cannot simply force itself on the present actuality; it must correspond to it, or as Jüngel revealingly puts it, the possible must "address" the actual. The latter phrase is a clue to the linguistic nature of Jüngel's solution to the problem. The human character of history is reaffirmed by the claim that language is the intersection within the present actualization of history of the actualities inherited from the past and the possibilities approaching from the future.

Before looking more closely at the language issue we must pause to grasp the concrete significance of these very abstract statements. For language is not being invoked here initially as a natural anthropological possibility; a very specific kind of language is involved in the bestowal of historical possibility: the gospel of God's kingdom. Jüngel is not, of course, making the bizarre claim that the concrete confession of Jesus Christ as the "parable of God" has been heard from the beginning of human history. He is, however, claiming that the power whereby human language sets human beings free for real historical transformation (as opposed to simply recycling present actualities) is and always has been grounded in the address of God to humanity in the incarnation. In other words, Jüngel's discussion always presupposes the Barthian conception of the election of humanity from all eternity as the structural key to human being in time, indeed as the

---

43 Eberhard Jüngel, "Metaphorische Wahrheit: Erwägungen zur theologischen Relevanz der Metapher als Beitrag zur Hermeneutik einer narrativen Theologie," in *Entsprechungen*, 103.

44 Jüngel, "Welt als Möglichkeit," 227.

ground of possibility of creation itself. A brief christological "detour" is needed because God the creator is always to be grasped from the revelation of God the reconciler in Christ.

Thus this ontology of history, so important for the theological significance of the concept "creation," will remain completely obscure unless its radical christocentricity is recognized. God's revelation in Christ, mediated by the language-event of faith in the gospel, is the revelation of the true future of humanity. When Jüngel speaks of history he is speaking of those transformations in individuals and societies which have a future in God's kingdom, as opposed to those transformations which are grounded in mere shiftings and manipulations of the human actuality of the past, and which have no future, properly speaking. In the continuing event of the proclamation of Jesus as the inaugurator of God's kingdom, God's ultimate vision of human fellowship not only becomes visible but indeed is furthered. The gospel is the linguistic possibility which comes to humans. It frees those in faith to act historically in the kingdom and also illuminates those events and acts outside the realm of the church as either creations of God's possibility (unrecognized by those among whom they occur) or else the empty creations of the "old man" shaped completely by the past.

In short, Jüngel wants to define true history christologically as those acts which flow from the freedom granted to us by God, from our justification. In turn, the cul-de-sac of history is always the "work of the law," now redefined by Jüngel in ontological terms as the act springing from the false possibilities humans create for themselves, apart from God. When a person faithfully grasps the presence of God in the word of the crucified and chooses to act out of the realization of God's reign in history, then he or she is no longer bound simply to repeat the past but is freed for true relationship to the neighbor. This, ultimately, is the concrete significance of Jüngel's insistence on the primacy of possibility over actuality. Obviously, much more would have to be said on this topic to clear up its difficulties and explore its profundities, but such would require another book. Before leaving it, however, we must try to clarify further why language is so central to this discussion.

There will be much to say in the next chapter about the role of language in Jüngel's theology. Here a simple indication of the close connection of the concept of possibility with that of language will suffice. For it is an "event of language" (*Sprachereignis*) when the "claim of the possible" truly corresponds to "the language of actuality." In other words, it is by means of a word that the actual is confronted with the external possibility; this confrontation is not a collision, but is rather the bestowal of possibility on the actual within the actual's context.[45] This is a linguistic occurrence, a mediation through the linguistic forms of metaphor and narrative, and through the linguistic situation of address. Jüngel has many different ways of expressing this occurrence. He can say that in metaphor or parable (which is a narrative form of metaphor) there is an "expansion" of actuality which occurs without leaving the context of the actual (GGW 398 [291]). He can say that historical narrative liberates possibilities by participating in the historical mode of being, a mode neither arbitrary (to which pure fiction would correspond) nor absolutely necessary (to which corresponds the language of logical inference) (GGW 416-7 [305]). Finally, he can say that the linguistic situation of being addressed (as opposed to that of merely understanding an assertion) brings to expression the power of possibility.[46]

These statements are components of a theme which runs throughout Jüngel's work: the indispensible role of language in the mediation of human freedom. Language not only creates room for the possible within the actual, it also grants to the participant the freedom to actualize the possible.[47] This detour into the implications of the primacy of possibility for Jüngel's anthropology is necessary because in his anthropocentric doctrine of creation history, despite its close correlation with human agency, has ontological significance. The primacy of possibility is crucial for a proper interpretation of the basic character of being as we experience it: its ineradicably temporal character, or "transitoriness" (*Vergänglichkeit*). In fact, the pervasive misinterpretation of being in the history of thought can be traced largely to the inflated valuation of actuality at the expense of transitoriness which is the heritage of Aristotle.

---

[45] GGW 398 (291). Cf. Jüngel, "Welt als Möglichkeit," 229.

[46] Jüngel, "Metaphorische Wahrheit," 135.

[47] Cf. Jüngel, "Welt als Möglichkeit," 229-30.

Being as Struggle and Creation as a Work of Love

For Aristotle and the tradition inspired by him, the utterly actual is the highest ontological value; it is the "perfect." The transitory character of the perceived world could only be understood as a deficiency as long as the actual was simply equated with being. In a scheme where being and becoming are set into opposition, and where possibility or the potential for change is defined negatively over against the actual, then the transitory seems afflicted by possibility, for possibility is read as a tendency toward annihilation. Jüngel expresses this as the consequence of seeing actuality as what is "ontologically positive" (the "plus of being"). The stigma of nothingness which marks the transitory is only removed when, in contrast to the prevailing metaphysical inheritance, possibility itself is determined as the "ontological plus" (GGW 289-90 [213]). As has been seen, this revaluation of possibility is an implication of the Christian understanding of God the creator and redeemer. But Jüngel claims that this is also an implication of the fundamental characteristics of human experience: its historicality, and its linguisticality.

The primal error against which Jüngel protests is the identification of being with actuality, and of actuality with the present moment, the "here and now" (*hic et nunc*). If this is done, the present, indeed being itself, is reduced to a vanishing point between the no-longer-actual and the not-yet-actual. If, however, the linguistic disclosure of the present (which will be discussed shortly) is analyzed, it reveals two aspects of the putatively unitary present. Alongside the actual is the possible. In fact, it is only language or the word which grants historical possibility to the present; only in this way does the actual become historical in character (GGW 289-90 [213]). The fact that Jüngel goes on to make the discovery of the historicality of human existence the key to the structure of being in general is not a mere parroting of Heidegger; it is closely tied up with the doctrine of elected humanity as the inner ground of created being. The precise nature of the transition from the centrality of possibility in the freedom of historical existence to the centrality of possibility as a general ontological principle is difficult to define. But the fact itself of their connection in Jüngel's thought is manifest.

The turn from human existence to general ontology is not, however, of intrinsic interest from the standpoint of the current chapter. Wherein lies the contribution of these ideas to a doctrine of the creator? According to Jüngel, in order to be able to conceive of God properly it is necessary to think God in a way which is compatible with the transitoriness of the world, indeed "to think God and transitoriness together." The problem is that the legacy of Western philosophy reveals inadequate thinking about the nature of transitoriness as well as the nature of God. In fact, the dissolution of metaphysical theism as described in Chapter Three can be summarized as the convergence of these inadequacies: it is the traditionally negative evaluation of transitoriness which drove metaphysics to a position where God was no longer thinkable (GGW 276 [203]). Jüngel insists that God must be thought together with transitoriness, whereas traditional metaphysics felt impelled to keep them separate, to protect God from such contamination. To oversimplify somewhat, there is a necessary proximity between thinking God and thinking transitoriness for two reasons. Subjectively, the thought of God is only possible in intimate connection with faithful existence; to truly think God is a fully concrete and historical procedure, a function of a living response to God's revelation in history (GGW 275 [202]). Objectively, it is necessary because thinking God's unity with perishability means concretely thinking God's being as the unity of God's essence with the human existence of Jesus (GGW 284 [209]).

Implicit in the discussion so far has been the characterization of being in terms of a tension between two moments. Jüngel wishes to locate God in terms of this tension, for in this way the true relationship between God and the transitory world can be identified. The problem, however, has been a persistent misapprehension of the nature of this tension. To see being dialectically, as involving an inherent struggle or conflict, is in itself not new; but Jüngel refuses to accept the terms of this struggle as commonly understood. The position against which he protests identified actuality as the positive moment of being against which transitoriness and the possibility associated with it were marked with the stigma of annihilation (GGW 277 [204]). The drive towards nothingness comes to characterize becoming; in response, the attempt is made to construct an eternal present, a moment elevated beyond flux, a "fixed" or "standing now" (*nunc stans*) with its attendant mysticisms (GGW 285-9 [209-13]). Jüngel, on the other hand, eschews this cleavage between timeless being and annihilating change. Rather than simply identify transitoriness as the negative moment in being, he locates the struggle in transitoriness itself. Everything turns on identifying properly what is positive and what negative within transitoriness (GGW 285 [209]).

It was said above that Jüngel identifies possibility as what is "ontologically positive" within transitoriness; it was also pointed out that language plays a role in disclosing this. Anthropologically, the situation of linguistic address (the occurrence of "word") acts to constitute the here and now of the present precisely by pointing beyond it. In being addressed by another person (and, by analogy, by experience itself) the human being is removed from his or her immediate life-context and is enabled to see it both in its facticity (its actuality) and it its constitution by and openness for the future (its possibilities). The word is that displacement which discloses place. Far from simply identifying the present as the mathematical point of actuality, our linguistic being enters the present as an interplay of the actual and the relations of possibility which help to constitute it. Beyond the tautological here-and-now is our historical reality, which is understood as our reactualization of the past on the basis of possibilities received from the future (GGW 292 [215]).

The fact that the past may be reactualized in the present, and in response to the future, is for Jüngel the meaning of history and of the human person as an historical being.[48] This means that the possibilities of a thing or event do not disappear once that thing is no longer actual, i.e. once it is in the past, even though, as was seen above, the power to reactualize any possibility (even a past one) comes only from God's future. Even the fact of memory shows that the possibility of the past is preserved; possibilities still cling, so to speak, to what has been. Since for Jüngel possibility is identical with the capacity to become, he draws the conclusion following Kierkegaard's *Philosophical Fragments* that the past is not eternally fixed, but has the capacity to become again (GGW 292 [215]). It would require far more clarification than Jüngel provides to begin to understand this very counterintuitive conclusion except in the most vague and suggestive way. But the ubiquity of possibility as characterizing the past, present and future indicates that "the boundaries of actuality are not the end of being" (GGW 289 [213]). Transitoriness is the boundary of the actual. At

---

[48] Jüngel's dependence on Heidegger's anthropology is again in evidence here. Cf. GGW 291 note 54 (214), where he sees Heidegger's thought as a refutation of the Aristotelian primacy of actuality.

this boundary, being is no longer actual, but it still is, it does not cease to be. These are the considerations driving Jüngel's insistence that transitoriness *per se* can no longer be simply identified with the plunge into annihilation. And the prevention of this false identification is the prerequisite for a proper identification of nothingness, namely as the negative moment within transitoriness.

The true opposite of possibility is not actuality, but nothingness. It is impossibility, the inability to become (GGW 293 [216]). As the negative moment of the transitory it is not the inevitable result of transitoriness; it is that which must be overcome by the positive moment of possibility. The transitory (*Vergänglich*) passes away (*vergeht*) but only the destructive power of nothingness distorts this passing away into annihilation. As is perhaps inevitable, Jüngel's descriptions of the "tyranny" of nothingness take on a highly poetic, not to say mythological, flavor. Far from a simple lack or negation, nothingness is a "whirlpool," a "suction" into annihilation, a virulent force in its very negativity (GGW 293 [216]). This rhetoric in turn sets up the language of transitory being as a struggle. "Transitoriness is the *struggle between possibility and nothingness* . . . between being and nonbeing" (GGW 294 [217]). For our purposes the main point is that Jüngel's revised modal conceptions of possibility and actuality, and the reconceived dialectic of being which springs from them, finally enable a more precise determination of the being of God the creator.

Transitory being as the site of the struggle between possibility and nothingness — this is the locus of God's being. With this statement the ultimate foundation has been reached of Jüngel's ontological doctrine of God the creator and redeemer of creation. This is the result of a radical understanding of a theology of the crucified one, a theology which takes seriously "God's self-identification with the dead man Jesus," as Jüngel likes to phrase it. This is the first point in interpreting his claim: adequate understanding of God's relation to creation springs only from apprehending the meaning of Jesus' death and resurrection. The christocentric nature of creation in Barth and Jüngel has already been discussed; now that the basic outline of the struggle or dialectic of being has come into view, it must be tied more closely to the fate of Jesus. In this context, Jüngel's first insistence is that although God the creator must be understood as the source of the struggle within being, God's involvement in the cross of Christ prevents us from inferring that as its source God must somehow be removed from the struggle itself, profoundly untouched by it (GGW 295-7 [217-9]). The cross reveals not just the fact that God is creator, but also the pattern or mode of God's creative activity.

The meaning of the death and resurrection of Jesus as a process of divine self-identification and self-determination is this: "God is one who involves himself with nothingness" (GGW 296 [218]). The two events together, the fact that it is the dead man who is resurrected, help explicate God's self-involvement in the struggle. For Jesus' death and resurrection as divine events mean that God does not simply reject nothingness or destroy it, but rather God incorporates (literally, in the *corpus* of Jesus) nothingness into the divine life and history. Jüngel points out that the annihilation of nothingness would be meaningless. Since nothingness is defined by him as "sheer indeterminacy" or, more metaphorically, as "lack of place," then God's victory in the struggle with nothingness must be seen as a "neutralization" of it by determining it, by giving it a place. And that place for him must be God's own being (GGW 297 [219]).

A purely negative understanding of God's neutralization of the power of nothingness should be avoided. The emphasis in Jüngel does not fall on God's successful defense against the threat of nothingness, but instead on God's creative transformation of nothingness. Jüngel always understands God's creative act in terms of defining, of determining, of limiting. The positive creative significance of delimitation begins, as any Christian doctrine of creation must, with God's own being. For God's appropriation of nothingness is not just the delimitation of non-being but also an act of self-delimitation. On the cross God has suffered and thereby claimed death; this amounts to a self-denial, a "No" that reveals that God can open up space within God's being for the otherness of creation.[49] In an article devoted exclusively to this theme, Jüngel brings out the analogy between creation as an act of self-imposed divine limitation, and the acts of self-limitation belonging to God's essence in the form of the trinitarian relations. This clarifies to a certain extent the notion behind the

---

[49] Jüngel, "Tod des lebendigen Gottes," 120. Cf. Eberhard Jüngel, "'Meine Theologie' — kurz gefaßt," in *Wertlose Wahrheit*, 8.

analogy of relation discussed in the first section: "Creation 'repeats' God's eternal being."[50]

God's creative self-limitation in turn determines the mode of God's relation to creation. Not only does God initiate a self-withdrawal in order to grant time and space for creation, but God also continually engages that creation by granting transformative significance to the limits within the world and of the world.[51] The absolute negation characterizing annihilation springs from its annulment of every relation; by contrast, God's limiting of the world and of human beings is always a way of concretely relating to them. On the level of the human individual, God on the cross has appropriated death in such a way that, in the resurrection, death becomes a meeting point between God and the person suffering death; at the limit of human possibility, the new possibility of a relation to God is granted.[52] But this operates on the level of a general truth as well; God does not simply abolish nothingness, but determines it, giving it the function of concrete negation. As such it operates to energize possibilities within the world.[53] Indeed, for Jüngel limitation is implied in every act of relation.[54] The utter lack of delimitation, nothingness, is also the utter absence of relationship. It can readily be seen why Jüngel insists on a positive moment in the transitoriness of temporal being: transitoriness serves to limit the actual.

---

[50] Eberhard Jüngel, "Gottes ursprüngliches Anfangen als Schöpferische Selbstbegrenzung: Ein Beitrag zum Gespräch mit Hans Jonas über den 'Gottesbegriff nach Auschwitz,'" in *Wertlose Wahrheit*, 154.

[51] Ibid. On the importance of the concept of "limit" see Jüngel, "Grenzen des Menschseins," 355: Limits are "the divine harmonious ordering (*Wohlordnung*) of being corresponding to the divine beneficence (*Wohltat*) of creation."

[52] On the interpretation of death see Eberhard Jüngel, "Der Tod als Geheimnis des Lebens," in *Entsprechungen*, 327-354; and more extensively, Eberhard Jüngel, *Tod* (Stuttgart: Kreuz-Verlag, 1971).

[53] GGW 297 (219). Cf. Matthias Raden, "Hermeneutik der Entsprechung oder Hermeneutik der Nichtentsprechung: Eine Gegenüberstellung der theologischen Hermeneutiken von E. Jüngel und P. Ricoeur," *Evangelische Theologie* 48 (1988): 217-32 at 220: "As an act of *divine self-correspondence*, the limiting of worldly actuality is a positive possibility of God. God himself *is* the actuality of limiting, in that he limits the actuality of the world through himself."

[54] Jüngel, "Grenzen des Menschseins," 355.

Conclusion

The fundamental point to be made concerning God's creative encounter with nothingness as revealed in the fate of Jesus is that it provides an ontological key to the profound mystery of the Johannine utterance concerning the divine being: God is love. As always in Jüngel's thought (and here, too, he follows Barth) God's being is not to be distinguished from God's act. If God truly participates in the events of Jesus' death and resurrection, then "God must now be defined as the one who can suffer in his being the power of annihilation without being annihilated" (GGW 297 [219]). At several points in his writings Jüngel explores the phenomenon of love in rich detail. But only a brief indication of its formal characteristics is required to show the connection between God's involvement with nothingness and God's being as love. Abstractly speaking, love is a self-determination for the sake of an other; one chooses not to continue being oneself without the freely-granted presence of another. Obviously, this renunciation of self-grounding and self-containment entails the gravest risks; it is a choice to have one's being outside of oneself, a risking of a kind of death for the possibility of an incalculable enrichment of being. Hence Jüngel defines love as a dialectic of "being and nonbeing for the sake of being," or of "life and death for the sake of life" (GGW 298 [220]).

Now the idea of God's self-involvement with nothingness reappears in a sharper light. If in the cross of Christ and in the act of creation God is involved with nothingness there is no question of an extraneous act which leaves God's being unaltered. If God has truly "defined himself" in the life and death of the man Jesus, as Jüngel repeatedly says, then this self-definition can only be understood as a self-determination of God's own being, not the mere imparting of information. God's very being is at stake in the cross; God "defines himself with his being."[55] Only in God is there the ontological freedom to put one's own being totally at stake, to freely enact that being. But God's creative involvement in nothingness for the sake of the otherness of creation therefore means that God not only has love but is love. God is paradoxically a totally free act of total love; freedom as a "constituent moment of love" means that no conflict exists between this utter freedom and this utter being-for-another.

---

[55] Jüngel, "Vom Tod des lebendigen Gottes," 119.

Jüngel does not hesitate to draw the unavoidable conclusion: as that love which submits to nothingness in order to allow the being of another God is *suffering* love. "God suffers with the suffering and so gives that suffering importance for the course of the world, an eternal worth." The crucified God is the almighty God: "Only love is omnipotent."[56] But the fact that God defines God's self in the encounter with nonbeing must not be taken to mean that nonbeing is something primal alongside God. Jüngel says though it is true that the statement "God is love" is made on the basis of the event of Jesus, God's being is already love antecedent to that event (GGW 299 [220]). Analogously, God does not become love in response to nothingness. Nothing that has been said of God's suffering love should obscure what must also be said of God's eternal self-origination. As the eternal Father, as the ground of being and nothingness God precedes the distinction being/nonbeing (GGW 523-4 [381-2]). It might be said that because God is, being is, and because being is, nonbeing "is" as well. For all its chaotic power, nothingness remains derivative. As a result, Jüngel summary statement of the matter centers on two balanced statements: "(1) God is the one involving himself in nothingness and as such is love but (2) God is love from himself, and not first through the nothingness in which he involves himself."[57]

According to Jüngel's assessment of the epistemic path of theological thought, all these statements about the creative being of God are guided by a faithful apprehension of the cross and resurrection of Christ. Both the act of creation and the being of the creator are interpreted along these lines; moreover, that act and that being are not allowed to fall apart, leaving creation as a contingent act more or less arbitrarily connected to an eternal being isolated in absoluteness. The God who undergoes death in Jesus is none other than the God who always, eternally, has been creatively involved with nothingness. God's encounter with and victory over nothingness in history, in the

---

56 Jüngel, "Gottes ursprungliches Anfangen," 161. Cf. idem., "Die Offenbarung der Verborgenheit Gottes: Ein Beitrag zum evangelischen Verständnis der Verborgenheit des göttlichen Wirkens," in *Wertlose Wahrheit*, 180.

57 GGW 301 (221). Cf. GGW 302 (222): "The distinction of God and nothingness is not the logically neutral distinction between being (*Sein*) and nothingness, but the event of a distinguishing in which God relates himself by means of himself (*mit sich selbst*) to nothingness."

cross and resurrection, illumines creation itself to be an encounter with and victory over nothingness as well (*creatio ex nihilo*). Thereby God's being is grasped precisely in terms of a creative transformation of nothingness. Jüngel therefore proposes a definition of God's being as "*a se in nihilum ek-sistere.*"[58] Unpacking this formula will serve to conclude this chapter by recapitulating its insights and connecting them with the conclusions of Chapters Three and Four.

Some prominent strands of the Christian tradition, particularly those influenced by neo-Platonic motifs, have understood God as eternally "overflowing" being. With his definition Jüngel is aware that he is taking up this tradition in his own way (GGW 302 [222]). It consists of three elements: a verb (which in good Heideggerian fashion Jüngel articulates to suggest an etymology — *ek-sistere*) and two prepositional phrases as directional modifiers. The normally static verb "to exist" is broken up to reveal a dynamic or directional element: God's being "stands out." But everything which exists likewise "stands out", at least in some sense. The distinction in God's existence must be suggested by the additional phrases; they signal the peculiar mode of God's existence.

Of course, God has always been understood as self-originated, as "from himself" (*a se*). But the proximity of the verb "ek-sist" again brings out in the phrase connotations of movement and direction which are ordinarily latent; God's being has its point of origin, the *terminus a quo* of a journey, in itself. By the construction of this phrase Jüngel wants to suggest that God's being is dynamic and that it has a history. The implied metaphor of the phrase is that God's being is in movement, it "travels a path"; to use a mathematical metaphor, God's being is less like a static point and more like a vector, having directionality and not just magnitude.

The first modifying phrase thus signifies the direction God eternally comes from, while the second indicates that toward or into which God's being is eternally moving: "into nothingness" (*in nihilum*). This is the expression of God's creative transformation of nothingness, which as was seen is grounded in the divine being as love. To say that

---

58 GGW 303 (223). Jüngel speaks of the expansion and "overflowing" of God's being as the eternal "diminishing" (*Verminderung*) of nothingness. The parallels to this type of language in Schelling and Tillich are pointed out in O'Donovan, "Mystery of God," 267.

God's being is an "ex-isting into nothingness" is intentionally ironic in light of metaphysical custom, since existence has been understood precisely as a "standing out of nothingness" (*extra nihilum sistere*). The contrast is suggestive, redirecting the understanding of existence from the notion of an escape or flight *from* nothingness to the idea of a creative plunge *into* it. Thus, to give Jüngel's translation of his own Latin, God's being is a "Going-out-of-himself into nothingness."[59]

Each of the three elements contributes something essential to defining God's being. The verb "ex-sist" strikes the key note of a dynamism or motion in God's being. The phrase "from himself" stresses the moment of freedom in God's being, while the phrase "into nothingness" indicates the orientation of that being to the other in love. Theologically, it is a further stage in the task of "thinking God," one which renders more concrete the concept of the "more-than-necessary" which emerged from Chapter Four. In terms of the elements discussed there, the groundlessness (i.e. self-groundedness), event-character and freedom of the more-than-necessary are all secured in this definition of God's being. The formal character of the more-than-necessary as a self-grounded event of freedom is materially identified with God's creative and victorious submission to nothingness for the sake of the other.

Finally, this ontologically expressed definition of God's being as love can without much difficulty be seen as a further elaboration and development of the basic idea of divine simplicity. It is because God does not just "have" love but is love that the distinction of essence and existence dissolves. "The essence of love is to exist lovingly"; if God is love then God's essence is identical with overflowing, self-imparting existence.[60] No given, fixed essence could be salvaged from the encounter with the transitory because God's identity is eternally enacted in that very encounter. Moreover, one can now see that the possibility of God's historical existence with the human being Jesus is grounded in God's being itself, in that "ek-sistere" which is love. God can exist as Jesus because God eternally ek-sists as love. And this eternal act of "ek-sistence" is precisely God's identity, God's essence.

---

[59] GGW 303 (223): ". . .wir das Sein Gottes als Aus-sich-heraus-Gehen in das Nichts begreifen."

[60] GGW 410-11 (300): "Liebe ist wesentlich liebendes Existieren."

"With this ontological concept of the divine being we have grasped the essence of God *as* existence" (GGW 303 [223]).

CHAPTER SIX

FAITH AND GOD'S EXISTENCE AS WORD

The vision of theology as the thinking of faith in Chapter Two raised the question of the idea of God presupposed in such a conception. The crucial construals of language and of faith which were briefly sketched there must now be explored more fully and their close connection with Jüngel's notion of God's being must then be clearly indicated. In so doing, this chapter will provide the final set of concepts necessary for understanding God's being as Jüngel sees it, and will usher in the material dogmatic conception which integrates all of the previous discussions, which have been noteworthy for their formality and abstraction. That dogmatic concept is the trinity. But for Jüngel the true understanding of the triune God is only possible when the phenomenon of human faith is understood. Faith in turn cannot be interpreted apart from the proclamation of the crucified Jesus, understood as the word of God which first makes faith possible. Therefore I will turn first to a discussion of the basic elements of language which are presupposed throughout Jüngel's discussions of faith and of God. Then I will highlight the event of Christian faith in its correspondence to the God revealed in the word of the crucified. Finally, I will link these analyses together in a discussion of God as event of word and ground of faith. That discussion will at the end present the incarnate word as the culminating development of Jüngel's model of divine simplicity.

Word, Address and 'Ekstasis'

As was pointed out in the introduction, Jüngel's ties to the theological movement known as hermeneutical theology or the "New Hermeneutic" are very close. It is therefore not surprising that language plays a central role in his theological and anthropological views. God is identified as "one who speaks"; human beings, in turn, are defined by the word insofar as language in the form of addressing event enables both self-presence and the social presence of selves to one another.[1] Language occurs as a topic throughout Jüngel's writings in many different contexts. No attempt at a summary will be made here, much less a complete presentation of his theory of language. Our concern is entirely with those central linguistic concepts which are necessary to introduce Jüngel's notion of the encounter of God and humanity in faith as an "event of word." For the proper understanding of faith as an event involving human beings, a sketch is needed of the central part played by language in Jüngel's anthropology. But this will require an explication of the related concepts of word-event and language as address, concepts which themselves presuppose an understanding of those linguistic forms which are critical in Jüngel's theological project: metaphor and parable.

One of the momentous intellectual developments of recent times is that shift in the understanding of language whereby metaphor has migrated from its formerly peripheral position as a mere rhetorical device into the very center of language. In an important essay on the theological significance of metaphor, Jüngel sets up a fruitful opposition between Aristotle and Nietzsche in order to dispel the notion of metaphorical speech as "inauthentic."[2]

For Aristotle, a statement like "Achilles is a lion" involves the replacement of a true and proper description with a word based on an implicit analogy whose impact depends on its contrast with conventional understanding.[3] Although Jüngel admires Aristotle's analysis of the effect of metaphors and the sources of metaphorical creativity, he is dissatisfied with the way metaphor is banished from the linguistic determination of truth in definition and dialectic.[4] For

---

[1] On the former see, for example, GGW 210 (157). For the latter point, see GGW 232-4 (172-3).

[2] Jüngel, "Metaphorische Wahrheit," 108-9. The modern discovery of the importance of metaphor is of course one of the most widely remarked and discussed phenomena of recent intellectual history. One excellent study which may be singled out from the enormous literature is Paul Ricoeur, *The Rule of Metaphor: Multidisciplinary Studies of the Creation of Meaning in Language*, trans. Robert Czerny with Kathleen McLaughlin and John Costello (Toronto: University of Toronto Press, 1977).

[3] Jüngel, "Metaphorische Wahrheit," 105.

[4] Ibid. 131.

the tradition following Aristotle, metaphor serves the need for variety and ornament but has no role in "true" speech since it is a "deviation from purity and perspicuity."[5] Implicit in this is an understanding of truth as true judgment, the coherence of the mind with that which is, with the actual or real (later defined as *adaequatio mentis et rei*). The assertion or proposition becomes the privileged locus of truth as the linguistic formulation of that coherence.[6] From what has already been said about Jüngel's privileging of possibility over actuality, it might be predicted that he would dispute this notion of metaphor as inauthentic by attacking the notion of truth it presupposes.

Nietzsche points the way toward a more adequate understanding of metaphor by arguing that in fact all language is metaphorical. The notion of truth as the correspondence of mind and reality is a sheer illusion; words belong "to the immanence of subjectivity," and thus their use always involves a "transfer" between incommensurable realms.[7] All words are thus metaphors in that there is no "proper" identification between language and reality. Without accepting Nietzsche's reduction of truth to a deception born of the human drive to self-preservation, Jüngel takes up his line of thought insofar as it leads to a rethinking of the primacy of judgement and assertion in the notion of truth.[8] Jüngel agrees that "language lacks ultimate definitiveness" (or unequivocalness, *Eindeutigkeit*).[9] Typically, he wishes to expand the idea of clarity from a linguistic property, that of precise speech, to a characteristic of the linguistic situation, that of human communicative interaction. On this level, metaphorical and colloquial speech are revealed in their proper

---

[5] Ibid. 107. See also p. 112, where he speaks of "lying in the service of the truth."

[6] Ibid. 113. Cf. p. 104.

[7] Ibid. 117. The word "transfer" refers to the original meaning of "*metaphora*."

[8] The tendency to devalue judgment and assertion has been criticized by Wolfhart Pannenberg, *Theology and the Philosophy of Science*, trans. Francis McDonagh (Philadelphia: Westminster Press, 1976), 169-177.

[9] Jüngel, "Metaphorische Wahrheit," 105.

authenticity, their contribution to communicative clarity as an event, regardless of their deviation from literal, assertorical form.[10]

But how does metaphor connect with an expanded understanding of truth? Aristotle, despite his denigration of non-assertorical truth, correctly recognized the role of metaphor in "broadening the horizon of being."[11] In the assertion, language reflects reality, the actual state of things; but in metaphorical language what is already known is known in a new way, an unexpected and richer way. In this case, Jüngel argues that in fact language does not passively reflect a presence or actuality already achieved, but that "beings *become* present (not just *are* present)."[12] There is thus an interaction between language and the actual in which the possibilities available to the actual are brought to light and put into play (GGW 290 [213-4]). And this is nothing other than "the event of truth, in which beings allow themselves to be uncovered . . ."[13] This view of language has important anthropological implications which will be examined shortly, but for now the point is the fundamental contribution of metaphor to language as the expression of its wealth of possibility and as the mediator between what is and what can be.

Jüngel calls this richness of "possibilities of signification" in language its "parabolic dimension."[14] Metaphor and parable are closely connected: "The parable is regarded as an extended metaphor, or the metaphor can be called an abbreviated parable. The difference consists of the fact that a parable narrates while a metaphor coalesces the narrative into a single word" (GGW 396 [290]). The view that metaphor somehow contains an implied narrative is striking, but it follows from the highly temporal structure of language-formation, for which metaphor, as Jüngel sees it, is crucial. The individual linguistic forms are the result of a "language-history, which is the history of

---

10 Ibid. 106.

11 Ibid. 127.

12 Ibid. 129.

13 Ibid. 142. Cf. Heidegger's famous notion of truth as "uncovering": Martin Heidegger, *Being and Time*, trans. John Macquarrie and Edward Robinson (New York: Harper & Row, 1962), 261-2.

14 Jüngel, "Metaphorische Wahrheit," 135.

man's relations to the world."[15] Language is a movement; while the assertion temporarily arrests this movement by tying language to the present actuality, metaphorical speech is always implicitly narrative because it expresses the constant movement of language. It represents the possibilities of new word- and concept-formation through its linking of present actuality to future possibility. It is in narrative that the temporal structure of language is most clearly reflected, and as the quotation above indicates it is narrative which ties together metaphor and parable.

It is sufficient to note at this point the mutual interconnection of metaphor, parable, and narrative, particularly because it calls attention to the transcendent quality of metaphorical language. It transcends the present in its striving for the future. But this takes place within the present; metaphor cannot lose contact with what is precisely because it functions to bring future possibilities into connection with the present. Jüngel calls this a mode of truth "which contradicts reality" but "nevertheless avoids lying."[16] The core of the language of Christian faith, indeed of all religious language, is precisely this metaphorical process: transcending the actual from within the context of the actual. The language-form of metaphor "participate[s] in the truth in which the actual leads beyond its actuality without becoming false."[17] The metaphorical process enriches the present by transcending it toward the future; I will call this kind of identification through displacement "ekstasis." It is a theme which resonates in many areas of Jüngel's thought, as will soon become clear.

Jüngel's approach to language always presses inexorably from questions of linguistic form (metaphor, parable, etc.) to questions of the linguistic situation or event. Indeed to understand the centrality of metaphor for language it was necessary to place it in the context of the "event of truth." Jüngel also has another set of concepts for describing the central event of language: that of the word-event or the situation of

---

15 Ibid.

16 Ibid. 105.

17 Ibid. 143.

"address" (*anreden, ansprechen*).[18] The former term has a clear lineage in the New Hermeneutic, particularly represented by Jüngel's teacher Fuchs.[19] From Jüngel's varied usage (he nowhere explicitly defines "word-event," evidently presupposing its familiarity to the reader) it is not clear whether the address-situation is identical with the word-event or merely one type of word-event among others, but in this brief exposition I will treat them as basically the same.

The inadequacy of a treatment of language based on the isolated word is discussed in terms of a traditional approach which he calls the "hermeneutic of signification."[20] This latter understands words as conventional signs which serve to indicate things beyond themselves. In itself, such a view can certainly contribute to an understanding of language; problems arise only when it is taken as an exhaustive explanation, when "language is understood only in terms of its communication-function [i.e. its function of conveying information]" (GGW 6 [6]). Although he first discusses the problems arising from such a reductive view of language in the context of speaking of God, Jüngel implies that its inadequacies are not just theological. This view is problematic because it makes it impossible to understand the impact of certain linguistic forms such as the parable; it drives a wedge between content and form, reducing language to a conveyance, a vehicle whose relation to its content is accidental.

A variety of linguistic phenomena, from common vernacular to poetic and sacramental speech, point to a different theory of linguistic signs (GGW 9-12 [9-11]). What do a poem, the official proclamation of a judge, and an insult which finds its mark all have in common? In each case, it can be said that the words are the mode of presence of that to which they refer. If the hermeneutics of signification were the whole story, then words would always refer to something beyond language,

---

[18] Jüngel sometimes speaks of truth itself as a language-event. See Eberhard Jüngel, "Vorwärts durch Annäherung?", *Theologische Literaturzeitung* 91 (1966): 328-339 at 336.

[19] Ebeling tends to use the term "*Wortgeschehen*" while Fuchs prefers "*Sprachereignis*," and is followed in this by Jüngel. On Fuchs' understanding of this term see Ernst Fuchs, "Was ist ein Sprachereignis? Ein Brief," in *Zur Frage nach dem historischen Jesus* (Tübingen: J.C.B. Mohr [Paul Siebeck], 1960), 424-30.

[20] GGW 3-9 (4-9). Jüngel cites Augustine as the classical representative of this tradition. Cf. Jüngel, *Gottes Sein*, 18.

something which had its own mode of presence independent of its being referred to linguistically. The examples enumerated above are cases where the language, or rather the event of the words being spoken or read, in some sense simply *is* the presence of the referent. The sign-referral function is not really excluded but transcended.

> To be sure, the words here are also *signa*. But they do not necessarily signal something which is absent with respect to the sign. Under certain conditions, words can allow something which is present in the words, or rather with or through them, to occur (GGW 11 [10]).

In other words, in these cases there is no longer an ontological dichotomy (and therefore an accidental relationship) between the sign and the thing it refers to. The referent is taking place in the act of its being referred to. Jüngel refers these cases to the "addressing" function of language, an essential function distinct from that of signifying.[21]

The phrase "under certain conditions" in the citation is important; this function of language is not subject to analysis in terms of the syntax of utterances abstracted from the situation of their occurrence. The word of address is inseparable from the event of address. This event is characterized by the unique effects of the word upon the one addressed. It must be kept in mind that the signifying function of language is not simply put out of play in such a situation. The basic model of two people speaking to each other by both referring to some common topic holds good in the situation of address, but there is a difference in the way they relate to this topic. In what Jüngel calls "informative communication," that model of speech which tends to be assumed when language is reduced to its signalling function, the words are simply accidental vehicles. Once the information has been conveyed the words are superfluous. But in the address-situation, the self which is addressed about something is brought into relation to that thing solely through the act of being addressed about it and therefore through the words of address (GGW 231 [171]).

---

[21] GGW 11-2 (10-1). Cf. note 17: "Speaking linguistically, we have to do not only with a 'perlocutionary act' in Austin's sense, but rather with a perlocutionary-*attractive* act, whose *telos* does not lie outside the act, but instead is effected by the latter and incorporated into it — comparable to the entelechic structure of *praxis* as distinguished from *poeisis* in Aristotle."

Jüngel insists that the relationship to the referent initiated in the address-situation is one which affects the "being" of the person addressed. In other words, that person's self-identity and existence are to some extent at stake. This is opposed to the idea that only the consciousness is affected, an idea that Jüngel associates with the model of speech whose hegemony he wishes to dispute. That rejected understanding is one in which language is merely the communication of information and comprehension is reduced to an "input" into conciousness (GGW 12 [11]). By contrast, in the situation of address the whole being of the person is, as it were, interrupted in its normal relations, and drawn out of itself into relation with something else. I will return to these difficult concepts in a moment, but they reveal the profound importance for Jüngel of the event of address for understanding both human beings and language. Borrowing the terminology of Fuchs, he explains that "such acts of speaking which permit a person to be drawn out of himself are what we would call *language-events.*"22

Thus, the situation of address involves a word- or language-event. There is clearly a connection revealed here between this language-event and the "event of truth" discussed previously. Jüngel sees the notion of metaphor as truth-event to be an alternative to an "understanding of words as isolated signs with significance."23 In fact, I think the argument can be made that "truth-event" is simply a kind of description of the "language-event" itself. If, as Fuchs says, language "gathers together subject and object," then to speak of the event of truth is to focus particularly on the objective side of this process, on the way in which the object as referent is illuminated and rendered present in the language-event.24 Metaphor can now be seen to be so fundamental because it "preserves the addressing movement of language."25 The language-event, understood either as truth-event or address, is the basis of language. Truth as event in this special sense is more fundamental than truth as a property of assertions: "[T]ruth as language-event is the ontological locus of the proposition, not vice-

---

22 GGW 12-3 (12). On the idea of address as "interruption" cf. GGW 221 (165).

23 Jüngel, "Metaphorische Wahrheit," 140.

24 For the Fuchs citation see Jüngel, "Vorwärts durch Annäherung," 331.

25 Jüngel, "Metaphorische Wahrheit," 143, cf. p. 135.

versa."[26] Properly speaking, truth is not a function of utterances at all, but is a function of the interaction of the utterance and the situation in which it is uttered.[27]

Given these interconnections between the metaphorical structure of language and its essential character as language-event, one would expect that the "ecstatic" nature of the metaphorical process will be replicated in the language-event of address. Moving from what has been said about the event of truth to examine the event of address will clarify this formal similarity. On the one hand, Jüngel speaks of metaphor as "truth which contradicts reality without lying"; on the other, he describes the language-event as an affirmation "which surpass[es] the real without removing us from the context of the real."[28] In the case of metaphor, the literal meaning of a word is displaced by means of a transgressive connection to another semantic field, but in so doing the literal meaning is not rejected but receives a positive access of meaning. Similarly, in the address-situation the self is removed from its actual context and brought into relation to something outside itself in a linguistic event. The self is not destroyed; its relation to its context is disrupted, resulting in a new self-identity. This ecstatic linguistic process has fundamental significance for Jüngel's anthropology, which can only be briefly indicated here but which will serve to connect the discussion of Jüngel's reflections on language with his idea of faith.

The event of address is of supreme anthropological importance; human being is essentially lingual (*sprachlich*) being, for which addressing and being addressed is decisive.[29] Theologically, this is

---

[26] Jüngel, "Vorwärts durch Annäherung," 336.

[27] Eberhard Jüngel, "Gott — als Wort unserer Sprache," in *Unterwegs zur Sache*, 80-104 at 97-8.

[28] Jüngel, "Metaphorische Wahrheit," 105; GGW 289 (213).

[29] GGW 216 (161). Cf. GGW 229 (170). Jüngel regards it as a decisive advance that Fuchs moved from Bultmann's talk of the fundamental "questionability" of human existence to its fundamental "linguisticality." See Jüngel, "Vorwärts durch Annäherung," 334. I take it to be the case that "language" should be taken in the broadest feasible way throughout this discussion, to include any act of symbolically-mediated, interpersonal communication in which an "event of address" could occur, including sign language, etc. Obviously, this view of human existence implies that those persons who are fundamentally impaired linguistically or communicatively are *ipso facto* impaired relationally, and therefore in their very humanness. The troubling questions raised by the existence of linguistically-impaired persons would

crucial for understanding faith as correspondence to the word of God. As will be discussed later in this chapter, the impact of God's word affects a person's very being precisely because that being is fundamentally linguistic in nature.[30] But even apart from the special occurrence of God's word, language is central to any understanding of the human person because the relations to self and other which constitute the person are ultimately linguistic relations: "[H]uman being is a linguistic disposition to one's own and to other being."[31] One should not make the mistake of regarding thought as more primal or original, and language as derivative. Thought is "the principle of order for language" but not "the principle which constitutes speech." Temporally, thought and speech coincide, but materially speech has the priority.[32] Nietzsche stated epigrammatically, "Man exists as a transfer from being into language."[33] In his own way, Jüngel agrees, but Heidegger is clearly a more important influence on his characteristic statements.

It is language or, more precisely, the event of being addressed linguistically, which enables the mode of self-presence characteristic of human existence: "[L]anguage discloses our *being-there (da-sein)*" (GGW 230 [171]). In an important passage which merits citation at length, Jüngel follows Heidegger in pointing to the indispensible role of language in expanding human consciousness from a pointillistic series of "presents" defined completely in terms of "here and now":

> [T]he ego is put into a relationship with its own being here and now through the word which addresses it. Every addressing word approaches the addressed self in such a way that it lets this self come to itself. In listening, I relate myself to myself and approach myself with the word which addresses me. I am here and now, and yet in that I listen I come to myself at the same time. One might say that the point of "now" expands itself. It has a future and becomes thus the present . . . [The addressing word]

---

have to be dealt with if Jüngel's suggestions were to be expanded into a full-scale theological anthropology.

30 Jüngel, "Gott — als Wort unserer Sprache," 101.

31 Jüngel, "Möglichkeit theologischer Anthropologie," 216.

32 GGW 344-5 (253). Cf. GGW 410 (300): "[I]n general language presents itself as the more original phenomenon over against thought or consciousness."

33 Cited in Jüngel, "Metaphorische Wahrheit," 139.

relates the "here" and "now" to each other in a specific way. It is now here, and at the same time it is beyond the identity of "here" and "now." It gives the "now," so to speak, space beyond the point of "here" and it gives the "here" time beyond the point of "now." The word is what first discloses the present (GGW 231 [171-2]).

There is fortunately no need to completely unpack these very Heideggerian sentences in order to make the requisite observations. What is central is that by means of the ecstatic process inherent in the event of address, the self is put into a new self-relation through a linguistic displacement.

The word, in its transcendence of the "being-here" which characterizes mute things, points toward something which is beyond the self, which is "absent" vis-à-vis the self. The undifferentiated spatio-temporal point of immediate experience (here-now) is disrupted by relating to something which is not here and now. This "existential *distancing* of the ego into the absent" enables the continuity of temporal experience because it distances the self not only spatially but also temporally, either into the past or the future (GGW 232 [172]). This in turn makes it possible to experience the present as present, i.e. as the particular mode of human existence (*da-sein*).

> It is the *ego as spirit* which becomes present to itself in that it works through this experiential distancing. Spiritual presence is the most original capacity of the ego, to be fully present through the surpassing of the state of being-here which is identical with the state of being-now (GGW 234 [174]).

The basic point of Jüngel's language-centered anthropology is thus the ecstatic structure of existence enabled by the language-event of address. "In language, the ego is already and always outside of itself and at the same time deeply oriented to itself" (GGW 224 [167]).

A number of important consequences follow. First, the human person is not the presupposition of language but is rather constituted by language. This is what lay behind the claim of Jüngel mentioned previously that address affects not just the consciousness but the being of a person; language cannot be reduced to the conscious and autonomous manipulation of signs. As a result of this discussion two factors in particular are revealed in their role in the constitution of human selves: temporality and sociality. The disclosure of the present through the linguistic mediation of past and future is identical with the bestowal of possibility on the actual discussed in Chapter Five. The primacy of the possible over the actual implies the primacy for personal being of mediated temporality over Cartesian self-presence. Closely related to this is the primacy of sociality in the constitution of the self. "Whoever calls man a being distinguished by its language, has also understood him as the ego within a lingual and living community."[34] The temporal and social aspects of the construction of the self are combined in the primacy of narrative for thinking about that self. Jüngel juxtaposes the human self constituted through its history or stories over against the metaphysical grounding of the self in the "I think."[35]

Language-Event as the Isomorphism of God's Word and Faith

A simplified sketch of Jüngel's concept of faith was presented in Chapter Two. Here the question of faith must be entered into again in a more specific way. What is of interest from the perspective of this chapter is the correspondence of faith and word. The fundamental structure of word as language-event, especially what I have termed its "ecstatic" character, must now be applied to a very particular content: the word of God. As indicated earlier, Jüngel speaks of faith as human correspondence to the word of God; he has in mind not something vague but a particular kind of isomorphism whereby the human person as a linguistic being participates in a special kind of language-event originating in the historical occurrence of Jesus of Nazareth. What is the "word of God" in this sense?

Formally speaking, God's word is that language-event in which God and the human person truly encounter one another. Jüngel wants to emphasize that faith's encounter with this word is not an "archaeological" affair, as if God's word were a "trace" of divinity, something that God has left behind. Rejecting this possibility involves

---

[34] GGW 234 (174). Cf. GGW 257 (190), where Jüngel says that the "community of subjects" is enabled by the addressing word.

[35] GGW 414 (303). Jüngel cites with approval the phenomenological philosopher Wilhelm Schapp, who in stressing the temporal structure of the self memorably says that conciousness is "entangled in histories" or "stories" (*in Geschichten verstrickt*).

an appeal to the understanding of language-event already outlined and its transcendence of the notion of word as an "informative symbol," detachable, as it were, from the one who utters it. Instead, God is in relation to God's word, and when the human person as addressee is also brought into relation to it, then God and that person are related, albeit in a special way: "God's word is then not something left behind (*ein Relikt*), over against which God goes his own way, distant and isolated; rather, this word is full of relationship, in every regard it is a relational word. In it, God relates himself to us . . ." (GGW 221 [164-5]).

The wording in the last sentence is important: the relationship is "in the word" and therefore is not immediate. According to Jüngel, God's presence in the word can only be understood as a dialectic of presence and absence, an idea the importance of which will become manifest later. But for now all that is needed is to see that God's proximity and distance are both preserved by a proper formal understanding of any word-event. "What is generally true of word and language is also characteristic of the word of God, which is that '. . . language does not directly unite the speaker and person or persons to whom he is speaking. The encounter always takes place within the context of a particular matter.'"[36] In other words, the encounter of the one who addresses with the one who is addressed is mediated by language in its act of intending or referring to some object; the event of address has an irreducibly triadic character. This understanding preserves the notion of God's distance or "withdrawnness" in the word, without falling into the trap of understanding the word as "detachable" from God the speaker. It also opens up a perspective on God's presence in the word which need not imply that God is the content of the word, its semantic or intentional object. The word does not convey information about God, as if it were a "vessel" which were separable in principle from that which it "contains" (GGW 222 [165-6]).

But if the primary effect of the word of God is not to convey information about God, how does it function as revelation? Again, restricting ourselves to the formal side of the event, we can say that for Jüngel the word of God has a performative character. After all, since the word of God is within the limits of our language, "it *does not need* to

---

[36] GGW 222 (165). Jüngel is quoting Gerhard Ebeling, *Einführung in theologische Sprachlehre* (Tübingen: J.C.B. Mohr [Paul Siebeck], 1971), 207-8. This book has clearly had a significant influence on Jüngel's approach to language.

inform us of reality within the world, and it *is not able* to inform us of reality beyond our world."[37] Instead, its role is to provide the proper function for the word "God" in our language, and it effects this by speaking of that concrete event where God and humanity are together in history, the event of Jesus Christ. Further explication of the role of the word of God must take into account this material character of the word; the word of God is the word of Jesus Christ.

Jüngel approaches the problem in this way. Language about God must be metaphorical; it can never be literal language since such language is by definition "worldly" and God is only properly spoken of when the fundamental distinction between God and the world is simultaneously expressed.[38] No direct transference from literal language about the world is possible. God is not an aspect of the totality of our world, say its "unity" or "ground," nor does God represent a second ideal or perfect world alongside ours. These two options (which Jüngel loosely terms "Spinozist" and "Platonist" respectively) both seek to create a direct bridge between worldly language and language about God. Against these attempts, Jüngel insists that for Christian faith God can only be spoken of in terms of "God as . . ." (i.e. metaphorically).[39] The difficulty here, though, is that metaphor normally brings together a subject and predicate both of which are known in some way beforehand. In the case of metaphorical talk of God, how does the subject "God" become familiar to us so that we can apply metaphorical predicates at all?

The solution is to ground our metaphorical language about God in what might be called a metaphorical event effected by God. God makes possible the proper understanding of the word "God" by identifying God's self with the worldly reality of the human being Jesus Christ. Indeed the decisive point, the fundamental metaphorical act, is the "identity of the resurrected one with the crucified one"; this basic metaphor is then interpreted by means of further metaphors.[40] In

---

37 Jüngel, "Gott — als Wort unserer Sprache," 95.

38 Jüngel, "Metaphorische Wahrheit," 145. My colorless phrase "simultaneously expressed" is intended to translate the more forceful German word "*mitgesagt.*"

39 Ibid. 144-5.

40 Ibid. 153.

this way, the event of Jesus functions as the "ground and limit of the choice of metaphors" used to speak about God.[41] Jüngel insists repeatedly on the Barthian axiom that to know the fundamental distinction between God and humanity one must look to where both are paradigmatically presented in their concrete relationship: Jesus Christ. In speaking of this man, of his life, death and resurrection, the word of God effects within human language a decisive separation of God and humanity. It functions within the limits of our language to indicate the limits of our language.[42] In order to see more clearly how the word of Jesus Christ effects the linguistic separation of God and humanity by illuminating their relationship, the role of the word of God in awakening faith must be discussed.

Jüngel understands the constitution or creation of humanity in terms of its being addressed by God. This primal address to human beings became an historical event in Jesus; but in a sense this address also "predates" that event because of the grounding of created history in the election of humanity discussed in the previous chapter. At any rate, Jüngel insists that it is only as primally addressed by God that human beings become capable of addressing and being addressed by other creatures (GGW 208 [155-6]). This primal determination or definition of human being by God is a determination to free correspondence to God. The adjective "free" is crucial. On the one hand, human beings are determined by God to respond to God's address, to shape their existence as a response to this other. But since God's address is the expression of God's love, the only proper response on the part of human beings is reciprocating love, which implies a free response. But the demand for a free correspondence to God implies *ipso facto* the possibility that human beings might not choose to correspond in the same way.[43]

Jüngel summarizes this state of affairs by saying that God's address determines us to self-determination (GGW 219 [163-4]). The reality of both determinations is vital for any understanding of

---

41 Ibid. 150.

42 Jüngel, "Gott — als Wort unserer Sprache," 96.

43 Eberhard Jüngel and Ingolf Dalferth, "Person und Gottebenbildlichkeit," in *Christlicher Glaube in moderner Gesellschaft*, vol. 24, eds. F. Böckle, F.-X. Kaufmann, K. Rahner and B. Welte (Freiburg: Herder, 1981), 57-99 at 65.

theological anthropology. Jüngel draws a distinction between our being as persons and our being as human. Personhood is grounded in God's address to us; it is our constitution as free beings who are challenged to determine ourselves in response to God's determination of us. "[Man's] being a person characterizes him as the addressee of this demand [of God on him], but is not itself already the correspondence intended by this demand."[44] In other words, the fact of our non-correspondence to God (i. e. our being as sinners) cannot eradicate our being as persons since our determination by God is absolutely prior to, indeed is the ground of, the humans we are as a result of our free choices. The human person is therefore the intersection of two "personal histories." There is first the history which makes us, which refers to our becoming persons (and which is the result of God's address); second, there is the history which we make, our becoming *as* persons, which is our realization of the possibilities open to us. "Only as a person is man human, but as human he is not only a person, but always also that which he as his own product has made of himself."[45]

This all-too-brief foray into Jüngel's anthropology is necessary to make sense of the two sides of faith as simultaneously a being defined by God's word and a self-definition (GGW 219 [164]). As the response of one's entire existence to God's address in the gospel, faith is of course the free response of our existence in correspondence to that word. But it is also the acknowledgement of our already having been decisively addressed by God; faith is the realization that the capacity to respond to God's address is itself a product of that address.

At this point the treatment of faith begins to resonate with some things said earlier with regard to the anthropological function of language. That resonance is due to the way faith and the word interlock: "[F]aith, what one might call the concave, has the same structure as the word of God, which is its convex" (GGW 244 [181]). The convex/concave image suggests a similarity of shape in which the structure of the self is imaged as a receptacle which corresponds to what it receives, God's word of address. The key can "address" the lock, as it were, because they share a common pattern. In this case the common pattern is ecstasy: the self is constituted by being decentered,

---

[44] Jüngel, "Person und Gottebenbildlichkeit," 65.

[45] Ibid. 69.

and God's word is the unsurpassible instance of decentering. Recall that the general phenomenon of the language-event involved an interpretation of the immediacy of self-relation (the latter being understood as a pointillistic identification of being with being-here and being-now). The result was the self-transcendence of the person in a new temporal consciousness, a projection into past and future made possible only through the mediation of self and other in the word. Since the word of God shares the general structure of the word-event, it not surprisingly operates in a radically intensified but nevertheless formally similar manner.

The word-event discloses the "present" to human existence by opening up the past and the future in a concrete way. Analogously, the word-event of God's word uniquely qualifies that disclosed present because it opens the self to a concrete past and future which actually constitute the self. The self is no longer addressed in terms of an other "in general" but in terms of that other which grants to the self its possibility of being. Note that it is no longer just the self-enclosed identity of here and now which is surpassed; the existential present opened up by human words of address is now itself surpassed so that "a completely new qualification of man's state of being present results, which one could call eschatological spiritual presence."[46] A different kind of "present" results from a different kind of "distancing" into past and future, what Jüngel calls a "total distancing" or an "eschatological outdistancing" (GGW 235 [174]). It does not surpass the ecstatic distancing of ordinary language-events in some quantitative manner, as if the self were simply distanced into an infinitely remote past or future. The self is instead removed into that "history within which . . . God . . . has expressed himself," that is the event of Jesus Christ. It is "a distancing into the concrete past represented by his death on the cross and into the concrete future of Jesus Christ represented by his resurrection and parousia" (GGW 236 [175]).

The complexities of a complete hermeneutical theory of the word of God are barely touched upon, but it suffices to clarify the way in which faith and God's word interlock.   Explicating the concave/convex image cited above, Jüngel says: "Just as the word surpasses our being-here and being-now, faith too *permits* the

---

46 GGW 235 (174). This presence is "eschatological" in that it is a "presence defined by God."

surpassing of our being-here and being-now" (GGW 244 [181]). The active side of this equation, the "convex" of God's word, has already been discussed. Faith as the receptive or "concave" side must now be explicated. Jüngel's basic idea here is that faith represents a renunciation of self-grounding. What does this mean?

Once again Descartes and the modern traditions rooted in him are invoked as the problematic legacy which theology must overcome. "The understanding of man and his world based on the Cartesian 'I think' states that man secures *everything* through himself, and that this constitutes his humanity: the human ego exists for itself and to that extent for everything else which is secured through its being represented by the human ego" (GGW 242 [180]). It is important to note that Jüngel is not simply offering a blanket condemnation of this intellectual development. Part of the very definition of modernity and of modern humanity is that in this period the mental certainty of the world, the construction of the object through the logically secured representative faculty of the Cartesian subject, has metamorphosed into a mastery of the world through technological manipulation. The world is "produced" and is thus secured by human beings. This development is irreversible, and the theological debate with Cartesianism would be "irresponsible" if it attempted such a futile *tour de force*.[47]

It is not the securing of the world *per se* that Jüngel wishes to question, but the attempt to do so on the basis of a securing of the human self. As producer of the object the human person is secured as producing subject. But this must not be understood as an exhaustive securing, as a securing of the human person as human. A fully-secured person would in fact not be human at all; it would be a "robot-like *Doppelgänger*," a "horrifying caricature of man." The reason is that "man is truly human in that he is able to place himself in dependence on someone other than himself" (GGW 242 [179]). Jüngel typically indulges in a bit of word-play when he speaks of an ability to depend on someone else (*sich verlassen auf*) as involving a forsaking of oneself (*sich verlassen*). In

---

[47] GGW 241 (179). Obviously, in the context of those theologies influenced by ecological concerns this statement will be controversial to say the least. However, in itself it implies no hostility to such concerns; it simply accepts human responsibility for the state of the planet as a fact which could not be altered even if an anthropocentric view of nature could somehow be overcome.

short, trust in another is fundamental to being human. The discovery of this anthropological fact is traced to the constitution of the person by God's address revealed in the event of God's word. We are human persons in that God has addressed us, indeed has granted us a participation in the divine being. As a result, Jüngel draws the anthropological conclusion: "I am human in that I let someone else be there for me" (GGW 243 [180]).

Another way of approaching the point Jüngel is making is suggested by a contrast between notions of presence: the kind of dialectic of presence and absence discussed here as opposed to the notion of presence described earlier in discussing Descartes' notion of truth and being. The decentered, destabilized self ("de-secured" in Jüngel's terminology) opened up by the encounter with the other which occurs in the event of language experiences the presence of what is, of the other self and itself as well, as a gift. The privileged stability of self-representation must be problematized in light of the fact that absence is the space within which presence can be experienced as a gift.

The deep resonance of this theme of presence in Jüngel's thought is due to the close connection between interpersonal encounter and the event of faith which claims that the ground of all encounter with the other is God's address to humanity in Christ. Jüngel speaks often of the distance or absence which is involved in every encounter with another person, the necessary "withdrawn-ness" or space which can only be bridged by trust and vulnerability, in fact by one's being drawn by language out into that absence oneself. The contrast between this mediation of presence by absence and the drive for ultimate security and self-grounding implied in idealizing absolute self-presence is too striking to be ignored, even though Jüngel's nuanced approach to Descartes has little in common with the tiresome ritual demonization so common in contemporary theology.

Faith as trust in God is an acknowledgement that we *are* in that God is already "there for us"; the ground of our ability to trust in others is thereby revealed. Faith differs from trust in other people in that it involves a "total reliance" upon the creator of our personal being. The giftedness of human personhood is already the denial of the possibility of a truly human self attempting to ground itself in itself, to secure its identity in isolation from others. But this in no way inhibits the truly human freedom of self-definition. "Faith is, in fact, that self-definition of man in which man, on the basis of his being defined by God, renounces all self-grounding." The word of God is the revelation of the impossibility of self-grounding; faith is the determination to live freely on the basis of that impossibility. "[F]aith *can* renounce all self-grounding because self-grounding has already been surpassed by trust in God" (GGW 243 [181]).

As this renunciation, faith is said to be the "convex" to the word's "concave"; the event of faith and the event of the word are structurally similar. From the trend of the discussion it can readily be seen wherein the similarity consists: both involve displacement or "ekstasis." "Faith [like the word of God] does not allow one's being-here and being-now to continue in its directness" (GGW 244 [181]). In fact, rather than speaking of two events it is closer to Jüngel's conception to speak of a single event, that of the word, in which the believing person participates. Faith as the response to the event is enabled by and occurs in the context of the event itself. In faith the historical event of God's word finds a resonance, a response in the historical existence of an individual. The word of God tells the human person the truth about him- or herself; faith occurs when the decision is made to accept that truth and live on that basis.

The Being of God Revealed to Faith

There is another side to the word of God which has not yet been touched upon. "The 'word of God' is to be understood as the abbreviated formula of the state of affairs that God addresses us about himself and so at the same time about ourselves" (GGW 234 [174]). The notions of word and faith as outlined above must now be directed toward establishing a true knowledge of God's being on the basis of the occurrence of faith. Theological reflection demands a move from understanding the word which triggers faith to understanding the one who utters the word. Faith hears God's word and in so doing it knows God. As the model of address has shown, the word-event in which faith occurs is the mediation of a personal encounter. In hearing another's address, one's being is brought into contact with the being of that other. Therefore, if faith is modelled on the structure of the linguistic event of address, it must involve a real encounter with God's being: God must be thought of as with us, as in our midst.[48] The word which enables such encounter is accordingly that kind of word which occludes any absolute distinction between speaker and word spoken (GGW 221 [164-5]). An examination of the human encounter with God's word is a legitimate basis for drawing conclusions about the being of God; in fact, it is the final norm for talk about God in the context of Christian proclamation.

For his identification of God with God's word Jüngel appeals to the prologue of John's gospel: the word is *with* God from eternity, and in fact the word *is* God. The application of the model of human linguistic interaction should not be seen as one of those anthropomorphic analogies to which only a limited legitimacy is granted for the sake of its heuristic function. God's word is not just like human words, it is word *par excellence*, it is the only true, real and proper word, the archetype of human address. The word of God is "the addressing word in an absolute sense" (GGW 258 [190]). It should thus come as no surprise that the things which Jüngel wishes to say about the divine being on the basis of the divine address can be interpreted as extrapolations from or intensifications of the event of address. I will indicate three such conclusions before attempting to assess their contribution to an understanding of God's ontological unity.

The first statement Jüngel makes about the addressing God is that God must be understood as speaking freely, of God's own accord (*von sich aus*).[49] The suggestion here is that God is essentially one who speaks, that God's speaking does not presuppose another who has already spoken. In this God differs from human beings who, in their lingual being, are in effect always responding; human beings in their acts of address have always already been addressed, entering into a prevenient network of meaning. Thus human beings are initially recipients of the word of address and only on that basis do they utter

---

[48] GGW 13 (12). It is with this linguistic observation early in the book that Jüngel plants the first seeds of doubt with regard to God's being defined as absolutely superior, i.e. "above us" rather than "with us."

[49] GGW 219 (163), cf. 210 (157). I have opted for the more idiomatic translation of the phrase "*von sich aus*," which Guder routinely translates literally as "from himself" or some similar formulation. The phrase involves both connotations: God's word is free and unprompted on the one hand, and it represents a movement from God's being outward on the other.

addressing words in their turn.[50] Even so, the fact that they can be addressed at all presupposes their capacity as lingual beings to hear the word of address and respond to it. The peculiarity of faith is that here the very capacity to hear and respond to God's address is experienced as something only given in that event of address itself. As has already been stressed, "[t]he fact that man is addressed by God makes him a fundamentally addressable being" (GGW 208 [155]).

Jüngel's claim, therefore, is that God's address enables human beings to receive not only the divine address itself, but also any and every kind of address. The founding role of God in the constitution of humanity is already familiar from the earlier discussion of God's defining the human person to self-definition. But now the focus is not anthropology but the nature of divine being. The experience which faith has of the God who speaks is that of one who has always already spoken to us. God's address is the event presupposed in every event of human address. Initially, God does not respond to anything; all things respond to God's addressing word. Hence for faith God is the one who speaks in utter freedom, from out of God's own being, *"von sich aus."* For this reason faith knows God as the "absolutely addressing being" (GGW 219 [163]).

God speaks freely. But what does God say? The shortest answer would be that God speaks God's own being; God utters God's self. Probing the meaning of this will bring to light a second claim Jüngel makes concerning God's being. The first conclusion just discussed, that God speaks of God's own accord, could if taken in isolation leave faith with a purely abstract notion of God: we would not know what God is, we would only know that God is the one whose word awakens faith in us.[51] There is, of course, a distinguished lineage of "bracketing" the question of God's being in one way or another, from the "incomprehensibility" of God emphasized by the Greek Fathers, to Aquinas' unknowable divine essence, and on to Melanchthon's famous dictum about restricting knowledge to Christ's benefits. This tradition found echoes not only in the liberalism of Schleiermacher and Wilhelm

---

[50] Jüngel, "Metaphorische Wahrheit," 139.

[51] Cf. GGW 237 (176): "Is theology condemned to indeed be able to think our *relatedness to* God, but to have to terminate the question of the thinkability of God himself in each case with the tautological answer: 'God is — God'?"

Herrmann, but also in the dialectical theology of the latter's rebellious pupil Bultmann, a fact of which Jüngel is clearly aware.[52] If this traditional modesty is being transgressed, it is a remarkable fact in the face of such a cloud of witnesses.

Thought "thinks after" faith, and it is the nature of faith's encounter with God which prevents the false humility of an "*epoche*" with regard to God's being. The analysis of faith in terms of trust is decisive. Faith is trust in God; it allows God to "be there for us." As that word-event which radically distances the believer into the concrete existence of God on the cross, God's address has already been grasped as a participation in God's existence. But the form of this participation, what might be called "eschatological trust," is essential. "It is the essence of faith to let God be the one he is" (GGW 237 [176]). In other words, faith by its very nature cannot take God to be anything other than the one who is present in believing existence. The fact that God is there for faith is inseparable from what God is: God's existence is identical with God's essence. Hence faith participates in God's being but not in the manner of self-securing thought, which as was seen in Chapter Three cannot proceed to think God without positing an essence behind God's existence. Faith, however, is the "de-securing" of human existence in favor of that "certainty" which characterizes trust (GGW 228 [170]).

For Jüngel, the conclusion is unavoidable: "If faith participates in God himself, without penetrating God in such a way that it forces itself between God and God, then God's being itself must be thought as a being granting participation in itself, as a being which turns *outward* what it is *in itself*" (GGW 237-8 [176]). Although it is the nature of faith which demands the understanding of God's being, it is Jüngel's linguistic understanding of the faith-event which specifies how this is possible. Faith is awakened by God's word, and "it belongs to the essence of word to give a share in the being of the speaker by bringing that being to turn toward the other" (GGW 238 [176]). The notion of the word-event is predicated on language as a kind of "carrier" of a person's entire being or self; language cannot be reduced to the utilization of symbols by consciousness, as the practice of psychoanalysis illustrates. With human beings, language often betrays more of the inner person

---

[52] Cf. GGW 237 (176), note 7.

than is intended. But with God there is no reserve, no jealously guarded core of interiority; in the word God utters God's very self without holding back.

The proper unification of God's existence with God's essence, which amounts to an identification of God's act with God's being, drives Jüngel to the view that the gift of participation in God's being is no "accident" but expresses essentially who God is. For this reason, the idea that faith should limit its knowledge to God's gift and not press on to know God's being is put out of play from the start. To know the gift of God's being is to know God's being as gift, as a free self-donation.[53] In this sense, too, faith knows God as the "absolutely addressing being." In Jüngel's idea of the word of God is revealed the inner dynamic of God's being, a dynamic which can be expressed in a progression of tightly connected statements: (1) God freely (*von sich aus*) speaks, (2) God freely speaks God's self, and (3) God freely speaks God's self to us.

There is a third and final formal characteristic of the divine being which can be derived from analysis of the word-event of faith: God is only present to us as absent. The mode of God's being with us is always a dialectic of presence and absence, of proximity and distance. It is part of faith's certainty of God's presence that it is simultaneously an experience of God's "withdrawnness" (*Entzogenheit*). Two premises are involved in this important theme. First, the terms "absence" and "presence" when applied to God's being are relational; they refer to the way the believer experiences God's being with relation to his or her own being. Second, the usefulness of the terms presence and absence in theology is consequent upon the rejection of their character as strict alternatives; they must be carefully related, not dichotomized as mutually exclusive (GGW 70-1 [54-5]).

The interrelationship of presence and absence is derived from the ecstatic structure common to both the word-event and faith. On the one hand, when address occurs, the speaker and hearer are not brought into an immediate relation. Their "apartness" is preserved in that

---

[53] GGW 238 (176). This stance forces Jüngel into a somewhat delicate attempt to position himself with regard to Luther's doctrine of the hiddenness of God. For a fascinating and erudite interpretation which avoids a simple clash with the reformer on this issue, see Eberhard Jüngel, "Quae supra nos, nihil ad nos: Eine Kurzformel der Lehre vom verborgenen Gott — im Anschluß an Luther interpretiert," in *Entsprechungen*, 202-51.

they are brought together within the context of the word (GGW 222 [165]). The word locates them together outside of themselves within the context of a particular meaning. The one addressed is only present with the one who addresses when the one addressed is simultaneously absent from him- or herself. In the same way, the distance of the addresser is preserved even within the intimacy of encounter.

As has already been stressed, the encounter of faith with the word of God represents an intensification or radicalization of the word-event in general. The sense of existential presentness ("being-there", *da-sein*) which is mediated by the word is "surpassed" by a new sense of presence in the event of faith; the believer is "outdistanced" into a new, eschatological present identified with God's presence in the crucified Jesus. God's presence to the believer in the past of a dead man is a supreme example of the interrelation of proximity and distance. At the very least, God's "being-there" surpasses our "being-there" in that the dialectic which mediates the former unites moments of presence and absence which are marked by their extremity.

There are, accordingly, two sides to this event: our self-presence is surpassed not only by the unsurpassable distance of "eschatological outdistancing," but it is also surpassed by the unsurpassable proximity of God to us achieved in faith. God accomplishes this proximity through the radical disruption of our sinful self-presence, our drive to ground ourselves in ourselves. In putting me outside myself God is simultaneously "closer to me than I am to myself." This interplay of near and far, or of present and absent, is another way of saying that God cannot be known apart from faith. The being outside of ourselves which the act of faith in Jesus Christ involves is from another perspective identical with God's presence.[54] "Without a fundamental *extra nos*

---

[54] On this understanding what kind of divine presence can be accorded to those who do not participate in the word-event of faith, either because they have not been addressed by the proclamation of the Christ or because of a more fundamental language deficit of the kind discussed earlier? Jüngel provides no direct answer to this difficult question. In the former case, we may assume a kind of "anonymous" divine presence in the humanizing event of language in general; God's presence in language is visible and proclaimed as such in the gospel, but it is not limited to the gospel. In the second, more extreme case it seems that we must speak of a real impairment of divine presence, although insofar as such persons are persons, are brought into the network of loving human interrelation, it seems impossible to deny God's presence even where the rudiments of faith are lacking. But these are only guesses as to how Jüngel might begin to address problems like these.

faith knows of no *deus pro nobis* and certainly no *deus in nobis*. God is only *near* to us in that he distances us from ourselves."[55]

Conclusion

The language of God's word is, of course, an interpretive formula for conceiving God's self-revelation in Christ. Jüngel appeals to Bonhoeffer, who first wrestled with God's presence-as-absence in his intense reflection on the soteriological significance of the cross as played out in modern culture.[56] Developing this insight in a manner informed by Fuchs and Ebeling, Jüngel has attempted to understand God's absence from the world in linguistic terms, in accordance with the structure of address. The three conclusions about God's being reached above can be reformulated in such a way that they reflect their Christological origin. The first point, that God speaks freely or from God's self, means that God depends on nothing outside God's self in uttering; God neither presupposes a hearer to whom speech is addressed nor answers a previous address from another. In Johannine language, the "word was with God" from the beginning. The second point was that God's word is God's self, or conversely that God's being is self-utterance and self-disclosure. Again, to follow John, the word "was [and is!] God." Christologically speaking, this statement implies God's self-identification with and in the man Jesus, who as the event of revelation is identical with God's word.

The third and final point was God's presence in the mode of absence. Linguistically, this meant that God is only present as word or in the word; God's presence is that mediated presence in which the one who addresses and the one who is addressed are united in a common context of meaning. Christologically, it means that God is present in human history as a part of that history, in the human life and death of Jesus. God's presence to humanity only occurs as human beings are ecstatically transferred into the presence of the crucified Jesus. The

---

[55] GGW 246 (182). "The 'nos ponit extra nos' [i.e. the "ecstatic structure" of faith] is accordingly the structure of the experience with experience, which we had understood as the experience of God."

[56] GGW 82 (62). Following Bonhoeffer, Jüngel insists that divine "omnipresence" demands a particular understanding of the idea of presence lest it be misunderstood as a "massive intensification of worldly availability (*Vorhandenheit*)."

fact that Jesus' presence as God's presence is decisively revealed only after Jesus' death, and remains active in the community of faith only in connection with the "withdrawal" of Jesus, is a further expression of the pattern of presence as absence.[57] In fact, one may discern a dual pattern here in which the presence of the absent Jesus (resurrection of the crucified) corresponds to the presence of the absent God (the revelation of the living God in what is other than God, in a human history and a human death). These material correspondences of the word of the gospel in turn reflect the formal correspondence of addressing word and faith. Form and content cohere in the word of the cross since the pattern of letting a speaker be present as absent is common to both. "[T]hat which the word addressing us says about the God who speaks out of himself (God on the cross as our neighbor) and the structure of the relationship between word and faith are congruent" (GGW 247 [183]).

The role of faith is indispensible, because it is faith which directs thought to the place where God is available: the word. This is not really because faith imparts some new information, the clue to solving a puzzle. Faith is the presupposition for thinking God because it liberates thought from grounding itself and allows it to think in response to God's word. It was pointed out earlier that for Jüngel faith is allowing oneself to be defined by God as one who must define oneself. "Put anthropologically, faith is the emergence of freedom" (GGW 220 [164]). Jüngel implies that the liberation of thought from self-grounding presupposes the similar liberation of human existence as a whole, in which thought is embedded. Self-grounded thought cannot think God as God really is precisely because it cannot think God as the true ground of the self; in attempting to ground itself, thought has foreclosed the possibility of thinking God. Faith represents a disposition of the self towards God which "de-secures" the self, annulling self-grounding. Thus proper thought of God is dependent on grasping the actual relation of God to the person as revealed in the word. "The attempt to think God takes its departure from this relation between God and the self" (GGW 220 [164]).

---

[57] See Eberhard Jüngel, "Die Wirksamkeit des Entzogenen: Zum Vorgang geschichtlichen Verstehens als Einführung in die Christologie," in *Gnosis: Festschrift für Hans Jonas*, ed. B. Aland (Göttingen: Vandenhoeck & Ruprecht, 1978), 15-32.

The complex of ideas discussed in this chapter, centering on the role of language and faith in Jüngel's theistic conception, meet and coalesce around the figure of Jesus Christ. Faith's encounter with the word is rendered concrete when the content of that word is specified: God's presence in the crucified. That event as revealed to faith becomes in turn the locus wherein God is properly available for thought. More than this, the conclusions about God's being reached in the previous chapters of this study are now visible in the originary context from which they were abstracted. Chapter Four, the exposition of the ideas involved in God being "more than necessary" resulted in a God whose essence was precisely the radically free actualization of existence, pure self-grounded event. Chapter Five issued in a different perspective: investigating God's creative act in the light of its ground in the covenant brought to light God's eternal overflow of love, submitting to and conquering nothingness.

Faith and the word as corresponding events have issued in a third perspective on God's being. The gospel narrative of passion, death and resurrection, a largely submerged influence throughout the earlier discussions, has emerged as decisive for the shape of Jüngel's reconstructed concept of God. Jesus is that event of freely actualized existence in which God's being is defined (Chapter Four). The cross is the paradigmatic act of loving transformation, the creative plunge into suffering and negativity, which reveals the existence God has chosen (Chapter Five). In this chapter it has been shown that Jesus as the word of God is also the mode of God's being as self-impartation to us; God's existence is that history of language-events which grounds the ecstatic existence of faith, destabilizing the self-grounding subject. In each case, the existence of God which determines the divine identity is the existence of the man Jesus proclaimed as the Christ.

CHAPTER SEVEN

CONCLUSION

Before concluding this study it will be helpful to review briefly the course it has taken and the salient results.

Results of the Study

After the introductory chapter, Chapter Two utilized some early methodological reflections by Jüngel in order to expound his conception of the nature and task of theology. His basic scheme of reflection on faith in service of the historical propagation of that faith led to the conclusion that the theology envisioned here should be classified as a *Glaubenslehre*. Even so, the faith to be reflected upon has been conceived in historical and linguistic terms. Rather than defining faith in terms of a psychology of feeling or of primal trust, Jüngel ties faith exclusively to the word-event witnessing to Christ. Moreover, he understands the linguistic event of faith and its historical continuity as themselves modes of God's presence to and in the world; the interconnection of faith and the life, death and resurrection of Jesus constitute the trinitarian *oikonomia*. Taking seriously this idea of worldly divine presence drives Jüngel's reconstructed theism which is the burden of the remainder of the study.

The third chapter presented Jüngel's reading of the metaphysical theistic tradition of the West as a struggle to reconcile the unity of essence and existence in God with the demands of thought. Descartes clung to the traditional conception of divine simplicity, unaware that his new methodological foundation for reason was to subject that particular kind of simplicity to intolerable stress in the ensuing period. The threefold issue in Fichte, Feuerbach and Nietzsche demonstrated how in each case divine existence had to be sacrificed precisely because the traditional understanding of the divine essence was more or less taken for granted. The challenge for Jüngel is now plain: to conceive the unity and simplicity of God in a new way. God's existence is not to be dismissed but consistently affirmed, and it is the traditional divine essence which must be subjected to critique.

The remaining chapters show that these two tasks (affirming God's existence and rethinking God's essence) cannot be performed in isolation from each other; in fact, they are aspects of the single project of defining God's being in rigorous conformity with faith's witness to the event of Jesus Christ. Chapter Four approaches the problem from Jüngel's attempt to redefine God's relation to the world as "more than necessary." His dispute with the traditional set of ideas associated with God as a being of absolute necessity leads him to a complex retrieval of certain motifs of German idealism. Without accepting the totalizing frameworks of Hegel or Schelling, Jüngel nonetheless finds in their thought fruitful suggestions for his own (at this stage highly abstract) construction of divine being. I argued that the fundamental result of these reflections is the idea of God's being as radical ontological freedom. As the always free self-mediation and self-actualization of the divine being, God is a self-grounding event. These unique ontological characteristics preclude the traditional role assigned to God by metaphysical reflection on finite causality: the highest and necessary being.

Chapter Five took a different tack. It showed that Jüngel's statements about creation and about God as creator are permeated by his rethinking of God's being. On the one hand, he takes up Barth's christocentric and trinitarian understanding of the doctrine of creation; on the other he demands a new evaluation of the relationship between possibility and actuality. The primacy of possibility in turn involves a new perspective on the temporality and transitoriness of existence; the negative moment of the struggle in which all being participates must not be identified with change or becoming *per se*. The negative moment, the true enemy of being, is rather the absolute annihilation which destroys every possibility of relationship. It is this annihilation which is constantly overcome in the outpouring of God's creative being; we know and understand this victory of God the creator only from the victory of love on the cross of Christ. Jüngel draws from this a more precise definition of the unity of essence and existence in God's being: God's essence is "to exist from itself into nothingness."

Finally, Chapter Six probed the common "ecstatic" structure of language-events and of faith in God's word as a final element in Jüngel's conception of God's being. The examination of his views on language revealed a linguistic anthropology in which human subjectivity is constituted as temporal existence through linguistic interaction with another. The discussion of faith in turn expanded upon the reception of the word of the cross as God's word; this special case of the word-event involves an eschatological intensification of that displacement involved in the linguistic constitution of the person addressed. These conclusions supported yet another approach to the question of God's unity of essence and existence. At this point that unity reaches its most concrete expression in the definition of God as self-imparting word in the history of Jesus Christ. As the free utterance of God's being, revelation instantiates that groundless event and overflow of love spoken of in previous chapters. As the word made flesh and crucified, the existence of God is seen as one with the human existence of Jesus.

The common thread running through these reflections on Jüngel's theism should by now be obvious: God's identity, God's essence, is not something defined in abstraction from God's existence. The traditional metaphysical formulation, repeatedly criticized by Jüngel, understood the essence as that which could be salvaged from the torrent of change. Everything in a given being which exhibits change must be accidental, for the essential is precisely the persistent identity. Jüngel likes to quote these lines from Angelus Silesius: ". . . For when the world passes away, / so falls away the accident. The essence, that endures" (GGW 29 [24]). As is commonly the case, the metaphysical scheme reflects a prior evaluation of worldly categories; God as that which is highest in the order of being is invested with those properties deemed most worthy of such a being. From the stock of properties common to beings metaphysical theism typically selects those it deems excellent and applies them to God; conversely, other properties which imply inferiority must not be associated with the divinity, except perhaps where poetic license is granted.

Jüngel's point is not that God lacks true excellence, but rather that we must learn what is truly good and excellent in the world by looking at God. He could say with Paul that "God chose what is weak in the world to shame the strong" (I Cor 1:27, NRSV). An obvious example of this "revaluation of all values" is the triumph of the weakness of love on the cross, so beautifully celebrated by Bonhoeffer in his last writings. Thinking God within the context of the human existence of Jesus demands some rethinking of traditional notions of omnipotence; it must be understood not simply as triumphant, all-embracing causality but as the capacity for withdrawal, contraction, vulnerability. Only love is omnipotent.[1] But this kind of rethinking is also at work in the question of God's unity of essence and existence. To reorder that unity in the light of God's unity with the crucified Jesus Jüngel initially has to challenge not only the metaphysical tradition but also the values it took for granted.

His initial move on the metaphysical level can be seen in his attempt to disconnect the concept of contingency from the concept of accident; as was seen in Chapter Four, Jüngel insists that the essential need not be equated with static subsistence. The corresponding move on the evaluative level was examined in Chapter Five: the redefinition of temporality and transitoriness so that the process of becoming can begin to be seen in its true dignity. The flux characterizing temporal existence does indeed have its sinister moment, but Jüngel defines the destructive element in becoming not with the passing into the past of what is actual, but rather with the annihilation of the possible. These two disputes with traditionally accepted positions form the groundwork for Jüngel's own positive development of the old doctrine of divine unity.

That development takes the form of an inversion. It must be kept in mind that Jüngel is fully in accord with the tradition insofar as he, too, demands the ultimate identity of essence and existence in God (GGW 205 [153]). The problem lies in how this unity is conceived. Jüngel argues that the dominant procedure has involved a metaphysical determination of what God is (God's essence) on the basis of which is decided the kind of existence God must have. In other words, what God is dictates how God exists: essence determines existence. This study has repeatedly revealed a pattern in which this order is reversed. From every perspective, God's mode of existence is itself God's identity or essence. God's existence is not the actualization of an essence which could be abstracted from it and made the object of independent reflection. God's existence is an ultimate in itself; as ultimate freedom it is a perpetually new event. Since God's existence is a becoming with which God is identical, then "God's being is in [the

---

[1] Jüngel's discussion of Bonhoeffer in GGW 74-82 (57-63) draws on the documents collected in Dietrich Bonhoeffer, *Letters and Papers from Prison*, ed. E Bethge, tr. R. H. Fuller (New York: Macmillan, 1972). On the "withdrawal of omnipotence" see the brief comment in GGW 137 (103).

mode of] becoming."[2] Thus God's essence (*Wesen*) drops out of view as an object of reflection, to be replaced by language of God's being (*Sein*).

Two related points must be made with regard to this "inversion" effected by Jüngel. The first is that the notion of existence has undergone a shift in meaning which is presupposed by Jüngel's procedure. In a minimal sense, existence can mean the real instantiation of a thing as opposed to its mere concept or possibility; thus it does not pertain to what something is (*quod sit*) but only to whether it is at all (*an sit*). According to Jüngel, Descartes more or less unwittingly initiated a transformation of the idea of existence when he tied it so closely to representation by a thinking subject. As a result of the "metaphysics of subjectivity" the idea of existence became identified with the temporality and transitoriness of the human subject. As pointed out in Chapter Three, one resulting option for thinking about God was the denial of God's existence in order to salvage the traditional superiority of God's essence (Fichte). But Jüngel embraces the alternative: "to align oneself with the *consequences* of the Cartesian concept of existence in such a way that God would quite consciously be thought of as an essence exposed to transitoriness" (GGW 252-3 [186-7]).

The metaphysics of subjectivity has thus performed a great service for theology: "[I]n the horizon of the *cogito* the entire problematic of the presupposed divine essence had to emerge in all its sharpness" (GGW 167 [126]). Once this has been granted, however, a second point needs to be made. The blame for the disintegration of the idea of God cannot be laid entirely at the door of the traditional concept of God: the tendency of thought to distinguish essence and existence generally, particularly in the context of developments stemming from Descartes, is itself deeply problematic. Thought can avoid the disastrous disintegration of the concept of God only when it abandons the notion of "securing" thought in general. One could even speak of a dual legacy of the Cartesian revolution, one rejected by Jüngel (the attempt to "secure" thought through self-grounding) and

---

2 See Jüngel, *Gottes Sein*, vi-vii. The point of the phrase is not that God's being is becoming, as if God were in the process of becoming God. Nor is God's being equated with the process of becoming in general. Rather, "becoming" is here the ontological realm or locus where God has being. God's being is in becoming because it is freely self-actualized event.

another embraced by him, albeit with modifications (the identification of existence with transitoriness).

It should be noted in this context that Jüngel believes the theistic reconstruction required of the Christian theologian should also have consequences for thought beyond theology. "The two tasks of learning to think God anew and learning to think thought anew cannot be theologically separated from one another" (GGW 205 [154]). But as a theologian of the word Jüngel believes he must approach the latter task only from the former; it is on the basis of seriously rethinking God's being from God's unity with Jesus that thought in general is taught "to avoid positioning itself between essence and existence" even with regard to beings in general (*Seiende*). "In place of that it would be a matter of perceiving existence as what is essential (*das Wesentliche*) and thus laying bare (again) in thought that act of perception which preserves the original unity of existence (*Dasein*) and essence (*Sosein*)" (GGW 205 [154]). It is precisely that perception of original unity which has been disrupted in modern consciousness, shaped as it is by the Cartesian turn to the self-grounding of thought.

The implication here seems to be that the "rational distinction" of the essence of a thing and its existence which had been found so useful to reason from the beginning became, under the dominant influence of the metaphysics of subjectivity, a harmful compulsion. It must be said that Jüngel's picture of exactly how this is supposed to have occurred is obscure and quite impressionistic. Even so, enough has been said on this matter to see that he connects the Cartesian self in its attempt to secure certain knowledge of its own existence in time with the setting up of subjectivity as the foundation of existence in general.[3] As the arbiter of existence the very act of thinking was rendered increasingly incapable of grasping things in their concrete unity. Thought once limited itself to discovering the ground for the essence/existence distinction in the thing itself (the *fundamentum in re*); after the Cartesian turn, thought cannot even think a thing without *ipso facto* schematizing it in terms of that distinction (GGW 143 [109]). This, then, is Jüngel's reading of the problematic of post-Cartesian

---

[3] GGW 166 (125). "As the *res cogitans*, the self has become the *subiectum* (*hypokeimenon*) of all existence."

epistemology which theology must find some way to overcome on the basis of truly and responsibly conceiving God.

The Questioning of Metaphysics

This particular discussion raises a more general issue, that of the relationship between metaphysics and theological method as Jüngel sees it. As was discussed in the introductory chapter, Jüngel's insistence that the procedures of thought are always historically situated within and oriented by traditions makes him unwilling to treat metaphysics as a general possibility of thought (or method) in isolation from the actual historical course of Western philosophy. The tenor of the discussion so far, particularly where God's ontological unity is concerned, might suggest that Jüngel's strictures on the role of metaphysics in theology are only relevant insofar as metaphysics follows the paths laid out for it by Descartes or other objectionable trends. For example, process metaphysics certainly cannot be taxed with setting up an absolute God removed from all flux and transitoriness. Has Jüngel unjustly condemned metaphysics by identifying it exclusively with problematic historical developments which, at least in principle, can be transcended?

There is certainly some validity to this question, but the situation is actually more complex than this accusation suggests. In the first place, there is a certain tension discernible in Jüngel's most general statements about metaphysics. He has certainly been deeply influenced by Heidegger's reading and radical critique of the Western philosophical tradition. Not surprisingly, then, Jüngel tends to see the historical course of metaphysics as a more or less consistent development from initial principles leading to an eventual collapse or dissolution. He also echoes Heidegger when he talks of metaphysics as a "theo-onto-logic"; there is a particular complex of ideas relating God, being and thought which has run like a theme-and-variations throughout the metaphysical tradition, and whose dissolution heralds the dissolution of metaphysics in general.[4] It is undeniable that for Jüngel our intellectual culture stands "at the end of the history of metaphysics" (GGW xi [vii]).

---

[4] GGW 275-8 (203-5). Cf. the similar idea of metaphysics as "onto-theo-logy" in Martin Heidegger, *Identität und Differenz* (Pfullingen: Neske, 1957).

This collapse is of enormous concern to theology because in adopting the concepts of metaphysical theism it had failed to subject them to theological critique; faith fell "under the dictate of metaphysics" (GGW 49-50 [39]). The collapse of metaphysics was intimately tied up with the "death" of the metaphysical God, a conceptual construction upon which Christian theology had become dangerously dependent. The theological traditions in which Jüngel was trained were therefore hostile to the metaphysical tradition on principle. "[W]e learned that one can only rule out atheism when one overcomes both the presupposition and the contestation [*Bestreitung*] of modern metaphysics —theism" (GGW 55-6 [43]). But it is accordingly the particular historical assumptions of metaphysical theism, especially the location of God in absolute superiority to the transitoriness of worldly processes, which must be absolutely rejected. That in and of itself would not entail the absolute expulsion of metaphysical language or concepts from theology.

On the level of the general relationship of theology to metaphysics Jüngel insists that in fact theology must make use of metaphysics, but only critically, that is in a way which does not compromise theology's freedom. He sums up his position in an important passage which bears quoting at length.

> That a potential leave-taking of theology from metaphysics nevertheless cannot lead simply to a "metaphysics-free" theology should not remain concealed from a critical and self-critical theological consciousness. For even if thought were supposed to put metaphysics behind it by simply handing it over to itself, it will only be able to preserve its freedom if it does not refuse to make critical use of the metaphysical traditions. The questions of metaphysics are not all already suspect, even if its answers are. And with the posing of a question (*Fragestellung*) the phenomenon possibly violated (*vergewaltigte*) by that question is not thereby already settled (*erledigt*). The discussion (*Auseinandersetzung*) of theology with metaphysics for the sake of a free theology is still valid at least with respect to the answers, the questions, and the way the questions are posed in the metaphysical tradition; but now in such a way, that theology works for the freedom of a perfectly *ambivalent* relationship to this tradition (GGW 62-3 [48-9]).

The delicacy of this issue for Jüngel is amply attested by his careful, almost hesitant language. Note that taking leave of metaphysics is an issue not just for theology, but for thought in general (the language of "handing it over to itself" is Heidegger's). At all events, a "free" theology must still grapple with metaphysics for two reasons. First, it must critically utilize the traditions lest it unwittingly fall under their "dictate." Second, the "phenomenon" interrogated by metaphysics is not necessarily obviated by the rejection of the metaphysical problematic.

Perhaps the broad conclusion can best be formulated in this way. The issues and questions raised by the "metaphysical traditions" remain of indispensible utility for theological reflection. There is a wealth of insight to be gained from the historical struggles of thought to clarify and categorize the world of experience, to determine the ultimate contituents of reality, to explore the nature of temporal process, and to determine the relation of the human mind to the realities external to it and in which it is imbedded. Theology simply cannot dispense with these traditional questions, both because Western thinking still remains shaped by them and also because with careful and critical use they can aid theology in its task of conceiving the interrelations of God, world, self and faith.

But theology cannot accept the pretension of metaphysics to occupy a superior (because more encompassing) position to theology, from which it can determine the general concepts of God and world which theology must use. With regard to the particular questions dealt with in this study, Jüngel's reconfiguration of divine unity would seem to have definite consequences for theological positions which in his view remain too much under the sway of a metaphysical approach. This would even apply to a "post-classical" metaphysical position (such as a process metaphysics) insofar as it failed properly to conceptualize the concrete results of theological reflection. Jüngel's intriguing comments on an article by Schubert Ogden will serve as a brief illustration.[5]

---

5 Jüngel, *Gottes Sein*, 113-4.   Cf. Schubert Ogden, "Bultmann's Demythologizing and Hartshorne's Dipolar Theism," in *Process and Divinity: The Hartshorne Festschrift*, ed. William Reese and Eugene Freeman (LaSalle, Illinois: Open Court Publishing Co., 1964), 493-514.   Jüngel refers to the German translation: Schubert Ogden, "Zur Frage der 'richtigen' Philosophie," *Zeitschrift für Theologie und Kirche* 61 (1964): 103-24.   It should be stressed that the following

Following Charles Hartshorne, Ogden wants to draw a distinction between God's "existentiality" ("the abstract structure or form of his being [*Wesens*] which characterizes him as God and distinguishes him from every other being [*Wesen*]") and the "concrete actualizations" which are grounded by that existentiality. His basic point is that philosophy is capable of probing God's abstract structure on the basis of his concrete acts, which serve as "contingent illustrations" of the divine existentiality. Thus he speaks of a "phenomenology of the divine being." In other words, the distinctions drawn by Heidegger's "fundamental ontology" on the basis of analyzing human existence (ontic/ontological, *existentiell*/existential) are being applied analogously to God's being. Ogden regards the close correspondence between these Heideggerian concepts and the dipolarity of Hartshorne's theism as of great utility for theology.6

Jüngel replies that this phenomenological reduction to an abstract essence (existentiality) is forbidden at the outset by the concrete unity of God's being-in-act, which prevents a strict analogy based on the structures of human existence in general.7 That is, one consequence of Jüngel's identifying essence and existence in God's being is that the becoming in which God has God's being cannot be assigned exclusively to a realm of divine acts, while leaving God's identity or essence untouched. "God's being cannot be made a theme in abstraction from the becoming proper to this being; conversely, this becoming cannot be understood 'merely as . . . contingent illustrations' of divine being,

---

brief discussion does not in any way form a decisive confrontation between Jüngel and process thought, a philosophical tradition with which he is apparently not well acquainted. It is rather an illustration which suggests the lines along which such a confrontation would have to occur.

6 Ogden, "Bultmann and Hartshorne," 506.

7 This is essentially the same question which Bultmann puts to Ogden in his own, very brief reply to Ogden's article. Rudolf Bultmann, "Zur Frage einer 'philosophischen Theologie,'" in *Einsichten: Gerhard Krüger zum 60. Geburtstag*, ed. Klaus Oehler and Richard Schaeffler (Frankfurt-am-Mein: Vittorio Klostermann, 1962), 36-8. Ogden, in turn, replied to Bultmann in a footnote to the German translation of his (Ogden's) article. He attempts to trace Bultmann's opposition to the analogy between human and divine historicity to an abstract and insupportible opposition between human temporality and a timeless divine eternity. In my opinion, it is not clear from Bultmann's language that this charge is just. It does highlight, however, the importance of Jüngel's own work in attempting to work out a conceptuality of divine existence which, in his opinion, remains more faithful to Bultmann's intentions than Ogden's similar attempt.

indeed cannot be understood at all in differentiation from that being."[8] That God's being is as such God's act, and can only be considered concretely, is precisely the implication of that notion of radical ontological freedom which this study has discovered at the heart of Jüngel's various conceptions of divine being. There is nothing contingent about God's free act simply because it is the enactment of God's very being and therefore essentially identical with it.

It is noteworthy that this discussion occurs in the context of Jüngel's exposition of Barth's trinitarianism. He accordingly couches his reply to Ogden's position in terms of its impossibility in Barth's scheme, despite the fact that Ogden's article is not concerned with Barth at all! The significance of this curious fact will be clarified by the two following considerations. First, as will be discussed in a moment, the reconstruction of the divine unity of essence and existence is itself a conceptual explication and interpretation of the kind of trinitarian design elicited from Barth's dogmatics and fully supported by Jüngel. Hence, there is no reason to consider Jüngel's recommendation of Barth's position as anything other than a recommendation of his own position, broadly speaking.

Second, recall that Ogden has introduced Hartshorne's metaphysics of divinity in response to a perceived deficiency in Bultmann's thought. Bultmann's theology of faith lacks a coherent conceptual elucidation of God's reality; it is "anthropologically one-sided" and therefore extremely vulnerable to subjectivistic misunderstandings.[9] But there is then a striking symmetry between Ogden's intentions and Jüngel's at this point. In essence, Jüngel is offering his own interpretation of Barth's trinitarianism, as opposed to Ogden's dipolar theism, as the divine conceptuality which Bultmann's *Glaubenslehre* lacks. On this interpretation Jüngel is, as it were, disputing with Ogden for control of the Bultmannian legacy; each proposes a way of following up on Bultmann's true intentions in a more consistent fashion than Bultmann himself. But the theistic concepts offered by Jüngel point in a different direction than Ogden's, toward a trinitarian unity with becoming determined not from generic ontological

---

[8] Jüngel, *Gottes Sein*, 114 note 148.

[9] Ogden, "Bultmann and Hartshorne," 501.

analysis but from faith's identification of God with the concrete
history of the suffering man Jesus.

To sum up what is at stake in Jüngel's implication that Ogden's
proposal is a dubious continuation of the old metaphysical enterprise in
theology, the following two points are in order. First, what Jüngel
objects to both in Ogden and generally is the way in which God's essence
or identity is separated from God's actual existence. To be sure, the
scheme outlined by Ogden does not define a divine essence abstractly
and then attempt to deduce existence from it. It attempts to begin "from
below," on the level of God's temporal activity, and move from there to
the abstract essence behind the activity. But the result from Jüngel's
point of view is no better for it still results in juxtaposing a necessary
essence with acts which are accidental to that essence.[10] This bears a
strong resemblance to the view of Helmut Gollwitzer against which
Jüngel's entire interpretation of Barth's trinitaritanism is directed.
Gollwitzer wants to distinguish God's being-for-Godself as an
ontologically more foundational or original aspect of God's being than
God's being-for-us; God's will to love, God's gracious decision, must be
grounded in (and therefore separable from!) the divine "substance."
Jüngel's conception of God's ontological unity is intended to eradicate
this gap between divine essence and divine will.[11]

Jüngel's reasons for this spring from his interpretation of the
meaning of faith in Christ as God's revelation; it is a soteriological
interest which ultimately drives his conceptual revisionism. It has
been implicit throughout this study that Jüngel's reconstruction of
divine unity in dispute with the theistic tradition constitutes an
interpretation of Barth's trinitarianism. He is attempting a conceptual
elucidation of the trinity and its implications on two fronts. First, he
wishes to show that trinitarianism must uncover and overturn what

---

[10] Both Jüngel and Ogden can speak of a self-identification of God's self in
the history of Jesus Christ, but Ogden's understanding of this as a "decisive representation of God" demands a gap between the general metaphysical relationship
between God and the world (God's eternal essence) and any act through which we come
to know that essence in its concrete interrelation with us (e.g. the existence of Jesus).
God's essence is not "decided" or "executed" in unity with the human person Jesus as
in Jüngel's understanding; rather Jesus is a decisive but nevertheless contingent
"illustration" of a divine essence which is "locked into" performing a given
metaphysical function vis-â-vis the world.

[11] Jüngel, *Gottes Sein*, 103-6.

might be called the "deep structure" of the metaphysical theistic tradition, which (as the examples of Gollwitzer and Ogden show) still haunts reflection even in the schools of Barth and Bultmann. Second, he wants to connect the trinity intimately with an ontology of linguistic events and of faith which follows developments associated with Heidegger, Ebeling and Fuchs. This is the justification for speaking of Jüngel's thought as a "trinitarian *Glaubenslehre*." The attempt can now be made to delineate briefly how the identity of essence and existence in God as envisioned by Jüngel must be interpreted within the horizon of the doctrine of the trinity.

Trinity and *Glaubenslehre*

The doctrine of the trinity is an interpretation of revelation. It begins from the confession in faith that God was historically present in the human being Jesus Christ and continues to be historically present in the community's proclamation as the Spirit of Christ. As Jüngel interprets it the trinity is a formulation of God's being such that the historical event of God is not in conflict with nor divorced from the eternal freedom of God's being. "The grace of God's being-for-us must be able to model (*abbilden*) the freedom of God's being-for-Godself in such a way that this freedom (as the 'prototype' [*Urbild*] of that grace) becomes manifest (*anschaulich*) in that grace (as the 'likeness' [or reflection, *Abbild*] of this freedom)."[12] The shape of God's being is determined from the shape of the giving of that being in the historical life and death of Jesus. It is not thereby implied, of course, that God's being is somehow reduced "without remainder" to the human event of Jesus, as if the universe were somehow evacuated of the creator's presence and power for 30 years or so! The living and dying human being Jesus is chosen from eternity as the "path" of God's being, of God's loving self-relation, and thus also as the mode of God's loving relation to all human beings and the entire creation. This ability to enter into perfect self-relation through and with an other without suffering disruption is a central point of any trinitarian interpretation. The task of the doctrine of the trinity is thus to read the pattern of Jesus' history as the pattern of God's free being.

---

[12] Ibid. 108.

To explore the intricacies of Jüngel's trinitarian understanding in itself would require another monograph. The immediate task is merely to indicate broadly the connection of the trinity with the reconceived unity of divine essence and existence as set forth in this study. In each chapter the same result was arrived at from different angles: God's being must be understood as free self-actualization and self-impartation. God's essence is this eternal event, this relational occurrence. God's self-relation is not grounded in an "already" given self-identity. Just the opposite: the identity is grounded in the actualizing of the self-relation. But this unity of identity and actuality, of essence and existence, is precisely the ontological implication of the doctrine of the trinity. In fact, this unity and this triunity are both envisioned as reflections on the Johannine definition of the divine being: God is love.

Recall Jüngel's characteristic way of defining love: it is a self-relation grounded in an even greater selflessness or self-impartation. On the one hand, then, this is the pattern of divine actualization; to exist in just this way is God's essence. This is that "existing from itself into nothingness" which was discussed in Chapter Five: it describes a being which does not "have" love (i. e. as a possible actualization), but which "is" love (GGW 410-1 [300]). On the other hand, the notion of God's triunity is intended to formulate just this truth, that God does not love in the manner of human persons; God's identity is an eternal event of love. In trinitarian language, it is the Spirit which binds into a unity the Father's love for the Son and the Son's love for the Father. But in so doing it opens that event of love to participation by what is not God. Thus the intensity of God's self-relation is eternally "outdistanced" by God's relation to the other.

Jüngel explicitly affirms this close connection between the unity of essence and existence, the trinity, and the Johannine definition:

> The God, who is love, is precisely in his existence completely identical with this his essence. His existence is his essence. The doctrine of the trinity formulates just this. It does it in that it thinks the essence of God, which is love, as an essence constituted through relations, and [in that it thinks] the relations constituting the essence of God as the divine existence (GGW 508 [371]).

In other words, the divine essence or identity is in no way prior to or ontologically separable from the divine act of existence, since that act is the network of trinitarian relations which constitutes the divine identity. But this understanding of divine existence as triune self-relation (the "immanent trinity") is grounded in (and therefore epistemologically posterior to) faith's interpretation of the Christ-event, i.e. the "economy" of salvation.

The unity of identity and actuality in God cannot be grasped in terms of a necessary existence derived from an absolute essence precisely because faith knows God's existence from its occurrence in history. "In this existence of God with the human being Jesus, the divine essence takes place (*sich vollzieht*). Faith preserves the identity of the essence and existence of God in that it perceives God's being as a being with the human Jesus . . ." (GGW 259 [191]). The inner-trinitarian relationality is not to be understood as a special "existence" of God over and above God's existence in human history (with the latter understood, perhaps, as a particular instance of that more general existence). Jüngel embraces Rahner's thesis of the unity of the economic and the immanent trinity. Moreover, he interprets it in terms of Barth's language of "relapse" (*Rückschluss*); the immanent trinity is formulated by "stepping back" from the economic trinity and conceptualizing the Christ-event precisely as an event of the eternally free God.[13] Therefore, Jüngel's insistence on the unity of essence and existence in God is not reducible to a "speculative" formulation of God's immanent being, but is an attempt to conceive consistently the concrete life and death of Jesus as God's history. That unity is the implication of faith's claim that "God himself takes place (*sich ereignet*) in Jesus' God-forsakenness and death" (GGW 507 [370]).

Thus Jüngel sees the doctrine of the trinity as a function of a rigorous theology of the cross: "The doctrine of the trinity conceptualizes (*auf den Begriff bringt*) what is narrated in the passion story" (GGW 507 [370]). Jüngel's way of conceiving the unity of essence and existence in God is intended to present an understanding of divine being as historical in its essence, and therefore capable of identifying with the transitoriness of history, even death, while still corresponding to itself. The metaphysical conception of that unity (absolute essence/necessary existence) was designed to do the opposite:

---

[13] See Eberhard Jüngel, "Das Verhältnis von 'ökonomischer' und 'immanenter' Trinität," in *Entsprechungen*, 265-75. On the notion of the "relapse" see Jüngel, *Gottes Sein*, 62.

it sought to prevent any real contact with the transitoriness of history, a task it carried out with disastrous efficiency. Jüngel offers his alternative as a dispute with the philosophical and theological tradition necessary to secure the conceptual viability of a rigorously consistent trinitarian theology of the cross.

Nor should it be forgotten that Jüngel's scheme is also linked to the execution of theology as *Glaubenslehre*. In Chapter Three it was seen how Jüngel associates the Cartesian project of "securing" the subject with the absolutization of the existence/essence distinction. One consequence was the gradual erosion of the old metaphysics of divine unity. But the root of the problem lay as much in the new subjective point of departure as in the traditional problem of the absolute divine essence. For the rift between essence and existence was a product of the establishment of the subject and its representative faculty as the "*subiectum*" or foundation of existence. This in turn was necessary in order to secure the thinking subject as absolutely certain and impervious to doubt.

This historical background is the key to the close connection between establishing a theology of faith and recovering the unity of essence and existence. Recovering that unity will have to involve rejecting the self-securing subject which makes that unity impossible. Chapter Six pointed out that faith means abandoning the project of securing oneself (and therefore securing God) in favor of a radically "insecure" relation to God and others, that of trust. The "certainty" of faith (*Gewißheit*) is based on trust and is incompatible with securing; it is in fact a "desecuring" (*Entsicherung*) of the self (GGW 227 [169]). Faith rejects securing the self because it allows our existence to be dislodged or dislocated, removed into the concrete presence of God and given to us anew. Faith rejects securing God because it allows God's existence to be that presence-as-absence which is exposed to transitoriness in the life and death of Jesus. In both cases the attempt to evade the utter temporality and relationality of existence is rejected. The self-certainty based on trust is "the precise opposite of self-grounding through securing" (GGW 248 [184]). Therefore, Jüngel says, "[t]he unity without distinction of essence and existence cannot be secured through representation and does not exist in the mode of being-secured at all" (GGW 254 [188]).

This clarifies somewhat the liaison in Jüngel's thought between a vision of theology as a hermeneutic of the faith-event

(*Glaubenslehre*) and a demand that God be conceived in trinitarian terms. Theology can speak of God on the exclusive basis of faith in the crucified and resurrected Christ only because it believes that God has given God's self to be identified in and with the transitoriness of historical existence. But on that basis faith is driven to conceive God's relationality and historicality as primordial possibilities of God's being. To allow one's self-presence and self-understanding to be reshaped in encounter with Christ is at the same time to be drawn into the trinitarian interplay of relations which is God's being as love.

Jüngel's Contribution: Some Critical Considerations

In attempting to summarize the contributions, real or potential, as well as the problems which Jüngel's thought presents to systematic theology, discussion must be limited to the specific topics dealt with in this study.[14] To begin on a more general level, there are two theologically significant and closely related tasks which Jüngel's work as dealt with here has helped bring into focus. The first task is the retrieval and reconfiguration of the heritage of dialectical theology in the two great trajectories associated with Barth and Bultmann. In particular, he has attempted to combine what Robert Jenson calls Barth's "christocentric ontology" with the scriptural hermeneutics, linguistic analysis and anthropology of faith which made Bultmann and his followers so important.[15] This conjunction is fruitful for both traditions. It attempts to counteract the massive isolation from non-theological discourse and intellectual culture which was and is the constant threat to Barth's grand vision.

At the same time, Jüngel's theistic reconstruction is a defense and rehabilitation of the basic concerns of the Bultmannian school, which after its heyday in the Fifties and Sixties has become sadly neglected especially in English-speaking theology. Herein lies the second task which he has illuminated in his work: that of constructing

---

[14] Just how limited such a discussion is becomes clear when the many other areas in which Jüngel has written are brought to mind. He has made noteworthy contributions in scriptural interpretation, theological language, anthropology, ethics, ecclesiology and sacramental theory.

[15] For the phrase cited see Robert W. Jenson, "Karl Barth," in *The Modern Theologians*, 2nd ed., ed. David F. Ford (Cambridge, MA: Blackwell Publishers, 1997), 30.

a satisfactory doctrine of the Christian God on the basis of the interpretation of the phenomenon of faith. This is what has been spoken of as his trinitarian *Glaubenslehre*. It is an attempt to do justice to the very distinctive shape of the Christian God by locating the basic criteria for theological reflection in the phenomenology of ecclesial belief and especially in the hermeneutic of the New Testament within the context of that belief. This task is crucial in the current setting, in which alternate paradigms for theistic reconstruction (scientific cosmology, metaphysical systems, ecological and socio-ethical demands) jostle one another on a crowded and confused theological stage. Jüngel's own project need not imply the illegitimacy of these other concerns; indeed they are patently necessary, but they can only play their vital role when located within the context of understanding faith in Jesus Christ, not when simply imposed as absolute criteria. It should also be pointed out that Jüngel's location of trinitarian thinking within a theology of faith also helps to dispel the taint of speculation and supernaturalism from which some especially of Barth's more enthusiastic followers have never quite been free.

Before summarizing the more specific and positive achievements highlighted by this study, there are a number of critical questions which must be acknowledged for it cannot be said that Jüngel has set about the tasks just outlined in an uncontroversial way. Again, these questions must be limited to issues which arise from the study itself. There is first of all room for critique of the way Jüngel has dealt with philosophical and theological history. He certainly has a tendency to deal with broad trends, a practice which often leads to insufficient attention to variety and nuance, even conflict within a supposedly unified tradition. One might ask, for example, whether his reading of Descartes (which itself is heavily indebted to Heidegger) is accurate or fair in its particulars. Indeed, Jüngel displays throughout his work a heavy reliance on Heidegger's critique of the Western philosophical tradition; even if the overall paradigm is justified, more attention to the specialized literature on figures or periods would reduce the risk of biased or idiosyncratic interpretations. On the theological side, too, the enthrallment of tradition to an absolutist theistic model is perhaps not as total as Jüngel's treatment suggests.

A second group of questions must focus on particular conceptual complexes which are vital to his thought. From the standpoint of the philosophy of language there is surely a need to investigate thoroughly the presuppositions of his hermeneutic philosophy and anthropology, which again is greatly indebted to Heidegger, as well as to Fuchs and Ebeling. A flood of sophisticated work has been produced in the last quarter century in linguistics, semantics and philosophical hermeneutics; more engagement with this literature would be necessary to probe the weaknesses of his various assumptions, even presuming they are not fatal to his entire conception of the word-event.[16] Another question could be raised about the logical coherence of the unity of essence and existence. Is this ultimately a notion which makes any sense? In my opinion there can be no simple answer to this question, since it is tied up with particular conceptual definitions and basic metaphysical choices. But this raises a larger point, for the entire question of precisely how theological and metaphysical reflection relate to one another is answered in ways which are at once suggestive, tentative and vague.

Finally, there are those questions which inevitably arise in the very attempt to appropriate Barth's thought on a large scale. It is manifestly the case that Jüngel sees his project as an extension (even if a critical one) of Barth's achievement. A great deal of what Jüngel has to say both on the doctrine of God and on theological method therefore stands or falls with one's ultimate verdict on the viability of the Barthian project. Here the questions are too numerous and well-known to receive explicit treatment, but it is clear that the wholesale rejection of neo-Protestantism, the overwhelming concentration on Christology and revelation, the massive recovery of trinitarian discourse all remain as controversial as ever. The least that can be said is that the issue remains in doubt, and that it cannot be regarded in terms of a simple "yes" or "no." Jüngel's work itself should be seen as an attempt to deal with these critical issues while remaining broadly faithful to Barth's vision. As such, it takes its place within the debates on the nature of theology which are now occurring, and which in fact have been part of the Church's self-reflection from the beginning.

---

[16] Jüngel's student and erstwhile collaborator Ingolf Dalferth has put some very sharp questions to the entire tradition of German hermeneutic theology which further work in this area must attempt to answer. See Ingolf Dalferth, "God and the Mystery of Words," *Journal of the American Academy of Religion* 60 (1992): 79-104. Cf. Garrett Green, "Mystery of Eberhard Jüngel," 38. More generally, it should be remarked that Jüngel's extreme reluctance to deal seriously with English-language scholarship remains a weakness in his work as a whole.

The attitude throughout this study has been one of broad critical sympathy with Jüngel's approach. It is from this stance, informed by the critical reservations just registered, that I will conclude by acknowledging the particular contribution of his thought which has been my special concern. In contrast to the large projects mentioned before, for which Jüngel's thought serves as a paradigmatic approach, the more concrete issue at hand is the actual result of his reconstruction of Christian theism. This is probably Jüngel's central achievement: the most rigorous attempt yet to think through the conceptual implications for theistic thinking of God's identification in and with the historical life and death of the human Jesus. The result is a unification of the doctine of the trinity with a theology of the cross which neither the Patristic and Scholastic thinkers nor even the Reformers were able to accomplish due to persistent flaws in the doctrine of God, inherited traditions lodged in the doctrine like foreign bodies and insufficiently assimilated by faithful reflection.

The great value of Jüngel's project lies among other things in the thoroughness with which he sifts the theological tradition for its uncriticized theistic assumptions. The result of this excavation was the uncovering of a two-fold problem. On the one hand, theology allowed into its deliberations a doctrine of God's essence which defined the latter in terms of one or more notions of absolute metaphysical superiority; the divine essence was determined as an agglomeration of selected generic properties purged of perceived frailties. This absolute essence, defined more or less in abstraction from faith in the Christ, was granted necessary existence as the complement to its perfections. On the other hand, the Cartesian revolution of thought in a (at first unperceived) countervailing movement "relationalized" and "temporalized" existence by establishing it upon the representations of the secured human subject. The cultural "death of God" was intimately tied up with the intellectual disintegration of the God-concept which resulted to a large degree from the collision of theological tradition and post-Cartesian innovation.

It is Jüngel's achievement first of all to have investigated this problem and to have taken it seriously as an obstacle to the development of a coherent theological conceptuality. Even the signal contributions to theistic reconstruction of the dialectical theologians (especially Barth) were insufficiently aware of the historical matrix and continued potency of the classical theistic paradigm (GGW 271-2

[200-1]). This conceptual pedigree had to be brought to light; like a repressed memory, it had to be rendered conscious in order to neutralize the danger of its disguised return. This study has shown Jüngel's response to this uncovered legacy to be a complex strategy of appropriation and reconfiguration. Both the basic idea of divine simplicity (the identity of essence and existence) and the historicization of existence developed by post-Cartesian metaphysics were appropriated, but in a thoroughly reconstructed way: the absolute divine essence underlying the former and the absolutely self-grounding subject underlying the latter are rejected.

In their place Jüngel offers an anthropology of faith open to its own construction in the encounter with otherness, and a refashioned notion of divine simplicity in which relationality (a play of otherness) and temporality (an overflow into nothingness) are essential characteristics of the divine. The new divine simplicity unifies identity and actuality, finding contingency and history to be central to the divine identity revealed in the life and death of Jesus Christ. To speak of the living God is therefore no anthropomorphism; instead, we must say on the basis of this study that life is theomorphic. And is it not the implication of faith in the Crucified One that because only God truly lives, therefore only God truly dies? "[P]ropriisime *solus Deus* mortuus esse dici potest."[17]

---

[17] Jüngel, *Gottes Sein*, 80 note 25.

BIBLIOGRAPHY

PUBLICATIONS BY EBERHARD JÜNGEL

"Der Schritt zurück: Eine Auseinandersetzung mit der Heidegger-Deutung Heinrich Otts." *Zeitschrift für Theologie und Kirche* 58 (1961): 104-22.

"Die Möglichkeit theologischer Anthropologie auf dem Grunde der Analogie: Eine Untersuchung zum Analogieverständnis Karl Barths." In *Barth-Studien*. Gütersloh: Gerd Mohn, 1982. First published in *Evangelische Theologie* 22 (1962): 535-76.

Review of *Sein und Existenz: Die Überwindung des Subjekt-Objektschemas in der Philosophie Heideggers und in der Theologie der Entmythologisierung*, by Gerhard Noller. *Evangelische Theologie* 23 (1963): 218-23.

"'Theologische Wissenschaft und Glaube' im Blick auf die Armut Jesu." In *Unterwegs zur Sache: Theologische Bemerkungen*. Munich: Christian Kaiser, 1972. First published in *Evangelische Theologie* 24 (1964): 419-43.

Gottes Sein ist im Werden: Verantwortliche Rede vom Sein Gottes bei Karl Barth: Eine Paraphrase, 4th ed. Tübingen: J. C. B. Mohr (Paul Siebeck), 1986.

"Jesu Wort und Jesus als Wort Gottes: Ein hermeneutischer Beitrag zum christologischen Problem." In *Unterwegs zur Sache: Theologische Bemerkungen*. Munich: Christian Kaiser, 1972. First published in E. Busch, J. Fangmeier and M. Geiger, eds., *Parrhesia: Karl Barth zum 80. Geburtstag* (Zürich: EVZ-Verlag, 1966).

"Vorwärts durch Annäherung?" Review of *Ernst Fuchs: Versuch einer Orientierung*, by Jürgen Fangmeier. *Theologische Literaturzeitung* 90 (1966): 328-9.

"Die Freiheit der Theologie." In *Entsprechungen: Gott - Wahrheit - Mensch: Theologische Erörterungen II*. Munich: Christian Kaiser, 1980. First published as *Die Freiheit der Theologie* (Zürich: EVZ-Verlag, 1967).

179

"Das Verhältnis der theologischen Disziplinen untereinander." In *Unterwegs zur Sache: Theologische Bemerkungen.* Munich: Christian Kaiser, 1972. First published in E. Jüngel, K. Rahner and M. Seitz, *Die praktische Theologie zwischen Wissenschaft und Praxis* (Munich: Christian Kaiser, 1968).

"Vom Tod des lebendigen Gottes: Ein Plakat." In *Unterwegs zur Sache: Theologische Bemerkungen.* Munich: Christian Kaiser, 1972. First published in *Zeitschrift für Theologie und Kirche* 65 (1968): 93-116.

"Gott—als Wort unserer Sprache." In *Unterwegs zur Sache: Theologische Bemerkungen.* Munich: Christian Kaiser, 1972. First published in *Evangelische Theologie* 29 (1969): 1-24.

"Die Welt als Möglichkeit und Wirklichkeit: Zum ontologischen Ansatz der Rechtfertigungslehre." In *Unterwegs zur Sache: Theologische Bemerkungen.* Munich: Christian Kaiser, 1972. First published in *Evangelische Theologie* 29 (1969): 417-442.

Tod. Stuttgart: Kreuz-Verlag, 1971.

"Grenzen des Menschseins." In *Entsprechungen: Gott - Wahrheit - Mensch: Theologische Erörterungen II.* Munich: Christian Kaiser, 1980. First published in H. W. Wolff, ed., *Probleme biblischer Theologie: Gerhard von Rad zum 70. Geburtstag* (Munich: Christian Kaiser, 1971).

Unterwegs zur Sache: Theologische Bemerkungen. Munich: Christian Kaiser, 1972.

"Thesen zur Grundlegung der Christologie." In *Unterwegs zur Sache: Theologische Bemerkungen.* Munich: Christian Kaiser, 1972.

"Quae supra nos, nihil ad nos: Eine Kurzformel der Lehre vom verborgenen Gott—im Anschluß an Luther interpretiert." In *Entsprechungen: Gott - Wahrheit - Mensch: Theologische Erörterungen II.* Munich: Christian Kaiser, 1980. First published in *Evangelische Theologie* 32 (1972): 197-240.

"Gott ist Liebe: Zur Unterscheidung von Glaube und Liebe." In *Festschrift für Ernst Fuchs*, edited by G. Ebeling, E. Jüngel and G. Schunack. Tübingen: J. C. B. Mohr (Paul Siebeck), 1973.

"Theologie in der Spannung zwischen Wissenschaft und Bekenntnis." In *Entsprechungen: Gott - Wahrheit - Mensch: Theologische Erörterungen II.* Munich: Christian Kaiser, 1980. First published as *Theologie in der Spannung zwischen Wissenschaft und Bekenntnis* (Stuttgart: Evangelische Zentralstelle für Weltanschauungsfragen, 1973).

"Metaphorische Wahrheit: Erwägungen zur theologischen Relevanz der Metapher als Beitrag zur Hermeneutik einer narrativen Theologie." In *Entsprechungen: Gott - Wahrheit - Mensch: Theologische Erörterungen II.* Munich: Christian Kaiser, 1980. First published in P. Ricoeur and E. Jüngel, *Metapher: Zur Hermeneutik religiöser Sprache* (*Evangelische Theologie* Sonderheft, 1974).

"Redlich von Gott reden: Bemerkungen zur Klarheit der Theologie Rudolf Bultmanns." *Evangelische Kommentare* 7 (1974): 475-7.

"Das Verhältnis vom 'ökonomischer' und 'immanenter' Trinität: Erwägungen über eine biblische Begründung der Trinitätslehre —im Anschluß an und in Auseinandersetzung mit Karl Rahners Lehre vom dreifaltigen Gott als transzendentem Urgrund der Heilsgeschichte." In *Entsprechungen: Gott - Wahrheit - Mensch: Theologische Erörterungen II.* Munich: Christian Kaiser, 1980. First published in *Zeitschrift für Theologie und Kirche* 72 (1975): 353-64.

"Das Dilemma der natürlichen Theologie und die Wahrheit ihres Problems: Überlegungen für ein Gespräch mit Wolfhart Pannenberg." In *Entsprechungen: Gott - Wahrheit - Mensch: Theologische Erörterungen II.* Munich: Christian Kaiser, 1980. First published in A. Schwann, ed., *Denken im Schatten des Nihilismus: Festschrift für Wilhelm Weischedel zum 70. Geburtstag am 11. April* (Darmstadt: Wissenschaftliche Buchgesellschaft, 1975).

"Der Tod als Geheimnis des Lebens." In *Entsprechungen: Gott - Wahrheit - Mensch: Theologische Erörterungen II.* Munich: Christian Kaiser, 1980. First published in A. Paus, ed., *Grenzerfahrung Tod* (Graz: Styria, 1976).

Gott als Geheimnis der Welt: Zur Begründung der Theologie des Gekreuzigten im Streit zwischen Theismus und Atheismus. 6th ed. Tübingen: J. C. B. Mohr (Paul Siebeck), 1992. Translated by Darrell L. Guder under the title *God as the Mystery of the World: On the Foundation of the Theology of the Crucified One in the Dispute between Theism and Atheism* (Grand Rapids: Eerdmans, 1983).

"Gelegentliche Thesen zum Problem der natürlichen Theologie." In *Entsprechungen: Gott - Wahrheit - Mensch: Theologische Erörterungen II.* First published in *Evangelische Theologie* 37 (1977): 485-8.

The Freedom of a Christian. Translated by Roy A. Harrisville. Minneapolis: Augsburg Press, 1988. Originally published as *Zur Freiheit eines Christenmenschen: Eine Erinnerung an Luthers Schrift* (Munich: Christian Kaiser, 1978).

"Die Wirksamkeit des Entzogenen: Zum Vorgang geschichtlichen Verstehens als Einführung in die Christologie." In B. Aland, ed., *Gnosis: Festschrift für Hans Jonas.* Göttingen: Vandenhoeck & Ruprecht, 1978.

Entsprechungen: Gott - Wahrheit - Mensch: Theologische Erörterungen II. Munich: Christian Kaiser, 1980.

(with Ingolf Dalferth) "Person und Gottebenbildlichkeit." In F. Böckle *et al*, eds., *Christlicher Glaube in moderner Gesellschaft.* Vol. 24. Freiburg: Herder, 1981.

Barth-Studien. Gütersloh: Gerd Mohn, 1982.

"Zur Lehre vom Heiligen Geist: Thesen." In U. Luz and H. Weder, eds., *Die Mitte des Neuen Testaments: Einheit und Vielfalt neutestamentlicher Theologie: Festschrift für Eduard Schweizer zum 70. Geburtstag.* Göttingen: Vandenhoeck & Ruprecht, 1983.

"Die Offenbarung der Verborgenheit Gottes: Ein Beitrag zum evangelischen Verständnis der Verborgenheit des göttlichen Wirkens." In *Wertlose Wahrheit: Zur Identität und Relevanz des christlichen Glaubens: Theologische Erörterungen III.* Munich: Christian Kaiser, 1990. First published in K. Lehmann, ed., *Vor dem Geheimnis Gottes den Menschen verstehen: Karl Rahner zum 80. Geburtstag* (Munich: Steiner & Schnell, 1984).

"Glauben und Verstehen: Zum Theologiebegriff Rudolf Bultmanns." In *Wertlose Wahrheit: Zur Identität und Relevanz des christlichen Glaubens: Theologische Erörterungen III*. Munich: Christian Kaiser, 1990. First published as *Glauben und Verstehen: Zum Theologiebegriff Rudolf Bultmanns*. Sitzungsberichte der Heidelberger Akademie der Wissenschaften, Philosophisch-historische Klasse, no. 1985/1 (Heidelberg: Carl Winter, 1985).

"'Meine Theologie'—kurz gefaßt." In *Wertlose Wahrheit: Zur Identität und Relevanz des christlichen Glaubens: Theologische Erörterungen III*. Munich: Christian Kaiser, 1990. First published in J. B. Bauer, ed., *Entwürfe der Theologie* (Graz: Styria, 1985).

"Gottes ursprüngliches Anfangen als schöpferische Selbstbegrenzung: Ein Beitrag zum Gespräch mit Hans Jonas über den 'Gottesbegriff nach Auschwitz.'" In *Wertlose Wahrheit: Zur Identität und Relevanz des christlichen Glaubens: Theologische Erörterungen III*. Munich: Christian Kaiser, 1990. First published in H. Deuser *et al*, eds., *Gottes Zukunft—Zukunft der Welt: Festschrift für Jürgen Moltmann zum 60. Geburtstag* (Munich: Christian Kaiser, 1986).

"Das Entstehen von Neuem." In *Wertlose Wahrheit: Zur Identität und Relevanz des christlichen Glaubens: Theologische Erörterungen III*. Munich: Christian Kaiser, 1990. First published in R. Schröder *et al*, eds., *Wahrzeichen: Freundesgabe zum 50. Geburtstag von Wolf Krötke am 5. 10. 1988* (Munich: Christian Kaiser, 1988).

"Nihil divinitatis, ubi non fides: Ist christliche Dogmatik in rein theoretischer Perspektive möglich? Bemerkungen zu einem theologischen Entwurf von Rang." *Zeitschrift für Theologie und Kirche* 86 (1989): 204-35.

"Zum Begriff der Offenbarung." In G. Besier, ed., *Glaube - Bekenntnis - Kirchenrecht: Festschrift für Vizepräsident i. R. D.theol. Hans Philipp Meyer zum 70. Geburtstag*. Hannover: Lutherisches Verlagshaus, 1989.

Wertlose Wahrheit: Zur Identität und Relevanz des christlichen Glaubens: Theologische Erörterungen III. Munich: Christian Kaiser, 1990.

"Toward the Heart of the Matter." Translated by Paul Capetz. *Christian Century* 108 (1991): 228-33.

OTHER WORKS CITED

Bannach, Klaus. "Schellings Philosophie der Offenbarung: Gehalt und theologiegeschichtliche Bedeutung." *Neue Zeitschrift für Systematische Theologie und Religionsphilosophie* 37 (1995): 57-74.

Barth, Karl. *Kirkliche Dogmatik*. Vol III/2. Zollikon: Evangelischer Verlag, 1945.

Barth, Ulrich. "Zur Barth-Deutung Eberhard Jüngels." *Theologische Zeitschrift* 40 (1984): 296-320, 394-415.

Bonhoeffer, Dietrich. *Letters and Papers from Prison*. Edited by E. Bethge. Translated by R. H. Fuller. New York: Macmillan, 1972.

Buckley, Michael. *At the Origins of Modern Atheism*. New Haven: Yale University Press, 1987.

Bultmann, Rudolf. *Theologie des Neuen Testaments*. Edited by Otto Merk. 9th ed. Tübingen: J. C. B. Mohr (Paul Siebeck), 1984.

———. *Theologische Enzyklopädie*. Edited by E. Jüngel and K. W. Müller. Tübingen: J. C. B. Mohr (Paul Siebeck), 1984.

———. "Zur Frage einer 'philosophischen Theologie.'" In *Einsichten: Gerhard Krüger zum 60. Geburtstag*, edited by Klaus Oehler and Richard Schaeffler. Frankfurt-am-Mein: Vittorio Klostermann, 1962.

Busch, Eberhard. *Karl Barth: His Life from Letters and Autobiographical Texts*. Translated by John Bowden. Philadelphia: Fortress Press, 1976.

Dalferth, Ingolf. "God and the Mystery of Words." *Journal of the American Academy of Religion* 60 (1993): 79-104.

DUDEN: Deutsches Universal-Wörterbuch. Mannheim: Bibliographisches Institut, 1983.

Dupre, Louis. *Passage to Modernity*. New Haven: Yale University Press, 1993.

Ebeling, Gerhard. "Die Bedeutung der historischkritischen Methode für die protestantische Theologie und Kirche." In *Wort und Glaube*. Vol. 1. Tübingen: J. C. B. Mohr (Paul Siebeck), 1960.

————. *Einführung in theologische Sprachlehre*. Tübingen: J. C. B. Mohr (Paul Siebeck), 1971.

————. *Theologie und Verkündigung: Ein Gespräch mit Rudolf Bultmann*. Tübingen: J. C. B. Mohr (Paul Siebeck), 1962.

Fichte, J. G. "Rückerinnerungen, Antworten, Fragen." In *Sämmtliche Werke*. Vol. 5. Edited by I. H. Fichte. Berlin: Veit & Company, 1845. Reprint, 1971.

Fiddes, Paul S. *The Creative Suffering of God*. Oxford: Oxford University Press, 1988.

Frei, Hans. *Types of Christian Theology*. New Haven: Yale University Press, 1992.

Fuchs, Ernst. "Was ist ein Sprachereignis? Ein Brief." In *Zur Frage nach dem historischen Jesus*. Tübingen: J. C. B. Mohr (Paul Siebeck), 1960.

Geyer, Hans-Georg. "Gottes Sein als Thema der Theologie." *Verkündigung und Forschung* 11 (1966): 3-37.

Green, Garrett. "The Mystery of Eberhard Jüngel: A Review of his Theological Program." *Religious Studies Review* 5 (1979): 34-40.

Hartmann, Nicolai. *Möglichkeit und Wirlichkeit*. 3rd ed. Berlin: Walter de Gruyter, 1966.

Hegel, Georg Wilhelm Friedrich. *The Science of Logic*, 2 vols. Translated by W. H. Johnston and L. G. Struthers. London: Allen & Unwin, 1929.

Heidegger, Martin. *Being and Time*. Translated by John Macquarrie and Edward Robinson. New York: Harper & Row, 1962.

————. *Identität und Differenz*. Pfullingen: Neske, 1957.

————. *Nietzsche*. 2 Vols. Pfullingen: Neske, 1961.

Hoffmeyer, John F. *The Advent of Freedom: The Presence of the Future in Hegel's Logic*. Rutherford, NJ: Fairleigh Dickinson University Press, 1994.

Jeanrond, Werner. "The Problem of the Starting-point of Theological Thinking." In *The Possibilities of Theology: Studies in the Theology of Eberhard Jüngel in his Sixtieth Year*, edited by John Webster. Edinburgh: T & T Clark, 1994.

Jenson, Robert W. "Karl Barth." In *The Modern Theologians*, edited by David F. Ford. 2nd edition. Cambridge: Blackwell Publishers, 1997.

Kant, Immanuel. *Critique of Pure Reason*. Translated by Norman Kemp Smith. Unabridged Edition. New York: St. Martin's Press, 1929.

Kern, Walter. "Theologie des Glaubens, vorgestellt anhand von Eberhard Jüngel." *Zeitschrift für katholische Theologie* 104 (1982): 129-46.

Kierkegaard, Søren. *Philosophical Fragments and Johannes Climacus*. Edited and translated by Howard V. Hong and Edna H. Hong. Princeton: Princeton University Press, 1985.

Knudsen, Harald. *Gottesbeweise im Deutschen Idealismus*. Berlin and New York: Walter de Gruyter, 1972.

Küng, Hans. *The Incarnation of God*. Translated by J. R. Stephenson. New York: Crossroad, 1987.

Marion, Jean-Luc. *God Without Being: Hors-Texte*. Translated by Thomas A. Carlson. Chicago: University of Chicago Press, 1991.

Moltmann, Jürgen. *Der gekreuzigte Gott: Das Kreuz Christi als Grund und Kritik christlicher Theologie*. Munich: Christian Kaiser, 1972. Translated by R. A. Wilson and John Bowden as *The Crucified God: The Cross of Christ as the Foundation and Criticism of Christian Theology* (New York: Harper & Row, 1974).

Mure, G. R. G. *A Study of Hegel's Logic*. Oxford: Oxford University Press, 1950; Westport, CT: Greenwood Press, 1984.

O'Donovan, L. J. "The Mystery of God as a History of Love: Eberhard Jüngel's Doctrine of God." *Theological Studies* 42 (1981): 251-71.

Ogden, Schubert. "Bultmann's Demythologizing and Hartshorne's Dipolar Theism." In *Process and Divinity: The Hartshorne Festschrift*, edited by William Reese and Eugene Freeman. LaSalle, IL: Open Court Publishing, 1964. Translated by Ogden as "Zur Frage der 'richtigen' Philosophie," *Zeitschrift für Theologie und Kirche* 61 (1964): 103-24.

Ott, Heinrich. *Denken und Sein: Der Weg Martin Heideggers und der Weg der Theologie*. Zollikon: Evangelischer Verlag, 1959.

Pannenberg, Wolfhart. *Theology and the Philosophy of Science.* Translated by Francis McDonagh. Philadelphia: Westminster Press, 1976.

Paulus, Engelbert. *Liebe - das Geheimnis der Welt: Formale und materiale Aspekte der Theologie Eberhard Jüngels.* Würzburg: Echter, 1990.

Plantinga, Alvin. *The Nature of Necessity.* Oxford: Oxford University Press, 1974.

Prestige, G. L. *God in Patristic Thought.* London: William Heinemann, 1936.

Raden, Matthias. "Hermeneutik der Entsprechung oder Hermeneutik der Nichtentsprechung: Eine Gegenüberstellung der theologischen Hermeneutiken von E. Jüngel und P. Ricoeur." *Evangelische Theologie* 48 (1988): 217-32.

Ricoeur, Paul. *The Rule of Metaphor: Multi-disciplinary Studies of the Creation of Meaning in Language.* Translated by Robert Czerny with Kathleen McLaughlin and John Costello. Toronto: University of Toronto Press, 1977.

Roberts, R. H. "Barth's Doctrine of Time: Its Nature and Implications." In *Karl Barth: Studies of his Theological Method*, edited by S. W. Sykes. Oxford: Clarendon Press, 1979.

Robinson, James M. "Hermeneutics since Barth." In *The New Hermeneutic.* New Frontiers in Theology, ed. James M. Robinson and John B. Cobb, vol. 2. New York: Harper & Row, 1964.

Schelling, F. W. J. "Zur Geschichte der neueren Philosophie." In *Sämmtliche Werke.* Division 1, Vol. 10. Stuttgart: J. S. Cotta'scher Verlag, 1861. Translated and edited by Andrew Bowie as *On the History of Modern Philosophy* (Cambridge: Cambridge University Press, 1994.

Schleiermacher, Friedrich. *Kurze Darstellung des theologischen Studiums.* Edited by Heinrich Scholz. Leipzig: A. Deichert, 1973. Translated by Terrence Tice as *Brief Outline of the Study of Theology* (Richmond: John Knox Press, 1966).

Spangenberg, Volker. "Eberhard Jüngel." Translated by D. Sutherland. In *A New Handbook of Christian Theologians.* Edited by Donald Musser and Joseph Price. Nashville: Abingdon Press, 1996.

Stace, W. T. *The Philosophy of Hegel: A Systematic Exposition*. New York: Dover Publications, 1955.

Troeltsch, Ernst. "Über historische und dogmatische Methode in der Theologie." In *Gesammelte Schriften*. Vol. 2. Aalen: Scientia, 1962. Translated by J. L. Adams and W. Bense as "Historical and Dogmatic Method in Theology," in *Religion in History* (Minneapolis: Fortress Press, 1991).

Webster, John. Introduction to *The Possibilities of Theology: Studies in the Theology of Eberhard Jüngel in his Sixtieth Year*. Edited by John Webster. Edinburgh: T & T Clark, 1994.

Zimany, Roland. *Vehicle for God: The Metaphorical Theology of Eberhard Jüngel*. Macon, GA: Mercer University Press, 1994.

INDEX